THE LONG ROAD FROM PORTMAN SQUARE

A gambler's odyssey from Portsmouth to Paraguay

Ian Carnaby

Published in 2020 by Marten Julian
69 Highgate, Kendal, Cumbria LA9 4ED
Tel: 01539 741 007
Email: rebecca@martenjulian.com

A catalogue record for this book is available from the British Library.

ISBN: 978-1-8380647-7-8

Book Design: Steve Dixon

Cover Design: Ian Lambert

Proofreader: Ian Greensill

Illustrations:
Ron Pollard Illustration: Robin Evans
All other Illustrations: William Butcher

Photo Credits:
Roberto: PA Images/Alamy Stock Photo
Uncle Tom & Jim Old: Ian Carnaby
Bill Wightman: Mark Cranham, Racing Post Photos
Bobby Stokes: In That Number
Mick Channon: Mick Channon
Barbary Pirate: The Sport & General Picture Agency

Printed in the UK by Finger Prints

Dedicated to my wife Sue, whose abiding belief in happy endings has seen me through. I think.

Acknowledgements

My sincere thanks go to Marten Julian for supporting me all
these years, and to his daughter Rebecca and her husband
Steve for ensuring this book saw the light of day. Also, Ian
Greensill has done a quite magnificent job of editing copy
which must have had his reserves of midnight oil regularly
showing the warning light.

Going further back, I owe a great deal to Iain 'Jimmy'
Thomas, former sports editor at BBC Radio, and Valentine
Lamb, editor of *The Irish Field*. Sadly, both have gone on
ahead. However, retired racing journalist Jonathan Powell
and former *Racing Post* editor Bruce Millington are still very
much with us. They believed when others doubted.

I tend to remember things like that.

Ian Carnaby

Contents

Foreword

Ian's writing makes me feel nostalgic for a time I never knew.

He writes of the most colourful of characters – some shady, some eccentric – but always interesting.

He remembers places, events and, most notably, songs and movies. Then there are the horses. Not always the big names, but many drawn from the ranks of his much beloved low-grade sprint handicaps.

There are insights into how 'the game' has changed, of dusty betting shops and trips to the seaside at Brighton. Ian can draw his inspiration from years of watching life go by, dipping into its mysteries only to then hop back to his seat by the side.

This book is a joy and an absolute delight in every way.

Marten Julian

Introduction

There is a moment in the Sam Peckinpah film *Junior Bonner* when the apocryphal rodeo rider, played by Steve McQueen, is confronted by his businessman brother Curley.

Exasperated beyond measure, Curley says: 'I'm working on my first million, you're still working on eight seconds' – this being the time Junior, a veteran by now, needs to stay on the feared Brahma bull when it explodes from the pen.

The parallels with gambling are obvious enough. Junior will never envy Curley, a sharpish land agent who is making the most of the mass migration west to cowboy towns like Prescott, but he will inevitably end up with far less money.

The acceptance of the situation informs my earlier book *Not Minding That It Hurts*, which is a line from *Lawrence of Arabia*, of course. If we distinguish between everyday punters (not a word I like) and committed gamblers, there is no doubt the latter will suffer hurt sometimes. In the pages that follow I've tried to outline how they deal with it and, in my own case, hold down various jobs (some of them for weeks as opposed to years) along the way.

To this end I've used various newspaper and magazine columns written over the last 30 years rather than replicate anything in *Not Minding*. Sometimes I wonder if anything has changed at all. I was recently watching another Steve McQueen film, *The Cincinnati Kid*, and realised I was still transfixed by the way the run of diamonds, from eight to queen, sits on the baize tabletop before Lancey, played by Edward G Robinson, flips over the killer jack for a straight flush.

It's well over 60 years since my parents bought their only child most of the Christmas presents they could afford, only to hear him suggest a game of rummy. The cards fascinated me then and still do now. If I go past a games shop in Soho with various packs in the window, I'll go in and buy a couple, even with no reason to open them in the foreseeable future. Like my mother's best china, which barely saw the light of day, they'll be kept for best.

For a few moments the Kid, with a full house, was looking at a life-changing sum. A long way from Prescott, and even further from Tinseltown, the same is true of my friend Dave Nevison, but more of that later. We lesser gamblers may not come as close but we know the strange, empty feeling that can last an hour, a month, or the time it takes for a sudden burst of nervous energy to propel us back into the world of risk and the company of like-minded souls. Then, while the wheel is spinning, the jack of diamonds is waiting or Hemingway's bunch of skins is hurtling towards the furlong pole, we're not thinking about anything else, regretting anything else or checking the time. This is where we live.

As Junior says: 'Rodeo time. I gotta get it on down the road.'

Ian Carnaby

Part One

Early Days, Early Warnings

At the age of six I knew nothing about value betting, or waiting for the right time to strike or setting something aside for the proverbial rainy day. (The last one is still pretty hazy.) On the other hand I knew that the king of diamonds was the only monarch in profile, that the wind had blown Ashurst Wonder home at 50/1 in the Stewards' Cup and Bill Wightman would win the King George VI Chase with Halloween.

We lived at 72 Burlington Road, more or less opposite the Dell, my Geordie father having moved south – avoiding a life certain to be spent down the pit at the Isabella Colliery – when his younger brother Tom signed for Southampton from Blyth Spartans just before World War II.

Dad worked shifts at Pirelli in Eastleigh, right through to his death in 1970. He was no gambler, indeed he saved with quiet determination, but he followed the horses on a daily basis, favouring some remarkably slow beasts trained by Eddie Magner, among others, often referring to them as 'pit ponies'. (I thought I'd never hear that again but there are no certainties in racing. A couple of years ago Victoria Jones, daughter of Champion Hurdle-winning trainer Arthur, came up with exactly the same description when saddling a couple for Malcolm Brisbourne at Brighton.)

Ashurst Wonder and Halloween were bound to be backed in Southampton because they were trained locally by Les Hall and Bill Wightman respectively. The latter will turn up here and there from now on. No apologies; he was my hero and that's all there is to it.

In 1954, we still had over six years to wait for betting offices to open. In the Portswood district of Southampton my Aunt Em and I would sidle up to a bus inspector called Ern, who ferried bets to the bookie Johnny Denton in Belmont Road.

On the way to home games at St Mary's I still drive past the house where Johnny plied his trade. Belmont Road, with its long row of middle-class Victorian houses, changes little with the passing of the years. Ken Russell, who made his name as a somewhat controversial film director, lived at number 31 from the age of three. It was his starting point when a local television station set out to make a programme about his early years in Southampton.

Ken and I went to the same school, Taunton's, and used the same hairdresser's, the Elite in Portswood. There were three barbers there and the middle one was called Mr Shearing. I know, I know, you couldn't make it up but these things happen. The *Guardian*'s health correspondent for many years was John Illman.

There was nothing illegal in off-course bookmaking; it was only the street runners – not that I ever saw Ern, a heavily built man, break into a trot – who attracted the attention of the police. (They weren't 'the fuzz' or 'the rozzers' at that stage, not in Portswood anyway.)

Those placing the bets generally went by a nickname, Aunt Em favouring 'Lucky'. I think it best to move on without comment, though I note that many years later Lord Lucan opted for something similar.

I am an only child and there were just the three of us in the house in Burlington Road. But my parents came from large families and everyone, bar an uncle on my mother's side, played the horses. It was all favourite jockeys, horses travelling a long way (in fairness, that was often far more relevant than it is today), interesting bookings and, in my dad's case, talented young apprentices just starting to make an impression.

It was doubles and trebles to small stakes, turning the evening paper sideways for the later races in the stop press and waiting for the evening results on the radio. It was the upstart Piggott annoying senior figures like W H Carr in the weighing room, Operatic Society winning the November Handicap at Manchester and my Uncle Ted cleaning up at Southampton greyhounds, where Alf Ramsey used to favour trap 1 during a wartime stint with the Saints. It was all of this and more, much more, but somewhere along the way my dad, a genial but cautious man who eventually put enough together for us to move across town, was bound to feel uneasy.

Maybe we all remember certain milestones when it comes to betting. He didn't like the pound I had on one trained by Eric Cousins at Haydock before we set off for a home game, even though it won at 4/1. The first £5, £10 and £20 bets all won as well, but a few years down the line, when he was gone, the first £50 wager on Sir Noel Murless' Whortleberry at Newmarket went down by an inch or so to one of Harry Wragg's.

None of this matters very much, except to me, and details of bets struck are seldom interesting to others. What DOES matter is appreciating the difference between those who study the horses every day and risk a few coins, accepting a relatively minor, inevitable loss overall as part of their hobby, and those who believe that anything is possible and the game is there to be won.

My dad couldn't fathom why anyone would have a pound on. It wasn't that he thought a pound was all that much; it just seemed crazy to him because, when it came right down to it, THEY WERE HORSES. And you either see what he meant by that, or you don't. I've had some great days and some fairly dreadful ones, the kind of setbacks that would have rendered him speechless. Not learning from well-intentioned homespun wisdom ('how do you know the horse felt like it today?') is painful but for most of my life I couldn't imagine living without risk. It shouldn't have become a constant companion but there it was, a shadow entirely independent of the sun.

Uncle Tom

Stewardess, Rytols Rocket and The Other Fred

I attended Taunton's in Southampton, a 200-year-old grammar
school which became a sixth form college in the late 1960s.
I could write a bit and act a bit and the Cambridge Entrance
Exam sort of fell into my lap, including as it did a short story
which had to end with the words 'and there was nothing
left but the footprints in the snow' together with a logic test.
Churchill College – the great man having died in 1965 – had
easily enough engineers and needed more Arts people.

At school I ran sweepstakes on races like the Stewards' Cup
and the Wokingham. There was also a card school in the
evenings but, if pressed for the single most significant factor
in what was clearly becoming a gambling life, Portsmouth
Greyhound Stadium would win by a country mile.

I loved Target Road, Tipner and when a couple of friends (one
of whom had a car) tired of the weekly visits, I travelled by
Royal Blue coach from Bedford Place in Southampton.

1967 was the year that George Curtis, trainer of the great
Ballyregan Bob, moved from Portsmouth to Brighton,
his place at Pompey being taken by his brother, Charlie.
Tragically, the latter was killed two years later when his
car skidded off the road on the way back from a meeting at
Crayford.

I remember many of the greyhounds from those evenings at
Tipner. Stewardess may have been the best but I had a soft
spot for Rytols Rocket out of trap 4 and the canny Broken
China, who features in the short story 'Stevie and Me' in *Not
Minding That It Hurts*.

But when it comes down to it, it's the places and the characters that fascinate me as much as the sport and the betting. Among the bookies there was J Clark of Brighton, though I believe his daughter took over; Southampton's Fred West, who never thought his name would become famous; and old Albert Martin, who used to bet 'without'. We took this to mean without the favourite, though Bill Francis, a lovely man and general manager for many years, told me he thought Albert was betting without any money.

And nothing changed, for ages and ages. The Herb Alpert tape must have nearly worn out with 'Tijuana Taxi' just pulling away from the kerb when 'Ladies and gentlemen, you have three minutes to the off' cut in. There was a roulette table in the main stand and people bet in old half-crowns, not chips. I won, and won again, and then lost. There was a vast, twinkling Tote board at one end of the track and a little bar offering scalding oxtail soup in plastic cups at the other. 'Mind, now, it's piping hot,' the lady said as you danced up and down.

I wrote about it all in the *Sporting Life* and Bill Francis invited me down. The stadium still had several years left but there were clear signs of wear and tear and it finally closed in 2010. We should be grateful for small mercies; it outlasted Park Royal, another favourite venue, by over 40 years. George Curtis did a stint at the London track when he was just starting out and I fitted in a couple of visits before the axe fell in 1969.

I never thought I'd be writing about it all 50 years later …

NO '20-MINUTE' RULE IN KENTISH TOWN
Racing Post April 2015

There was a day, over 50 years ago, when my dad fell foul of the '20-minute' rule. He had two winners, up and down as we used to say, at 100/6 and 33/1 with the double thrown in for good measure, but the races were only 15 minutes apart.

My mother had to tell him the bad news. The bet was in a Ladbrokes shop, though two or three of them in Southampton still carried the Charles Malizia name. I used to teach his daughter French in the posh part of town and she must be fluent by now with a place in Biarritz, probably, and an afternoon lover, Jacques Brel in the background and all the rest of it. This is where you and I have missed out, I think, or one of us has.

My mum didn't follow the rule whereby Ladbrokes or Charlie needed time to lay off a bet with a few pounds running on to a 100/6 shot but at 14 I could see how it worked, and it wasn't in our favour. One way and another we probably helped Ladbrokes on their way to the sunlit uplands, no question.

Nothing much fazed my dad and he just smoked another Capstan Full Strength, or half of it and put the other half behind his ear, like the old miner he was. I never thought to ask why he called it a 'doofer' and it was only a year or two ago that someone told me it meant 'do for later'. I've never managed to get all the way through *Finnegans Wake*, but at least I know what a 'doofer' is.

My parents differed in their approach to betting in that she settled for sixpences whereas he went for the whole two bob, or ten pence in newfangled money. Also, while he relied on Eddie Magner, she waited for the jumps to resume in August and followed Dick Francis, who had a tipping column in the

Sunday Express and was very well informed when it came to the first meetings at Market Rasen and Newton Abbot. Her other guiding lights were Captain Heath in the *Daily Mail* ('a woman's paper' according to my dad) and horses with recent form figures of 020. This was the holy grail.

"See, boy, they were trying with it the time before last and it didn't quite work so they had to cover it over again. Today's the day." As a young man starting out in life, this is the sort of advice you need; in fact, there is no reason for anything to surprise or disappoint you because, where the wicked ways of the world are concerned, your card has been well and truly marked. Sometimes I wonder how things would have turned out if I'd stayed with 020.

"I missed out on Biarritz but I once had a lover in Kentish Town," my friend 'Marvel' Mason said. Marvel made a fortune from American comics but worked through it slowly and efficiently. At first I thought he'd struck lucky on a rare visit to north London – a come hither smile on the Holloway Road, a chance encounter in a Walthamstow hostelry – but then I remembered there used to be regular trips from his office in Basingstoke.

"Of course, that was long before the heart murmur and the pills," he went on. "Things can happen at the right time in life; that's the way I look at it."

Quite so. I don't like to think of Marvel having a sudden heart scare in flagrante delicto, especially in Kentish Town, where I'd need an enhanced picture of the relevant page in the A to Z, always assuming there was a panicky phone call from a distressed lover with Al Martino in the background. Marvel has always been very big on Al Martino; 'Spanish Eyes', that's his favourite.

"I bet you're thinking about Malcolm Saunders," he said. "Ginzan 14/1, Sarangoo 33/1. He's one of your trainers, isn't he?"

You could say that, I suppose. I was nursing a glass of Barolo in San Carlo in Bristol a while back and Malcolm saw me through the window and came in for a chat. All I needed to do was ring him up; he'd have said the horses were working well and I'd have rung Wilsons straightaway.

Of course, my dad was long gone by then. But sometimes I link different eras in my mind and imagine him writing out the bet (he thought telephones were only for posh people anyway) and handing it to my mother before starting the 2 to 10pm shift. One way and another, Ladbrokes can count themselves lucky.

FLOATING AWAY WITH BROTHER RAY
Racing Post June 2013

No one thinks of Isambard Kingdom Brunel as a gambler, though he certainly was in some respects.

There are things you promise yourself you'll do once more. I wouldn't mind another go at following Donald Sutherland's troubled and erratic path through Venice in *Don't Look Now* (without the tragic outcome) and I have a Geordie friend who's more than happy to show me around Blyth, my father's birthplace but a town I haven't visited in well over 50 years.

It's a while since I've been to Newton Abbot, as well. One should always go by train, taking in the thrilling stretch along the sea wall at Dawlish where, in inclement weather, it seems that relatively little stands between the passenger and a watery grave. Brunel wasn't bound to choose a route hugging the sea for that part of his Great Western adventure but the risk probably appealed to him. Not for nothing was there a pub in Bristol called the Reckless Engineer.

In the days before summer jumping, Newton Abbot and Market Rasen got everything going again over August bank holiday weekend. My mother, a devotee of racing over the sticks, used to follow Dick Francis, who wrote a tipping piece in the old *Sunday Express*. Given his contacts he could hardly go wrong and there were many early winners while most people were still concentrating on the Flat. I cannot recall my mother ever expressing an opinion on Devon Loch or the early thrillers (far superior to the later ones, I think) but Dick's tipping made him a hero in our house.

I think of her whenever I go past Pepperbox Hill just outside Salisbury because she used to work at Plaitford on the old A36. If you spend a lot of time travelling between Bristol and Southampton you should rest awhile at Pepperbox Hill, especially when the bluebells are out. The view is pretty stunning, as well – a timely reminder of how much unspoiled countryside there is around the old city.

Some races linger in the memory. Where Salisbury is concerned they include Vernon Cross' Red Abbot fighting back to win the City Bowl half a lifetime ago and the one-eyed Striker pulling half a furlong clear in a mile seller. Herbert Blagrave simply didn't run horses in sellers but he did that day and 15/8 should have been about 2/5. Most of all, though, I think about Albert Finney and the Downton Handicap in 1990, won by the actor's Brother Ray, whom he also bred.

Certain bets, even down to the staking, take root the night before the event. There's the name in the *London Evening Standard* (when the paper cared about racing and printed the cards) and there you were in the Greek restaurant with a day off beckoning. You were in gambler's paradise.

From London I always chose the Andover route, passing very close to Toby Balding's old yard at Weyhill. These days Weyhill is little known outside the racing community but when Daniel Defoe visited Weyhill Fair in the early 18th century he called it 'the greatest fair for sheep that this nation can show'. As Tom Fort notes in his fascinating book about the A303, there were horses, cattle and pigs, Surrey hops and a travelling circus. Upstairs at the Weyhill Fair pub, a mural depicts the early scene from Hardy's *The Mayor of Casterbridge* when the drunken John Henchard sells his wife to a sailor for five guineas at the 'Weydon Priors' Fair.

Brother Ray started 15/8 favourite in a 20-runner handicap. He was 6lb higher for an easy Warwick victory six days previously but people tended not to worry about things like that when Epsom trainer John Sutcliffe junior was involved. The horse was none too well away but Michael Wigham brought him with a long, sweeping run on the outside to get up by half a length. Sutcliffe made hardly any mistakes when the money was down and Finney could hardly have chosen a shrewder operator.

Several years later, following his retirement, I interviewed Sutcliffe for a magazine called the *Sports Adviser* but Finney politely declined. "No, no, I don't think so, old love, do you?" he said. It was a pity because he had many good stories to tell. He was born in Salford, where his father was a bookie. Legend has it that, when his dad died, the funeral procession got lost in the back streets and ended up alongside the old Manchester racecourse.

Albert narrated the Mill Reef story, *Something to Brighten the Morning*, and invested heavily and successfully in US Triple Crown winner Seattle Slew, even though several experts advised him the horse had an uncommercial pedigree.

It would be fair to say he always backed his own judgement, including when directing himself in the film *Charlie Bubbles* (1967), which is off-beat but quite poignant in its way and takes him, as a rich but blocked writer, back to Manchester and his estranged wife and son. But the boy is too young to sit through an entire United game without losing concentration and Albert looks at him sideways, realising the relationship needs a lot of work and the trip has not been a success.

In the end he just floats away in a hot-air balloon, which many considered something of a cop-out, though I thought it reasonable enough. Mind you, if you choose to disappear like that, better make sure you get it right first time. Explanations might be tricky otherwise.

BLACK COFFEE, RED LETTER DAYS
Sporting Life May 1996

I was going to write this on the train from Bristol Temple Meads to Paddington but Luke Harvey got on at Didcot Parkway and that was the end of it. Work deferred for at least an hour and a half.

Lately I've done most of my writing and thinking on trains, although publicans should not despair. Incidentally, if you are of a mind to get down to some hard graft on the rattler and need plenty of space, I recommend carrying a few empty miniatures of Smirnoff vodka.

Spread them around on one of those foldaway tables alongside, dangle your binoculars from the little red knob in front and you will find that no one takes the vacant seat, even on very busy mornings.

At Swindon, a black man in a black hat got on. He had black hair, a black suit, black shirt and black tie. When the trolley came along, he asked for a black coffee. And the girl said: 'No, really?'

Which went totally unremarked by the other passengers but I thought it was great. I was going to tell Luke about it but he was deeply into the Worcester card and looking for a few Goodwood pointers for the Racing Channel.

When it rains in the south and west, and Goodwood and Salisbury race on the same day, you could lose everything, I suppose.

Especially if you know nothing about the draw. Official form publications fall short when it comes to emphasis, I feel. 'At Salisbury, when the going is soft, low numbers may have an advantage.' May? MAY?

'At Salisbury, when the going is soft, rest assured the little chaps in brightly coloured clothing will veer right across to the stands' side and do their level best from there.' See? Tell it like it is.

Pat Eddery once led the field across in appalling ground and I remember saying on SIS that it was probably one of the shrewdest, most tactically aware manoeuvres ever executed on the British Turf. I backed it, I think.

There was an interminable stewards' enquiry but all was well in the end and the Bristol bailiffs had to wait their turn – not that I'd ever let worries of that sort influence my professional judgement.

Things are going along quite well in Nailsea and Roger, mine host at the Queen's Head, has swiftly acknowledged and forgotten – well, nearly – the £200 he'd have won on across-the-card favourites if Kamari (4/5) and Willie Carson had held on at Lingfield. His lingering regret concerns the shortfall on turnover from the regulars. Apparently they all stormed off into the night – not the easiest of things in Nailsea, where you'd soon run out of places to storm to – when Willie was caught on the line. Roger estimates the damage at around £35.60, not that he's analysed it in detail.

"They would definitely have stayed in here, spending their winnings until 11 o'clock," he said, whistling through his new teeth. They cost just over two grand, as well, but what a player. £200 no problem but £35.60 a real pain in the derrière. All perfectly understandable.

Gamblers view things differently, of course. Françoise Sagan, who wrote the poignant short story 'Aimez-Vous Brahms?', once found herself playing chemin de fer at the Clermont Club in Mayfair.

They were so pleased to see her that chips were no problem. Having signed this piece of paper and that, and without seeing a single card in her favour, she asked, discreetly, how she stood. The deficit was £80,000.

This is one of my favourite gambling stories. To pay off this debt, she realised she would have to give up her flat, ask her mother to take care of her son and spend two years working exclusively for the taxman and the Clermont. She called for more chips.

A couple of hours later she had cordially discussed the Epsom Derby with the player on her left and the delights of Florida with the player on her right. Her deficit was down to £50 and she paid it, sweetly, on her way out. If you want the full story, it's in her frank account *With Fondest Regards*, published in 1986.

I love Françoise Sagan and often think about her when I'm on the forecourt at Paddington Station at 2am. I was going to tell Luke about her, too. But, as I say, he was pretty busy.

STIFFKEY BLUE COMPLETES THE LIST
Racing Post January 2014

It's funny what you think about in the middle of the night: house prices in Midsomer, horses named after places in Norfolk, Rory Delap's long throw.

You may not have noticed this but DCI Barnaby, played by John Nettles, and Rory, now with Stoke City, both use their arms in order to move forwards because the air gets in the way otherwise. They wear well, though, and John looks much the same as he did in *Bergerac* all those years ago.

I think about a lot of things I've missed. There was the old-style music hall revue in a West End theatre in 1964 called 'Nights at the Comedy' and one of the turns was a man hitting himself over the head with a tin tray while singing 'Mule Train'.

I wish I'd seen that and I wish I'd been in Paris to see Sea-Bird II win the Arc in 1965. I'd have followed it with a trip to the Folies Bergère, which would probably have had the edge over an afternoon meeting at Alexandra Park followed by Raymond Revuebar in Soho, though I've never found a horse at Longchamp to match Thames Trader at Ally Pally.

Sometimes, when there is little prospect of any sleep around 3am, I try to remember where everyone was sitting in my class when I was 16. I do quite well because the ones at the front and the back are dead easy; it's the handful in the middle I can't quite place. I know their names, indeed a couple of them still owe for the sweep I ran on the 1965 Wokingham won by Nunshoney, but they've probably forgotten.

The Norfolk thing didn't go on long enough, though there are several names – Hethersett, Blakeney, Morston, Norwich and Stiffkey to get you started. Given that he went on to win the 1962 St Leger by four lengths, with Derby winner Larkspur unplaced, Hethersett (a faller at Epsom) must have been one of the unluckiest losers of the Blue Riband there's ever been. As I backed him steadily from the moment he won the Brighton Derby Trial, the incident didn't do me a lot of good, either. There was a partial recovery when his son Blakeney obliged at Epsom seven years later, though I'm still not sure how Ernie Johnson wriggled between Willie Shoemaker and the far rail.

I wonder if Ernie would give that one up in favour of Barry Hills' Rheingold denying Roberto in 1972 instead of missing out by inches. He must have replayed the race a thousand times in his mind and it's covered in great detail in Barry's autobiography *Frankincense and More*. In the end, though, there is no denying genius on the most important occasions and Lester's ride on Roberto, especially the rodeo-style, whip-cracking finish, is simply from another world.

I interviewed the great man on several occasions but certainly wouldn't claim to know him well. All I would say is that today always mattered far more to him than yesterday and the iron in his soul left precious little room for sentiment. You've hardly ever heard Lester refer to winners, even Classic winners, by name.

"That other horse doesn't go," he told me when Epsom hero Teenoso was forced to miss the Arc. "I'm trying to sort something out." Priceless.

Anyway, Stiffkey took me a while, though I vaguely remembered a six-furlong sprinter called Stiffkey Blue. I thought it must be named after a Tory politician, though in fact it's a cockle. My time is never wasted.

The Reverend Harold Francis Davidson was the son of the vicar of Sholing in Southampton, which is how I started to piece things together. Not quite a chip off the old block, he nonetheless became the rector of Stiffkey at one point and claimed to have saved the souls of more than a thousand fallen women.

Unfortunately, he also photographed actresses in their pyjamas and was ejected from a nudist camp in Harrogate. Show business was more his thing and he returned to music hall in Birmingham before exhibiting himself in a barrel on Blackpool prom for pennies. Finally he moved to Skegness and appeared in a cage with a lion called Freddie who attacked him and inflicted fatal injuries.

He is still highly regarded in Stiffkey, apparently. I am sorry to have missed him.

MISSING MY CHANCE WITH DORIS
Racing Post February 2017

I miss Doris Constable.

Or at least, I miss the sign outside her house – Doris Constable: Pianoforte Teacher. Given that she lived right in the middle of Southampton's red-light district, a worldly-wise teenager might have taken her occupation with a large pinch of salt. I certainly did until a policeman who had seen most things in life told me years later that Doris was actually a much-respected music teacher who never allowed the various comings and goings outside to disturb her concentration. This was a constable who knew his Constables.

Well, the sign has gone – so too Doris, I imagine – and the area is a good deal more salubrious than it used to be, like London's Shepherd Market. It helps to know how all the streets connect – no problem here – because they offer the easiest way out of town after games at St Mary's.

Sometimes a day goes so well that you wonder why you were ever cynical about anything. My colleague Jonathan Powell arranged for the late Robert Alner to attend the West Brom match, having discovered that he was an Albion fan whose boyhood hero was the striker Derek Kevan.

After his sad, life-changing accident a few years ago, a trip like this was a major undertaking (to say the least) for the Gold Cup-winning trainer. There was the special mobility vehicle, complete with carers and a large oxygen cylinder, plus the wheelchair itself, of course, which had to be manoeuvred up to the box in the Itchen Stand. West Brom's record goalscorer Tony 'Bomber' Brown popped in, together with a few old Southampton players responding to a request from Mick Channon. They included the uncompromising left-back Denis Hollywood, who took few prisoners and appears more than once in Mike Summerbee's autobiography. This may be because the former Manchester City star still has the bruises.

Robert spoke calmly and lucidly with the aid of a voice box. At least I was able to thank him for the times he helped out with comments on horses to follow and all the other things we tend to take for granted. I had the utmost admiration for him and something Jonathan said has remained in my mind.

"He talks to young people in the same position, you know. He says it's them we should be thinking of. 'I've had most of my life but they've still got to live theirs,' he said to me."

Taking all of this into account I probably wouldn't have minded too much if Shane Long had saved it for the Baggies near the end. I still don't know how he missed, although following his move to the Saints I have a clearer idea.

Anyway, I drove Jonathan back through the darkening streets, past Doris's old place and out along Empress Road, where I took one of my driving tests nearly 50 years ago. I'm not bitter or anything though I suspect I'd have had a better chance if the instructor, an RAF type with a handlebar moustache – Whistler, that was his name – had given me some last-minute instructions instead of speculating on whether a beautiful black streetwalker who happened to be passing had somehow fallen pregnant. He seemed to know her quite well. It was an interesting area.

I remember handing the British School of Motoring a Barclays cheque when Richmond Sturdy completed a rare evening double but during my Jockey Club days I banked at Coutts. The arrangement was short-lived because they'd never come across anyone going overdrawn without express permission before. I don't think there were many gamblers on either side of the counter.

I encountered similar difficulties at other banks as well, with sympathy at a premium, though there was a memorable conversation with a chap called David Moisson at Lloyds, I think, in Covent Garden. Not only did he cash a cheque during Royal Ascot week but then, asked about his own well-being, he said: "Oh, you know how it is, Mr Carnaby. It's banking, isn't it? Dead men's shoes, really." I liked him very much.

I'm not saying I miss those days, but every now and then a distant bell rings and I wouldn't mind a day and night given over to risk. Failing that, I must find a new hobby or start learning the piano. It had to be Doris, though, I think. 'Au Clair de la Lune' in the early evening with roars of approval from the houses on either side.

TURKISH DELIGHT FOR THE TOTE?
Sporting Life October 1993

A man I only ever bump into at the furlong pole at Salisbury has written me a charming letter. He made some critical (and valid) points about the Tote Jackpot, but this is the bit which has stayed with me.

"Perhaps you or one of the Young Turks at the *Life* could take it up with the Tote. No offence, but not even our best friends would call either of us young any more!"

No, I suppose not. The truth always hurts. I wouldn't mind but I'm not sure I was EVER a Young Turk. An amiable, slightly confused Turk, perhaps, but not a young one.

I still had the letter with me when turning out for the pub quiz team on Monday night. This had never occurred to me before but if you can say, without a moment's hesitation, that Jay Silverheels played Tonto in *The Lone Ranger*, it means you're at least middle-aged. (Funny thing about old Jay. I saw him again recently in an Audie Murphy picture. *Drums Across the River*, it was called. He played a quiet, dignified Indian. Good to know some things never change.)

I don't mind these gentle reminders that one is well into the second half, so to speak, but I'd prefer the process to be a gradual one. I have to say there's nothing gradual about four of my favourite trainers calling it a day one after the other. What makes it worse is the fact that, whilst Messrs Wightman, Elsey and Fairhurst have all kept the Carnaby boat afloat at one time or another, I was only just getting to grips with John Sutcliffe.

Of course, my big mistake has always been the assumption that trainers exist in a kind of time warp. I never learn, which is why it hits me so hard when they go. When John Meacock and all those horses with strange Persian names departed the scene, I took it as a sign that my salad days were over. No more Vakil-ul-Mulk, no more Qalibashi, no more Karkeh Rud, with more coconuts by his name than a Bounty advert before his glorious Windsor triumph at 33/1.

I've come to realise that I associate every single phase of my life with some trainer or other. If you asked me about the mid to late 1960s, I'd mention Terry Paine, Channon wide on the left, working as a board man in Ladbrokes and going to see 'adult' films at the Southampton Classic. But there would also be room for Bolton trainer W Carr, or Willie as I learned much later on.

He was brilliant. All of his horses had a Constable connection and some of them were out of the mare Flatford Mill. They were hardly ever seen in public but he used to slip them in somewhere or other at bank holiday time. They were generally about 25/1 so I suppose he made a year's money in one hit.

The Country Lane was probably the best of them. She was quite a madam and sometimes tried to kick her rivals at the start before thrashing them in the race. Carr let her out so rarely that she needed a double dose of pleasure. I was just starting to fathom his methods when ill health forced him to retire.

Once, when I was 15, I went to the Classic on the proceeds from one of his winners. Those French 'X' films were something else. Strange to think we queued all round the block in the pouring rain for a glimpse of something available in any newsagent's today.

There was always a bluesy saxophone on the soundtrack and the volume would increase as the vital moment arrived. Then everything went a bit fuzzy. This was partly because the projectionist at the Classic was a sadist and an incompetent although, in fairness, those of us still in our macs were giving off quite a bit of steam in the crowded auditorium.

None of those French films has ever come round again. I never thought I'd see another Manolete, either, but 30 years after Ryan Jarvis trained a horse named after one of the most famous of all Spanish bullfighters, Steve Norton has a two-year-old with the same handle.

I may be cracking up because I can't remember who used to ride the original Manolete. It was either Eric Eldin or Stan Clayton. No doubt I'll soon pull myself together. As long as no one else retires, that is.

SUPREME CLARET ROLLS BACK THE YEARS

Racing Post November 2018

I could never quite imagine another dog like Broken China running out of trap 3.

He was an unlucky greyhound who often found trouble but on this particular night he timed his run to perfection and caught the one dog close home. 1965 sounds about right. Portsmouth Stadium, Target Road, Tipner. 9/2, I think, and a significant step along the road towards obsession.

I was wandering along The Cut between Blackfriars and Waterloo the other day after lunching with Brendan Brophy, who was due to be guest speaker at the school reunion dinner in Southampton last night. If you have stents (I have three) you owe Brendan a drink because, in the early nineties, he designed the building at St George's Hospital in Tooting which saw the introduction of the Philips biplane system – the angiogram through your groin or armpit which checks the width of your arteries. He also advised Sheikh Mohammed and his father on matters pertaining to the Deira Tower in Dubai but the racing bug missed him; remarkable for someone who lives at Tattenham Corner.

Anyway, it was about 3.45pm with time to spare before the 4.30 back to Bristol, so I went into the Betfred shop halfway along The Cut and took a shine to Supreme Claret in trap 3 at Monmore. I'm not saying I follow greyhound form all that closely these days but names mean a lot to me and I loved hers, so a score at 9/2 made perfect sense. Yes it did. She broke fast, tracked the front pair and found the best turn of foot to get up and beat the one dog. And of course, 53 years on, it all came flooding back, though Broken China had a bit more white about him as I recall.

Punters don't come in off the street and have twenty on a greyhound these days, so the winning slip was closely examined and held up to the light before being fed into some sort of machine (a big black one) which confirmed that, general misgivings notwithstanding, it was indeed valid. Not a word was spoken and my thoughts went back to Terry, the Ladbrokes manager in Pound Tree Road, Southampton in the old Broken China days. His whip action with a rolled-up *Sporting Life* rivalled Lester's on Roberto and his vocal encouragement when his nap went clear was fully reciprocated on the other side of the counter.

May Birch, a large, fearsome lady until you got to know her better, ran the place, more or less. "Yes, what is it now, Rothschild?" she'd say to some timid two-bob merchant. They loved her to bits. Sadly, we've lost that rapport between staff and customers.

Supreme Claret won on 31 October, a matter of hours before my favourite month, even if this particular November brings with it a 70th birthday. Good things are already starting to happen, with Count Meribel winning at Carlisle last Sunday.

The horse went with Jim Old when he joined Nigel Twiston-Davies a while back. He'd never jumped a fence in public but won this novices' handicap chase under top weight of 11st 12lb, which makes you realise what we're missing now that Jim no longer trains in his own right.

In the heavier gambling days – and nights – I'd sometimes need certain pieces of music the following morning, though I didn't know at the time that J A B Old was very fond of Kurt Weill's 'September Song'. It turns up on Radio 3 now and again, like George Butterworth's 'The Banks of Green Willow', which has a soothing effect. Butterworth, encouraged by Ralph Vaughan-Williams, had much more to offer but fell to a sniper's bullet at the Somme in 1916.

I have two of Jim's Siegfried Sassoon books here. The Great War poet lived until 1967 and adored cricket, even if his fielding (he favoured mid-on) at Heytesbury House in Wiltshire left something to be desired. His thoughts may have been with friends and colleagues from a long, long time ago.

'Dreaming of things they did with balls and bat

And mocked by hopeless longing to regain

Bank holidays, and picture shows, and spats,

And going to the office in the train …'

I imagine I perked up a bit by the time Brendan did his thing last night. You can't have an MC with a catch in his voice. Not in November, anyway.

EYES DOWN FOR A FULL HOUSE
Racing Post January 2014

Wandering in my favourite cemetery recently, I was struck by how simple and straightforward the epitaphs are.

Mine is unlikely to include anything about bingo, although many years ago I was a reserve caller at Kemp Town in Brighton. Unfortunately, it was like sitting on the subs' bench every week; by the time they tell you to get ready the moment has passed and you fail to do yourself justice.

I knew all the lines, needless to say. I even knew that 'Kelly's Eye, number one' referred to the one-eyed Australian outlaw Ned Kelly and 'five and nine the Brighton line' dated back to the five shillings and ninepence (about 29p) it cost a Londoner for a day return to the races, or something rather more exotic, on the old London, Brighton and South Coast Railway. The regular caller, an old sweat whose breath hinted at Woodbines, brown ale and peppermints, said it was because it took the train 59 minutes. I may have done more research but he could do a funny Charlie Chaplin walk, told end of the pier stories and the punters adored him. He was also a much better caller ('either way up, six and nine, 69!') and encouraged me, the way you do when there's nothing to fear.

My mother sometimes sat next to Benny Hill's mother at the bingo. "He's very good to her, you know," she said.

"How do you know that?"

"Because she said so." There was a long pause. "Yes, he's VERY good to his mother." I started buying flowers on a regular basis soon afterwards.

Eyes Down has always meant a great deal to me, ever since the great Bill Wightman days, when the old horse won nine times for him. I'd like another go at calling, though things have probably changed. Is 'all the eights, two fat ladies, 88' politically correct? Almost certainly not. It's probably vanished, like the *Dandy*, full racecards in the *Guardian*, most of the Italian restaurants I loved and Mr Golly from the Noddy books. Political correctness gone mad, as they say.

Jimmy 'Marvel' Mason has yet to recover from the closure of the *Dandy*, which he considers a national disgrace, but backing Richard Hughes for the jockeys' title helped ease the pain and a sizeable bet on Deputy Dan at Chepstow means there is now a large Famous Grouse alongside the Guinness. I'm not sure how this affects the heart murmur but he looks very well and even the roulette seems to be working.

The bar – more like a hotel lounge, really – on platform three at Bristol Temple Meads station is excellent and the Rioja well above average. When I raised an eyebrow at the Famous Grouse, Marvel tapped his nose and said: "Twenty-three and the neighbours," as if that explained everything. (Which to roulette players the world over it does, of course.)

"You can't compare bingo and roulette," he said.

"Why not? You leave home, you go to the usual place, you have a couple of drinks and hope your numbers come up. The only difference is that with roulette you choose them yourself. I'm not criticising. I'm happy for things to be random sometimes. It's a kind of therapy."

Marvel, more of a Dostoyevsky man – more of a *Hotspur*, *Eagle*, *Adventure*, *Viz* and Dostoyevsky man – will not have this at any price. He believes in sequences and I like him so much I judge this a poor time to ask about his reasons for backing Deputy Dan, who sounds like Desperate Dan, legendary star of the *Dandy* these many years but gone now.

"I got 7/2 about Hughes, you know," he went on. "I thought Ryan Moore would make all the right noises but not be all that bothered when it came down to it."

Well, I thought much the same myself, and I'm pleased one of us made it pay. In my teens, the first thing I asked my father when I got home from school was how the Lester Piggott and Scobie Breasley battle was going. Scobie edged home in the end, much to my chagrin. Years later when I interviewed Lester (an impossible dream), I came to realise that big races meant immeasurably more to him than titles. I blushed for my younger self.

"Life is a series of small setbacks and then a real cracker, right at the end," Marvel said, catching the barman's eye. "How old were you, anyway?"

"About 13, I suppose."

"Ah. Unlucky for some, of course. Another Rioja?"

A PERFECT GENTLEMAN

Sporting Life November 1995

I was 47 last week. ("Really? 47? Golly, you don't look it." Slight pause. "You USED to! Ha ha!" I've heard it.)

Before I went to the Southampton v Bolton game, my first as a 47-year-old, I received a copy of Alan Yuill Walker's book *Months of Misery, Moments of Bliss*, the biography of retired Upham, Hampshire trainer Bill Wightman.

In the course of the match, when I was thinking of going on to give Francis Benali a hand at left-back, I heard that Bill, now 81, is not in the best of health. And it made me think of many things.

But for the great W G R Wightman, racing would not have gripped me at such an early age. It just so happens that I was born in the year, 1948, that he laid out Final Score to win the Lincoln.

Mickey Greening was booked to ride, off 6st 11lb, and the owner went in early, and heavily, at 66/1. Unfortunately, the ground came up firm and Final Score had to wait for Hurst Park a fortnight later, when he duly romped in.

After the Bolton game the Southampton president, John Corbett, came into the boardroom. He was 90 yesterday and looks wonderful. Apart from riding many point-to-point winners – his family also bred the 1951 Grand National winner, Nickel Coin – he part-owned a mare in training with Bill called Halview Pet, who won on her hurdling debut at Newbury. The other partner all those years ago was the late Herbert Blagrave, not only a hugely generous philanthropist and successful owner-trainer himself later on, but also president of the same football club.

Eyes Down was possibly the first name I ever saw written on a piece of card in my father's spidery, rambling hand and when Import won the Wokingham in 1976 I danced a jig in Marylebone High Street. In the end I was in trouble far more often than I got out, but if anyone could have forced a draw on my behalf it was Bill Wightman.

Walker's fine book touches on the trainer's three and a half years as a Japanese prisoner of war. A six-footer, he came home weighing 7st 12lb and is understandably reticent about the darkest period in his life. But an indomitable spirit shines through.

"I had one tremendous asset because I had no dependants, no encumbrances if you like.

"Men with wives and children did nothing but worry and there were more deaths as each successive Christmas passed. At the finish, we were burying 15 men a week, a friend every day. If they had not dropped the bomb, thousands more British prisoners would have died."

Walker is strongest of all on lineage, both human and equine. The reader learns exactly how and why certain horses were purchased, and there is detailed analysis of arguably the best three-mile chaser never to win the Cheltenham Gold Cup – Halloween.

Mick Channon has contributed a generous foreword. He was still in his first spell at Southampton when Bill saddled Cathy Jane to win for him at Lingfield. Later on, Cathy Jane was mated with Import and produced the Tote Gold Trophy winner, Jamesmead.

Anyone who worries what happens to racehorses when they retire will take comfort from these pages. Wightman always tried to find good homes for his stalwarts and several lived out their final years at Ower Farm before being buried there. I think this piece best sums up the man:

"When I was younger and a horse was seriously injured, I was much more inclined to say that he should be put down, whereas being a prisoner of war I learned to accept a lower standard – it made me more compassionate.

"I know it sounds corny but my primary concern has always been for the welfare of the horse."

It doesn't sound corny to me; it sounds typical. And even if you stripped away every atom of my bias towards his and my part of the world, I would still be quite certain that Bill Wightman is a great man.

Bill Wightman

Part Two

Marylebone Offers
A Welcome Release

Dad would have backed Bill Wightman's Import in
the Wokingham in 1976 (a truly magnificent year with
Southampton winning the FA Cup) and we'd have celebrated
together, though I'd have kept quiet about how much it meant
to me – and I don't mean because it was trained by Bill. It was
the first major financial recovery, the race viewed through a
Radio Rentals shop window on Marylebone High Street with
an Irish gentleman of leisure assuring me Taffy Thomas had
got there 'by half a head'.

He and his friends from the homeless hostel on Marylebone
Road liked a drop – Carlsberg Special for preference – in the
little park at the top of the High Street and I'd chat with them
sometimes, returning as the months and years went by until
the group changed and changed again so that I was the only
'original' left.

Having started off as a trainee at the Jockey Club in Portman Square nearby, followed by several years in the wine trade at York Gate on Marylebone Road, I knew the High Street as well as I knew Burlington Road. The Baker & Oven, the Alpino (where a seven-card stud game sometimes materialised as if by magic in the afternoons), the Hellenic Greek restaurant lower down, the H Backhouse betting shop (Crazy Horse, more coconuts by his name than you'd see at a seaside fair between the wars but a snip at 11/2 with G Lewis riding for R C Sturdy in a Folkestone seller), the butchers Wainwright & Daughter – a rare shop sign indeed – and Odin's, which Peter Langan opened before the better-known Langan's Brasserie in Stratton Street off Piccadilly. Quite possibly mad, he set fire to himself with fatal consequences many years ago. Odin's has closed and, sadly, the brasserie is under considerable pressure in this Covid-19 year.

Betting offices are feeling the pinch, as well. As I write this in 2020, with FOBTs (fixed odds betting terminals, or pure chance 'machines') having been downgraded, they are slowly fading away, although Saturdays in what we used to call working-class areas remain much the same. I have worked in betting shops, bet in them and broadcast to them. And along the way I've met some very interesting characters, as will soon become apparent. The six I chose for a *Racing Post* feature on the 50th anniversary of the shops' opening had to earn their place in a VERY strong field …

SIX FAVOURITE SHOPS
Racing Post May 2011

Ladbrokes, Pound Tree Road, Southampton

Anyone fearing the demise of betting shops should go to
Pound Tree Road in Southampton, where Ladbrokes and
Coral's sit side by side with Paddy Power opposite.

Over 40 years ago, Ladbrokes had things to themselves and
I worked as a board man during college vacations. In those
days of 'blower' commentaries, when everything finished fast
and the final furlong was about a mile and a half, Terry the
manager rode a mean finish from behind the counter and so
did I.

It was a magical time. There was a man who received good
information from Portsmouth Greyhound Stadium and we
latched on to his bets, duplicating them in a Coral shop half
a mile away. They all won but I suppose we became greedy
and had too much on one day. The dog lost and the man never
came in again.

Terry loved an old mare called Nicolina, who used to run
in the Stewards' Cup on Tuesday without a mention but
then turned out again in another six-furlong handicap at
Goodwood on the Saturday and won. The whole shop backed
her and Terry rode one of his strongest finishes. A while later
her trainer Roy Pettitt hit hard times and sold his story to a
tabloid, saying he'd perked her up with something illegal.
I never believed a word of it. I just think she came right
between Tuesday and Saturday. Even if it means missing the
train and I'm fed up because the Saints have lost, I'll still go
out of my way to walk up Pound Tree Road. It's home.

Ladbrokes (formerly Charles Malizia), St Denys Road, Southampton

Several of the Ladbrokes shops in Southampton used to be owned by a man called Charlie Malizia. I have no excuse for the way things have turned out because I saw things from the other side of the fence early on when I went to his smart house in Bassett Green to teach his daughter French. Stop it, now.

The St Denys shop was close to the old Palladium cinema and both have gone. My Aunt Em would take me to see films like *Shane*. All I ever really wanted in life was to say, "No, Joey, I gotta be going on," like Alan Ladd at the end when he's sorted everything out. Of course, he's been shot as well.

When the shops opened it meant Aunt Em and I had no need of Ernie, the bus inspector who doubled as a bookie's runner for Johnny Denton. With a name like that Johnny should probably have been a riverboat gambler falling slowly and fatally in love with Barbara Stanwyck, but he was just a bookie. Ernie had his regulation issue bus inspector's mac, which was lopsided – money in one side, money out the other.

When I was an old 13 I could get from school to St Denys Road in time to hear the last race. I suppose the best-ever day was John Meacock's Karkeh Rud winning at 33/1 at Windsor, and that sublime moment when you realise the felt tip number one really is against his name on the marker sheet and he really is double carpet. And the worst day was Abbotsbury Abbot winning at 50/1 because I hadn't noticed him. So I named my house Abbotsbury House and the sign grows older with me and I think of St Denys Road, when I was happiest.

Laurie Wallis, 1 Jesus Lane, Cambridge

Long gone now, but a truly extraordinary place where the Indian restaurant-style flock wallpaper suited quite a few of the patrons and there were rude drawings on the wall, including one of a woman in the advanced stages of physical ecstasy. I wish I could draw like that.

Needless to say, there were budding thespians and a young man who was writing a novel. Jeff Connor was there and so was I and so was David Ashforth now and again, though he also used a Jennings shop nearby. Behind the counter we had Foxy, Moonface and Nice Man, all of them interesting for different reasons. Moonface had a condition which could only be soothed by vast quantities of Lucozade and he was permanently appalled by results. "How can THAT win? What are the stewards doing?" he'd say, to general amusement.

They didn't really like Tote bets in there but you could get four shillings (20p) on one of Ron Smyth's first-time out hurdlers if Nice Man was on. I had my first £20 bet in Jesus Lane on a filly called Benita, a two-year-old trained by Jack Waugh. It must have been around 1969, I suppose. The word was all around Cambridge for her but, remarkably, she didn't start favourite for this Lingfield maiden because one of Staff Ingham's, Abigail Hill, was fancied even more strongly. She missed the break, though, and Benita won at 9/4. To draw £65 was a handy sum in those days and it stayed locked up for a while.

One Saturday, Captain H Ryan Price had two in a multi-runner three-year-old maiden – 42 runners, Lingfield or Newbury. Anyway, Lester was on one and D Coleman was on the other. Not David, needless to say, but when it bolted in at 33/1 we discovered it was Des Coleman, a crack Australian who was on his way to take up a retainer in Ireland.

A couple of years later I was working for the late Ken Allday, Jockey Club Controller of Programmes at Portman Square. "Ryan Price doesn't back them, you know. He just does it to poke the Jockey Club in the eye," he said. I believe Moonface had an opinion, as well.

H Backhouse, Thayer Street, London W1

This is a Ladbrokes now but it used to be H Backhouse and I gave them a minor pasting when Geoff Lewis won a Folkestone seller on Richmond Sturdy's Crazy Horse 30-odd years ago. All bookmakers apart from H Backhouse have beaten me over the years so I nurse considerable affection for them.

You cannot live as I have done without being removed from the payroll now and then and I do enjoy lunch. Funnily enough, though, I left the Jockey Club of my own volition, partly because I was the only gambler there and felt lonely. By the time I went I was making my way further and further up Thayer Street to Marylebone High Street but H Backhouse was perfect. Not only did I win, but it was just beyond the Hellenic Greek restaurant, a favourite luncheon venue. With the Golden Eagle in Marylebone Lane serving Brakspear's it was possible to touch paradise for at least three good reasons and then I met John Watt, which made it four.

John, who died a few years ago, favoured the Hellenic for his Bell's Manager of the Month lunches. If Peter, the owner, had put all the photos of famous football people around the walls he'd have attracted many more customers. John was also PR man for Long John Whisky when they sponsored the European Champion Apprentice Award, won by Richard Quinn many years ago. Fellow Scots, they became firm friends and woe betide H Backhouse if 'Quinny' was on a couple of short-priced favourites. John would look out of the window of the Hellenic and murmur: "We'll have a little double on Richard, shall we?" He is a sad loss but I always raise a glass and cross the road to Ladbrokes or sit quietly in the Golden Eagle, accepting that you couldn't possibly do all these things in the average lunch hour.

William Hill, Shepherd Market, London W1

Between jobs and working as an itinerant board man in the early 1970s, I shared shifts in a Clerkenwell shop with a charming Irishman called Jim, who always backed Commutering in trap 1 at Harringay. He lent me a few books and one of them was *Goodbye Piccadilly, Farewell Leicester Square* by Arthur La Bern, which Alfred Hitchcock turned into *Frenzy*.

I already knew the William Hill shop in Shepherd Market, which features in the book, as does Ye Grapes, an excellent pub nearby. In addition, there was a Turf Newspapers shop presided over by the rudest man in England. In fact, he was so rude people couldn't quite believe it and would go back for a second bash. Sometimes I'd buy a book, sit in Ye Grapes, watch the working girls out of the window (though Shepherd Market is not the red light area it once was), then go and bet in Hill's. I knew a man who was besotted with one of the girls and she was nice to him, but that's as far as it went. I put him in a short story a while back.

I don't think I've ever lost in that Hill's shop. I used to have shares in horses trained by Gavin Pritchard-Gordon with my friend Arno Rudolf and one day a few years ago – a day given over almost entirely to betting, as I recall – I had a tip for one of Julia Feilden's called Don't Drop Bombs in a Brighton amateur riders' race. It won by miles and I believe it was around the three-furlong pole that Arno and I started dancing.

They had a bit of a sense of humour failure, to be honest, but we had a great time. I think I may go there again now.

Coral, Fleet Street, London EC4

During my Exchange Telegraph days in the late 1970s we used the Mecca shop in Fetter Lane but a few years later, whenever I met John Watt in Fleet Street, we used to go to the branch of El Vino by Blackfriars Bridge, so Coral was closer.

Like a lot of places in Fleet Street, it was more fun when the newspapers were there and it was managed by a really nice guy called Ronny Greenfield, who was fairly obviously on the punters' side.

I worked for BBC Radio from 1982 to 1985 and George Hamilton, a fine broadcaster who eventually went back to Ireland, wanted to do a feature on betting for Radio 4 at around the time of the Miss World contest. We pitched up bright and early at Ronny's Coral shop with Ladbrokes' PR chief Ron Pollard along as well because the Magic Sign were closely involved with Miss World at the time.

"I don't understand odds-on. What does it mean?" George said. So Ronny and I explained that a 3/1 on shot meant you were trying to buy money over something that was very likely to happen, though the payout wouldn't be great. Ron listened with interest to this and then said, in that wonderfully lugubrious way of his: "And it still has to win."

It was nice and sunny, the Coral part of the feature was safely in the can so they were happy and the day, a glorious Fleet Street day, lay before me. I said to Ron, "You must have some idea how Miss World will go?"

And in one of those moments that you take with you to the grave, he said: "Miss Venezuela. You should get 8/1. Don't have it with us and I haven't said anything."

I don't think he knew, I just think he was a very good judge. Miss Venezuela won so easily she'd still have made it even if the others hadn't bothered with swimming costumes. There are tips, and then again there are TIPS, aren't there?

TWO SCOOPS FOR THE MISSIONARY MAN
Racing Post July 2012

It's good to see your own looking happy.

Gazing at Jim Old's five mares, each with foal, my daughter Catherine entered another world, an altogether gentler one.

It probably runs in the family because the last time I saw anyone with a similar expression it was my father-in-law (who made it to 97 – never, ever, knock porridge) when Prince Charles came on the box. A vanished England was briefly ours, or his, once more. A devout Cornishman, he once expressed the desire to be up in the hills with his gun when the French brigands came up the Helston river in search of our fish. I said I thought they were more likely to be Spanish but, in his heart, he wanted them to be French.

It's been a good week. Geoff Lester's framed *Sporting Life* account of the 1996 Champion Hurdle is holding up well in Jim's office and the trainer's impression of owner Wally Sturt gets better and better. Not only that, but going to see him came a day after Henry Candy's Picabo won at Yarmouth, which paid for lunch.

My loyalty to the Wantage yard matches that of Richard Phillips, who worked as assistant to Henry and absolutely had to have Lenny The Blade, one of Master Willie's final offspring. Lenny was going to be called Afterglow, by Master Willie out of a mare we owned called Limelight (think about it) but the name was already registered so he became Lenny and eventually won at Newton Abbot before falling, fatally, at Chepstow. He was with Sarah Robinson in Somerset by then.

Richard rejects the suggestion that he bears a passing resemblance to the comedian Michael McIntyre. Well, no one is about to labour the point. On a scale of 1 to 10, where the Hills twins score the maximum, I can't rate Phillips and McIntyre higher than eight, just ahead of Giles Bravery and Dudley Moore. And whilst I may be a dead ringer for McGill, the original *Man in a Suitcase*, that doesn't count because you don't remember the programme anyway.

When Danedream triumphed last week she was the first filly to win the King George since Henry saddled Time Charter in 1983. That was a sad day in other respects because it saw the closure of the old *Sporting Chronicle*, whose principal writer was the late Graham Rock. I never saw him in anything other than a dark lounge suit with the trousers pressed like a man heading for a potentially life-changing interview. He was austere and friendly at the same time, and a fine journalist. Sometimes I think of him and wonder how he'd have reacted to someone calling a chance 'a window of opportunity'. Pain and bafflement in equal measure, perhaps.

Still, you've got to keep up. I think I can work out 'blue-sky thinking', I'm quite au fait with 'pushing the envelope' and I realise that when a politician says something that really gets on his counterpart's nerves, it's 'unhelpful'. I'm nearly there with 'zeitgeist' and I was always ahead of the game where 'vanilla' is concerned.

Vanilla has long been the working girl's term for the most intimate act in the most straightforward way. It would be hard to walk between the Victoria Sporting Club and Paddington Station in the small hours without realising this. But now, like 'marquee', it's reaching a wider audience. Soon, when you're in Pizza Express and it's dessert time, you'll be vaguely worried about asking for vanilla, not merely because it brings a blush to the waitress's cheeks but also because it pigeonholes you as an unadventurous person. (Which you're not, of course.)

It'll reach the betting shops, as well. Mercifully, my bet on Picabo was impressive enough to deflect any adverse comment, but just imagine being the sort of chap who habitually has £2 on the first favourite at 6/4, just to get off to a decent start. You think they're engaging in small talk behind the counter but what they're actually saying is: "Look out, here comes vanilla man." Should you overhear them you'll soon be out of your comfort zone (oops!), writing out Yankees and doubling up on the accumulator. You'll be completely skint, but at least you'll be rum 'n' raisin man.

I'm rather pleased that Glorious Goodwood coincides with the Olympics. Growing older brings little relief, apart from the saving on haircuts, but at least you don't have to feign interest. I hope the cyclists and Jessica Ennis win gold, but otherwise there's nothing to compare with the final perusal of the Stewards' Cup form in the Anglesey Arms at Halnaker.

When the entries for the Wokingham were published, Dandy Nicholls didn't have a horse in the top 40. Perhaps his revival will start at Goodwood with Victoire De Lyphar, or maybe those who backed James Fanshawe's Mac's Power last year will recoup with Hallelujah. Either way, I shall celebrate with an ice cream, trying hard not to notice that the girl is already reaching for one particular tray.

BRIAN, MARVEL AND DORIS – WINNERS ALL
Racing Post November 2017

"In the end, the age gap becomes frighteningly obvious," Marvel Mason says. "We should be grateful for racing and football because at least we can have a conversation. Otherwise young people might as well be aliens, don't you think?"

Well, I've never really thought of it like that but I suppose he has a point. We old-timers have our uses, though. There are three aliens playing the quiz machine in the Ring O' Bells in Nailsea and things seem to be going quite well although, as we know, it all speeds up when any sort of payout looks possible. "National Service!" one of them shouts over his shoulder. "Started off at two years, yes?"

"Eighteen months!" Marvel replies. "Became two years just before the Korean War." They believe him and survive by a second or two but the next tricky question flattens them because it was Danny Williams, not Andy, who had the original UK number one hit with 'Moon River' from *Breakfast at Tiffany's*.

"We could have won this, you know," Marvel says.

"Hmm. You knew the odd one out in the Kaiser Chiefs and Chumbawamba question, did you?"

Brian Hilton smiles. Eighty-two and possibly anaemic, this morning he was going to have an exploratory tube inserted where the sun don't shine but they changed their minds, probably because he's not strong enough for an operation in any case. He writes everything down following a stroke six years ago but the verbs seem to be missing.

"How are you, Brian?" Marvel says.

There is a long pause and much scribbling, followed by a couple of crossings-out. Finally he holds up the paper.

"No bum," it says.

Marvel, one of the nicest and most generous people I've ever met, is straight up and on his way to the bar for a large Captain Morgan but I tell him that Brian does indeed mean bum, not rum. We settle back and sip our Jameson's, a nasty head cold threatening to spoil Marvel's afternoon until Hard

Bought just gets up in the handicap hurdle at Thurles. This follows Martello Tower, Boom The Groom, Silviniaco Conti and Lancelot Du Lac. I've known him since he exchanged comics on Saturday mornings over 50 years ago and I could never have predicted a remarkable run like this. It's been going on for the better part of 18 months and there may well be hope for us all.

A large Jameson's Irish Whiskey, no ice, will dry up a head cold. As for an upset stomach, port and brandy in a two-to-one ratio will work the oracle, something I've known since working in Harlow New Town, where many of the pubs are named after moths and butterflies – the Willow Beauty, the Essex Skipper, the Poplar Kitten and so on.

No matter what anyone tells you, nothing cures a hangover except rest. A can of Tennent's Super lager followed by a large Hennessy will encourage the belief that you can write like Fitzgerald, ride like McCoy and make love like Errol Flynn, always supposing you can find someone at lunchtime, but there are no guarantees and the hangover will return in spades.

"The accordionist outside Waitrose has taken your advice," Marvel says. "He's doing a selection from *Oklahoma!* – 'Out of my Dreams' and the rest of it. 'Out of my Dreams' is perfect, just as you said. Before Christmas I told him to put everything on Silviniaco Conti but he probably doesn't bet. Let's face it, we'd struggle to do justice to 'Somewhere Over the Rainbow' if we'd just gone down the tubes. Did you back Martello Tower at Limerick, by the way?"

Well, I did, as a matter of fact, though I'm a sentimental gambler these days and I remembered an old horse called Martello Pirate trained by Richmond Sturdy, while there was something about the name that reminded me of James Joyce. There were originally 15 Martello towers guarding the short stretch of coast between Dublin and Bray and in *Ulysses*

Joyce has Stephen Dedalus renting the Sandycove one.

He also stayed there himself for a few days and *Ulysses* itself opens with a scene in the tower. Joyce shifted the date to 16 June, the day he first walked out with Nora Barnacle in Ringsend. I hasten to add that Marvel is more of a pragmatist and simply thought that, if it came to a tight finish in a three-runner race, Martello Tower was cracking value at 5/2. He was quite right, too, as his selection rallied gamely to beat Outlander by a neck.

A roar goes up around the quiz machine where quite a crowd has gathered. 'Que Sera, Sera' and the 1956 Oscar for best song are mentioned, which has Brian reaching for his pen and paper. Amidst a sea of smudges, crosses and arrows two words stand out quite clearly.

"I tell you, Brian, any day that starts with a cancelled probe in the dark and ends with Doris Day has to be pretty special," Marvel says. "God bless."

SPINNING A MIDWINTER YARN
Racing Post December 2012

December has always been kind to me.

I'm not saying there have been all that many winners but there are some happy memories – Halloween winning the King George, Bill O'Gorman's African Chimes obliging on the all-weather on a regular basis, Spunyarn turning up at Saint-Cloud. It's also the month of the Horserace Writers and Photographers Association annual lunch in London but I shall not dwell on this extended jamboree beyond saying that I have seen the Christmas lights in Bridgend.

Today, 2 December, is the anniversary of Spunyarn's triumph in France. It's only afterwards that you realise how certain something must have been. I didn't know Flat racing went on that long but Bill Wightman had it all worked out and even booked Yves Saint-Martin. Trying to get on at pari-mutuel odds (20/1) wasn't the easiest of tasks in 1967 but I managed it all right to some hopelessly inadequate stake.

I was only six but already fully engaged when Bill's Halloween won his second King George VI Chase. I never had enough on the winners, even in those days. More recently, when Scotch Imp, Glencroft and Chaplin's Club all won (at different courses) on the same day for David Chapman, I omitted to take a morning price about the last one, Chaplin's Club at Haydock, and watched as he went from 7/2 to 5/2 in one go. I must say I'd never seen that before and it was fascinating in a way; fascinating but quite painful. I was working at SIS and we had champagne. In theory we weren't supposed to bet, of course. I ask you.

Halloween in 1954 remains my favourite King George although Burrough Hill Lad beating Combs Ditch in 1984 was quite something. That was in my BBC Radio days and I drove from my parents-in-laws' place in Cornwall to Kempton. It was a proper Christmas that year, with snow on the ground and all the West Country meetings called off but Kempton survived.

It turned into the kind of race that would attract outsiders to the sport, even though there were only three runners. Burrough Hill Lad won by about an inch with John Francome at his very best. I happened to leave the course with John, Jenny Pitman and David Elsworth, who thought Colin Brown might have forced the issue the other way. John did not dismiss this out of hand but explained, in that amiable way of his, why things had worked out the way they did. It was principally about Burrough Hill Lad meeting the last fence perfectly and finding his stride a fraction of a second quicker. It was an enthralling battle.

Boxing Night is just about the perfect time to drive across London. Even if I weren't a sucker for Christmas I'd enjoy the lights with plenty of time to take everything in, though finding somewhere open for a drink wasn't all that straightforward in 1984. From Kempton you could be in Earl's Court quite quickly and I rented a tiny bedsit there in 1970 but everything had changed. I believe there used to be a dungeon where you wore a rubber mask and paid extra to be locked in a cupboard but that was no good if you only wanted a beer.

All the pubs around the BBC in Portland Place were closed, including the Stag's Head, one of Dylan Thomas's old haunts. I noticed the other day that the BHA had spotted and rejected the name Llareggub, the fictitious village in *Under Milk Wood* which, read backwards, gives you some idea of what went on there.

We're lucky the original copy, indeed at that stage the only copy, of his masterpiece survived because Thomas lost it during a monumental pub crawl. Fortunately a particularly determined BBC producer, Douglas Cleverdon, set about retracing the poet's steps and located the script in the York Minster, later The French House, on Old Compton Street. The Admiral Duncan staked a rival claim but this was probably wishful thinking. As a thriving gay bar, it became famous for much more sinister reasons when nail-bombed in 1999.

In the end I settled for the Horse and Groom in Hampstead, which has gone now. There was a barman there who bore a more than passing resemblance to Robert Redford and, I swear, was every bit as good-looking. It turned out he rode on the other bus, though, and I don't know when I've seen women look so disappointed.

No I don't.

LET THE TRAIN TAKE THE STRAIN
Sporting Life December 1994

It began with Party Politics and ended with a small game of blackjack, though not on the same day.

In between there was Dublin, Danoli, somewhere called the Irish Whiskey Corner and a long time in the air over Heathrow when I thought the engines had given up.

At Chepstow I stood between Master Oats and Party Politics after the Rehearsal Chase. Perhaps Master Oats will confirm the form in the Coral Welsh National, but to be close to Party Politics is to understand what makes steeplechasing such a compelling spectacle.

A great big tank of a horse, it's surprising the others turn up when they know he's coming. To my untutored eye, he blew a good deal harder than Master Oats and will be 4lb better off next time. He has at least one unconditional supporter.

Party Politics

It must often seem to readers that sportswriters float along on a wave of hospitality; a tidal wave in some cases and I have to plead guilty. But a typical Irish welcome contains all the temptations which may later be listed under 'mitigating circumstances'.

The reception and dinner at the Whiskey Corner included a tribute and presentation to Peter O'Sullevan before cabaret performed by a very talented harpist. She said at one point that she was 'going to stay with Andrew Lloyd Webber ...' By golly, the list is endless.

The coach journey from the hotel to Leopardstown the following morning was long enough to prompt thoughts of a restorative glass or two. Then, glancing up from the Sunday paper, I saw a lime-green train. There is so much of Ireland that is unfamiliar to me but one day I shall ride on the lime-green train and find out where it ends up.

Sunday was for Fairyhouse and a magnificent day's sport. The huge crowd had some to see Danoli and he was not about to let anyone down. Just as impressive was Sound Man, who put in a scintillating round in the Drinmore Novices' Chase and ran the opposition ragged. Cheltenham will exert its magnetic pull.

At certain times in my life, a very agreeable form of tiredness has made it seem perfectly reasonable to eschew routine tasks. On the early-morning flight from Dublin on Monday I should have studied the *Guardian*'s Media section to check the jobs. I couldn't face it, though, and settled instead for *The Irish Times*' sports supplement, where I learned that Sligo Rovers had remained unbeaten.

When we were in the air all that time over Heathrow I thought of making a will or working out the Ludlow seller. But we came down eventually and embarked upon one of those stimulating dashes along the M4 where the cabbie very nearly keeps the meter in constant motion. (I am not exaggerating here.)

The destination was the Royal Lancaster Hotel for the Horserace Writers Awards luncheon and naturally I was delighted that Alastair Down won and David Ashforth finished in the frame. Mind you, according to the official brochure, a heck of a lot of journalists attracted votes from somewhere or other. Indeed, the man on the *Nailsea Mercury* was quite miffed at being left out.

It seemed strange, visiting The Victoria, off Bayswater Road, BEFORE playing blackjack. It's one of those friendly hostelries with benches and trestle tables outside and I have been known to avail myself of the facilities when charting a similar course from the opposite direction.

But there were no problems on Monday. Accompanied by a good friend from SIS, I reached the target (oh, all right then, £300) and stopped.

My companion was stunned by this wholly unfamiliar restraint; another of the great form-book certainties overturned. The truth is, I couldn't bear to lose after such a fantastic couple of days.

Although it is inconceivable that I am becoming canny at this late stage, I decided to analyse everything fully on the last rattler home. But I fell asleep and dreamed of Jameson's 15-year-old, and Danoli, and Ireland, and the lime-green train going all the way to Sligo, just in time to see the Rovers.

A LONG NIGHT'S JOURNEY INTO DAY
Racing Post November 2012

They must sit over breakfast at Oliver Sherwood's and marvel at how clever their owners are. Or maybe it was the breeder Kenneth Parkhill who named Puffin Billy, by Heron Island out of Downtown Train. You will know that Puffing Billy was one of the first steam trains, built by William Hedley almost exactly 200 years ago.

'Downtown Train' was recorded by Rod Stewart after Tom Waits. Rod was crying after a recent Celtic match and I can't see anything wrong with that. I cry most weeks, sometimes during as well as after. As for classic Italian films, well, I'm damp-eyed in *Bicycle Thieves* when that chap has his bike nicked and his little boy looks up at him, wondering what the future holds, and I'm all over the place at the end of *Rocco and His Brothers*.

I've had a couple of winners lately, though. St Moritz at Nottingham came in handy and Morandi at Longchamp, though that was a month ago. I remember paying in, a novelty in itself, at a branch of the Royal Bank of Scotland near Fleet Street and it was very dark in there until a rather beautiful girl, possibly Iranian or Iraqi, flicked a switch.

"It is better for you with the light on, yes?" she said.

Well, I doubt that eyesight would be the main problem but it's nice to be reminded of the old questions so I just smiled and said thank you. Coming out of the branch I had an idea for the wee small hours, which is important because I'm running out of lists and sleep does not come easily.

I was pretty certain I could name all the pubs on Fleet Street itself but I decided to include betting offices and hostelries on Farringdon Road, all the way up to King's Cross. Obviously a man would need a livener in the Betsey Trotwood before researching the task and I have never felt any guilt over small rewards, especially when the day is still young. Betsey appears in *David Copperfield* and there must be areas of London where, even now, Dickens could come back and knock off a novel in a month or two but Clerkenwell would be unrecognisable to him.

The main reason I struggle with the idea of an afterlife is that I think it would go on too long and we'd be bored. I have lots of other reasons as well, but that's the main one. I only mention it because the other night, lying awake and trying to remember the sequence of betting shops in King's Cross itself, I actually fell asleep before 4am and had a strange dream.

For a start, heaven (or wherever) was at ground level and you had to go over a strip of coconut matting, as you do at Sandown and Ludlow. Then there was a door and when you entered all you could hear was Gorecki's 'Symphony of Sorrowful Songs', so naturally you'd fear the worst, but if you punched in a certain code you could have 'Blue Skies' by Irving Berlin instead.

The worrying thing was that it all seemed so routine. There was a tired-looking man, a bit like the Wizard of Oz, behind a desk supporting a huge book of loose-leaf pages.

"Oh, hello," he said. "This is your book. Everything you've ever done. It means you get over all the embarrassment on the first day. If I say we've had a bit of a laugh you mustn't take it personally. See these little golden stars? They're your winners. The glowing red dots are horses that didn't really feel like it on the day – not your fault, of course – and the shiny blue squares are those that were, um, how should we put it, 'not busy'. Does that make sense? You can rifle through if you want but I must warn you the blue ones can hurt your eyes. Take as long as you need and then off you go, through that little door over there."

"Are there any films?" I said.

"Yes indeed. The Old Man is very fond of *It's a Wonderful Life* and has it on all the time. He quite likes the idea of the two worlds coming together. And *Ghost*, that's another favourite."

"For the same reason?"

"No, he's just a big fan of the Righteous Brothers. Now you must excuse me; we're very busy today."

At which point I woke up sweating, my eyeballs on fire. All those blue squares, obviously. Yogi my bearded collie was barking for his wee so I sat on the front step and watched him. He is so old now I must stick around to look after him. He ambled back in and inclined his head, the way they do, as if to say, is everything all right? And I said: "Yes, of course."

Nothing but blue skies.

OF VICARS AND TATTERDEMALIONS
Racing Post July 2016

I do miss London, though I suppose the late nights had to come to an end.

During the Marylebone High Street years I sometimes found myself at the poker table in the Victoria Sporting Club. One night the players included not only a vicar but a brothel keeper from Penge, who relaxed over a hand of seven-card stud when the day's work was done. I gave the vicar, a player sadly lacking in divine inspiration, a lift back to Huntingdon when we emerged from the casino at 4am but the brothel keeper had his own car. Quite a smart one, I seem to recall.

A while back there was an excellent piece by Nicholas Lezard in the *New Statesman*, quoting from someone called Richard of Devizes, who gave his name not to a vulgar (though very funny) limerick but a series of travel pamphlets. He found in London 'stage players, buffoons, lewd musical girls, lustful persons, fortune tellers, nightly strollers, magicians, mimics, common beggars and tatterdemalions'. No, me neither, but it's a wonderful word.

'So (Richard goes on) if you do not wish to live with the shameful, you will not dwell in London.' He doesn't divulge his own tastes, though personally I wouldn't want to live in a city, or a world, without lewd musical girls or the occasional nightly stroller.

There's something about a well-turned-out vicar, as well. A while back there was a whole platoon of them in The Chase hotel opposite the grandstand on the Knavesmire. It was called The Chase in those days but it's something else now.

I made the mistake of referring to them in print as 'parsons' and received a charming letter from Ireland, pointing out that 'we were not parsons, but vicars fifty'. I wrote back, expressing the hope that they backed winners plenty, though I think they were there for a vicars' convention and missed the Ebor. It was still a very special race then, of course, not just another big handicap in the middle of a tumultuous Saturday.

I shall miss it myself this year, my elder daughter having produced a third grandson in Calgary. I believe the turf course may be open now, alongside the harness racing track. Meanwhile I continue to bring up our granddaughter from the Shanghai branch and at seven she is now word-perfect in 'Knees Up Mother Brown' in readiness for her first home game at St Mary's. A man cannot do more than that and the silence from her teachers across the road is clearly down to grudging admiration. It's perfectly understandable.

To alleviate financial worries there should be more competitions with cash prizes. On Radio 3 the other day they played a few bars of a piece and asked you to identify the film it came from.

And the thing is, quite a lot of Radio 3 listeners wouldn't know that 'Rhapsody in Blue' by George Gershwin opens Woody Allen's *Manhattan*, so I'd have been 7/2 from 100/8 before you could say knife. But in these ultra-correct days we're expected to play for fun. For fun! Not: 'Go on then, £500 for the first person to ring up with the correct answer' – on a premium rate number, of course. For fun. I ask you. Even when I was 13 and running a sweepstake on the Wokingham it wasn't for fun; it was for a huge pile of sixpences. You remember sixpences.

I did make money over Gershwin once, though. Well, sort of. About 30 years ago he ran in a Chepstow handicap alongside stable companion Commander Meaden, who was the better-handicapped of the pair (I knew them both like the brothers I haven't got) and won at 20/1.

Running two in run-of-the mill handicaps has always fascinated me. A few summers ago I rang Malcolm Saunders to ask about Matterofact in a Goodwood apprentices' race. "Actually, the other one isn't bad," he murmured. 'The other one' was Crimson Fern, who hacked up at 8/1. She turned out to be pretty useful; I only mention it because her boy Titus Secret won easily at Bath on Wednesday.

I told David Ashforth all about Titus Secret on the way to Brighton the day before, but 2/1 favourite is not really his, or my, sort of price these days. Mind you, there was a time when we'd have been counting down the hours to Bath and we'd have been in like, well, in like Flynn I suppose.

Now, there was a man. Good old Errol. Legendary womaniser, gambler, brawler and, if only I knew what it was, a hell of a tatterdemalion, too.

ALBERTS HERE, ALBERTS THERE ...
Racing Post January 2018

I've been fond of quite a few Alberts.

Albert Finney, Albert McCann, Albert Stubbins, Able Albert, Albert Argyle, Albert Davison ... the list goes on.

Some of them have won me money. That was true of Able Albert in the 1984 Ayr Gold Cup, though the payout would have been quite something if Alakh and Pat Eddery had held on. Albert McCann was a hard-working Portsmouth inside forward with the bandiest legs you ever saw, his appearance in Southampton v Pompey matches invariably prompting enquiries as to the whereabouts of his horse. I backed the draw when he scored a memorable equaliser at The Dell in 1965.

It's hard to make money over the Liverpool centre-forward Albert Stubbins, unless you risk asking people what he has in common with Oscar Wilde, Marlon Brando and Marilyn Monroe. If they happen to know he's on the cover of the Beatles' *Sgt. Pepper* LP – the only footballer – you've given a few quid back. (Nothing new in that, of course.)

The weights for the Grand National were announced at Abbey Road Studios two or three years ago. Needless to say, there are many Beatles pictures around the walls, together with a large photograph of Fred Astaire. The other day I was reading about someone who had 'Cheek to Cheek' played at their funeral. It's a nice touch – 'Heaven, I'm in heaven' is the opening line – and well worth considering when the big day comes, or a few days before, perhaps.

Albert Quixall was the perfect example of a big fish finding things tricky in an even bigger pool. A leading light for Sheffield Wednesday, he joined Manchester United in the aftermath of Munich and performed well enough for them but was eventually overshadowed by the likes of Law, Charlton and Crerand. Even so, he picked up an FA Cup winners' medal in 1963 before moving on to Oldham.

The fictional Albert Argyle was a tally-boy (hire-purchase collector) in Jack Trevor Story's *Live Now, Pay Later* trilogy, played to perfection in the film version by Ian Hendry. It was a different world, needless to say, England in the late fifties and early sixties, all twitching curtains in suburbia and absolute silence when the tally-boy rang the bell. Albert generally found a way to keep everyone happy, though. The last in the trilogy is entitled *The Urban District Lover*.

I'm not saying I back horses for purely sentimental reasons, though Zoe Davison's Georgieshore at Leicester on Tuesday proved irresistible. The venue was significant because it was here that Zoe's father Albert – a scallywag, an unspeakable rascal or a supremely clever operator, depending on your point of view – landed a monumental touch with Great Things on Boxing Day, 1978.

It was the classic set-up: everything worked out in minute detail on one of the busiest racing days of the year.

"Dad ran two in the race and Great Things, who went off at 33/1, was ridden by Richard Rowe," Zoe said. "They hammered the other one, which wasn't 'off', of course, while Great Things was backed all over Ireland. The bookmakers weren't happy but paid out. The coup was worth six figures, a great deal of money in those days, but Mum and I never saw a penny of it."

Quite understandably, Zoe Davison has always distanced herself from her father and his activities. He was eventually warned off for six years in 1998 over his part in the victory of Will I Fly (at Leicester) four years earlier, the horse having won a claiming hurdle when officially trained by Anne Jermy in Wiltshire, though it seems highly unlikely that he ever left Davison's Caterham base.

Albert owed HM Revenue & Customs £2m when he died in 2011. They settled for £850,000 and his ex-wife Penny Ann managed to have her divorce settlement increased to £970,000. It's not bad, when you consider Albert concentrated on Leicester sellers and claimers. "I found him to be a charming rogue. I liked him," a divorce judge once said. "However, he told me many untruths."

"And the cares that hung around me through the week, seem to vanish like a gambler's lucky streak," Fred continues in 'Cheek to Cheek'.

Something tells me Albert never relied too much on luck.

SENSIBLE PUNTING AT EASTER
Racing Post April 2014

I can just about persuade people that football teams used to play three games in four days over Christmas – West Ham 2 Blackburn 8 and Blackburn 1 West Ham 3 just 24 hours later lingers in the memory – but they won't quite have 'Additional Runner' and I always resisted the temptation to give them John McCririck's phone number for confirmation.

Nowadays we're lucky if newspapers print all the cards but there was a time when they printed them without the winner. So you bought the *Southampton Echo*, turned it on its side for the late results in the stop press and there was this 20/1 shot – an interloper, there's no other word for it – with 'Additional Runner' in brackets after its name. Yours was probably second. In my early teens I believed in justice, fairness, that sort of thing; small wonder I very nearly became a cynic.

All right, a few other things have happened since and I'm not saying it was all down to Additional Runner but a man deserves a better start in life.

At least I'm not surprised by anything. Racing on Good Friday was bound to come about eventually and I have no strong opinion on that, though I remember when the only sound you heard on Good Friday morning was the Salvation Army band a few streets away and it was hard to buy anything more exotic than a box of matches.

It was a long day, but you knew they raced just about everywhere on Saturday and Easter Monday, the chubby-cheeked David East (nothing else about him was chubby) would be getting up on something for Herbert Blagrave off 7st 7lb at Kempton and Portsmouth staged two greyhound meetings, lunchtime and evening.

It was paradise, apart from the results, and the prices were set in stone. 100/6 was precisely that; there was something magical about it and you never worried about finding anything better because it didn't exist, just as you didn't think about jockeys' Christian names – they were just these tiny chaps R Reader, S Millbanks and L C Parkes, who were all very dangerous off 7st 7lb and seldom turned up in the same race.

I tried to pay for Easter this year with a solid each-way bet on Es Que Love, runner-up in the Abernant at Newmarket on Thursday. 9/1 was all right, unless you happened to be in The Barn at Nailsea, where the Chablis, very good, costs £6.70 for a large glass. This eclipsed my previous pub record, beating the George in Mortimer Street W1 with something to spare.

The George used to have a photo of the BBC football commentator Peter Jones on the door and I once stood next to Captain Sensible in the gents'. More of an Ella Fitzgerald and Frank Sinatra man, I must say the punk era passed me by, though the Captain seemed a perfectly reasonable sort of fellow. I remember he came to Cambridge and was holding court in a pub frequented by well-to-do hoorays who thought of themselves as authors and punters.

As I recall, he was merely passing an opinion on the line-up of the Soft Machine or some other people I didn't know when the owner came up and threw him out. I thought this rather heavy-handed, even allowing for the fact that the Captain was wearing a dress, a fetching tutu if memory serves. You wouldn't get away with that today. (Throwing him out, that is; no problem with the dress.)

The Cambridge days came and went all too quickly. I suppose one race at Newmarket stands out from all the others and that was Creek Alley bolting up in a multi-runner three-year-old maiden in the hands of Duncan Keith. The strange thing was, Peter Walwyn was just starting to send out a lot of winners, yet Creek Alley attracted hardly a shilling and paid £36.17s 6d on the Tote. That was just over 180/1 and meant a term's bar bills wiped out in one hit.

I was sorry to read about Duncan's passing. He was a very good judge of pace and should probably have added to Niksar's 2000 Guineas triumph in 1965 but thyroid gland trouble cost him the ride on Humble Duty in the 1000 in 1970. One of his very best front-running efforts for trainer Walter Nightingall came on Sir Winston Churchill's High Hat, who made all to deny the brilliant Petite Etoile in the Aly Khan Memorial Gold Cup at Kempton Park.

Remarkably, he started off by grooming carthorses in the Gorbals district of Glasgow and apprenticeships do not come much harder than that. Anyway, it impressed me and I backed many of his winners. Not only that, they all appeared in the morning papers.

STILL CALLING 'EM HOME IN LYME REGIS
Racing Post March 2015

I have yet to meet anyone who lost at Cheltenham.

Normally one takes the stories with a pinch of salt, never losing sight of the fact that gamblers tend to lose ten units, win seven back and miraculously break even, but most of my friends named quite a few winners beforehand. I even helped in a small way by advising a saver Yankee with Glens Melody taking the place of Annie Power in the Mares' Hurdle.

Of course, the latter was in the process of hacking up when coming to grief, but a £10 Yankee at 2/1, 4/6, 4/5 and 6/1 is half decent and Archie also had three doubles and a treble in his £40 one. Pity about Annie Power.

"I think he has a bottle of champagne for you," old Arthur Sears said.

"You can help me drink it. It'll make up for that terrible brandy I ordered when we were all coughing a while back. 'Distilled from iron filings in a factory somewhere along the Ruhr Valley,' is that right? You haven't lost your touch, Arthur."

"Well, not bad for 91," the old advertising man smiled, tilting his glass of fino sherry to catch the sunlight.

"I can't imagine going a single day without this, half a bottle of burgundy and a glance at the horses," he said. "I love that old Kingsley Amis line, 'No pleasure is worth giving up for the sake of two more years in a geriatric home at Weston-super-Mare.' I worked with him on one or two promotions, you know. He didn't know I lived in Weston! Anyway, they can carry me out of my own place, now that I've got this far."

Arthur backs cleverly named horses but it was a quiet Cheltenham for him, though Glens Melody is out of an Orchestra mare.

More prosaically, I settled for Faugheen and a bottle of Chablis. Champion Hurdle day is my favourite because everything is still fresh on the opening day and there have been few, if any, setbacks. I have only fond memories apart from the morning – Make A Stand's year, I think – when I took part in a local radio phone-in with a man of the cloth who was railing against all forms of gambling. Very gently, I reminded him that Jesus chastised the man who buried his talents in the ground but was all for the chap who went out to speculate and accumulate. There's no point in having all these books if you don't read them. I wasn't invited back for a couple of years.

Morley Street is a favourite memory, partly because of Raleigh Gilbert's course commentary. Raleigh can see Morley Street winning from some way out and is calling him home for all money, as Aussie Jim McGrath might say, only for the horse and Jimmy Frost to bear sharply towards the stands' rails. He's still going to win (probably) but Raleigh has to drop an octave and start the build-up all over again. I liked him very much. He was an old Africa hand, a bit lonely, I'd say, but a proper gent.

So was John Tyrrel, who broadcast the betting and results on Channel 4 many years ago. Wandering through the Guinness Village (not sure about the 'village' bit) on Champion Chase day I thought about him because the horse racing game, where you roll balls towards a series of holes and your horse moves forwards on a big board according to your success rate, has gone. It's a pity because it was run by a proper circus barker and attracted countless punters as well as the television cameras.

I only mention it because John carried on broadcasting long after his death some 20 years ago. In seaside fairgrounds up and down the country he announced the winner and the odds following every running of 'The Derby', his voice going out on a (by now) warped, looping tape. So, even though he was buried in Newmarket, his daughter Rebecca could take the children to listen to him in Lyme Regis and have their photograph taken alongside the booth where he operated. Rebecca wrote a lovely piece about it in the *Independent* several years ago.

"You should do it," Arthur said. "Just think, your voice could be booming out everywhere from Selsey Bill to Clacton."

"But not the Ruhr Valley?"

"Let's not run before we can walk," he said.

Part Three

A November Sort Of Person

There is no gainsaying the fact that Cambridge came and went all too quickly. Eric Eldin and Gaykart inches too good for Lester on Pretty Puffin and a handsome payout. The bus from Newmarket back to Cambridge in the fading light, Cherry Hinton shop girls, Parker's Piece in darkness, penny for the guy, mister, the gas fire, Proust and La Rochefoucauld. They fought a losing battle with racing for nearly 50 years but never quite gave up.

Gaykart warmed a bitterly cold day, the sort of day when you're ready for the jumps – the Mackeson, the Hennessy and, in my case, another birthday in between the pair. All three events seem to occupy their familiar November slot, though it would be inaccurate to say that nothing has changed. Guy Fawkes (something of a scapegoat really, a lookout man left behind by the others and by no means a leading player in the plot to blow up the Houses of Parliament) attracts less attention than Halloween these days and there have already been several valuable steeplechases by the time they line up for what used to be the Mackeson.

By sharp contrast it was warm enough but very wet when Bill Elsey's Galosh and Sandy Barclay led turning for home over a mile and a half at the Craven meeting in 1969. He 'turned' because in those days they still had the round, two-mile Sefton Course which rejoined the Rowley Mile just under four furlongs from home. When it closed they told us it was to encourage a healthier covering of grass. It must be growing very slowly. Given the conditions, Galosh was a highly appropriate winner and Barclay rode a finely judged race from in front. Yellow colours, I seem to recall. Yellow colours, the Turk's Head on Trinity Street in Cambridge, the early-evening pint, the voices drifting across from King's, the reassuring rustle of pound notes.

There was also Peter Walwyn's Creek Alley and the day after the Craven when I couldn't bear missing Newbury and travelled to Berkshire on the train. Why spend the day studying *Tartuffe* when you can see Willie Carson winning on him at 100/6?

Years later the thought occurred that I might go back and turn an ordinary second-class degree into a first (perhaps) because I certainly knew a heck of a lot more about Proust by then, but there are regrets you have to live with. It took me too long to appreciate Cambridge and then my dad died in the week of my finals and everything changed.

Not that 1970 was all gloom. There was the little matter of Lester and Richmond Sturdy winning the Ebor with Tintagel II, who was probably a certainty. (We still believe in certainties at 21, yes?) Then the trainee job at the Jockey Club and a rather longer one in the wine trade with Gilbey's, followed by a brief South American adventure with the Stanley Gibbons stamp people. And all the while my thoughts drifted back to Marylebone High Street, Import and sundry other characters, both human and equine …

AN ITALIAN ADVENTURE

Racing Post January 2012

A 200/1 winner turns up – Lights Of Broadway on Monday – and you're bound to think of the times you came close to something similar yourself.

When Creek Alley won at Newmarket and paid just over 180/1 on the Tote, I thought Peter Walwyn should have been awarded an MBE there and then. I don't know why he had to wait so long for his achievements to be recognised whereas the actor Harry Fowler, who passed on a few days ago, was honoured as long ago as 1970.

In *Lawrence of Arabia*, Harry holds a naked flame to his bare arm, having watched Peter O'Toole do the same without flinching.

"Ooh, it damn well hurts!" he cries.

"Certainly it hurts," O'Toole agrees.

"What's the trick, then?"

"The trick, William Potter, is NOT MINDING that it hurts."

Which may well be the way lifelong gamblers come to view things in the end. It's also why, a few years ago, I called a modest collection of anecdotes *Not Minding That It Hurts*.

Young Albie, who must be about 66 now, would have celebrated Lights Of Broadway's victory with a couple of show-stoppers from the old days. His dad did a mean version of Al Bowlly's 'The Very Thought of You' in the Mecca shop in Paddington Street, W1. My own view, which I kept strictly to myself, was that a popular song here and there was unlikely to make much difference to the overall profit and loss account of the regulars but people can be funny sometimes and the management ended up having a quiet word with old Albie.

The Mecca became a William Hill and then disappeared, like the Ladbrokes in Mortimer Street not far away. This outlet was way before its time, a subterranean paradise with armchairs, drinks and counter staff who were not hostesses exactly, because you have to be very careful with a word like that, but certainly very charming. It didn't last long, needless to say, because there was no masochists' corner, nowhere for people to berate the stewards and jockeys. A man cannot complain properly sitting down, so everyone decamped to the shop in Great Portland Street, a Ladbrokes which has stood the test of time.

I was lying awake the other night, thinking about funeral music, some Brahms and 'I Apologise' by Billy Eckstine, perhaps, though you could ring the changes. I bet no one has ever thought of having their favourite racing commentary – "the mare's beginning to get up!" – instead of music. Or you could pre-record a final message so that just when everyone is looking forward to the Côtes du Rhône and salmon sandwiches and the staff are getting 'My Way' ready for the next chap, your face would come up on the wall and you'd say, with a wry smile, "I knew it would end like this."

People will never tolerate music in betting shops but I'd have said that about films in Italian restaurants until I went into a Pizza Express in Bristol the other night. On a large screen they were showing an old black-and-white picture with subtitles but no volume. After a while I worked out that it was *L'Avventura* with Monica Vitti, who went on to play Modesty Blaise. Unable to believe this, just as I can't believe there are virtual bike races we can bet on, or that Deauville starts just after breakfast, I went back a couple of nights later and *L'Avventura* was on again.

No one was paying the slightest attention but it struck me as a nice idea. I don't know if they're doing it throughout the chain or how often they change the programme, but I can see one or two problems. *Rocco and His Brothers* is just about the saddest film I've ever seen and I'd sit there transfixed, but it's no good if it's putting people off their Sloppy Giuseppe and special offer dessert. As for *Death in Venice*, with Dirk Bogarde mournfully eyeing young Björn Andrésen in his sailor suit, I think that might be the end of it.

The Adagietto from Mahler's 5th Symphony is used extensively in *Death in Venice*. It wouldn't do much for the atmosphere in Pizza Express but it's more or less perfect when you've had a bad day followed by a bad night. You can also use the snippets from Mozart's *Cosi Fan Tutte* in *Sunday Bloody Sunday* or simply put on a DVD of *Broken Flowers*, because the way Bill Murray acts is exactly the way you feel. Then you can listen to 'Her' by Stan Getz and it'll nearly be time for the first at Deauville.

Yesterday's results? Pah! A mere bagatelle. Just one of those things. "A trip to the moon on gossamer wings," as old Albie would undoubtedly have said. That's why he had to go.

FROM FRITH STREET TO MICHELDEVER
Racing Post May 2015

Of course, you need somewhere to prepare and somewhere to celebrate. Frith Street in Soho was always the starting point for Sandown, the Pope's Grotto in Twickenham lies within easy reach of Kempton and a winner or two at Pompey dogs invariably justified a visit to the Harbour Lights pub on the way home.

Frith Street was, and is, full of stories though it was even better when Ronnie Scott was still alive. Somehow he kept his famous jazz club going through the lean years. "When

I die, I want to be cremated and have my ashes scattered over my accountant," lives on in the memory, though my favourite, aimed at an unresponsive audience, went: "All right, let's all join hands and try to contact the living." He was a fine saxophonist and played the solo on the Beatles' 'Lady Madonna', but when gum disease claimed him and there was no prospect of playing any more, he quietly faded away.

Quite a few famous people lived on Frith Street – the young Mozart, at number 20 for a year or so from 1764, Samuel Taylor Coleridge, John Constable and William Hazlitt, while John Logie Baird transmitted the first television pictures from his workshop at number 22.

In the days when Mountain Call and D'Urberville were engaged in their fascinating battle for sprint championship honours, we'd drink coffee in the Bar Italia at the same address, number 22, before taking the rattler to Sandown. 'There's only one place we can go, It's around the corner in Soho, where other broken people go' – 'Bar Italia' by Pulp in 1995.

There weren't too many broken people there when I interviewed poker professional Barny Boatman. Just any number of mirrors and pictures of boxers all around the walls. Bar Italia was the most famous of the coffee bars but it faced competition from Moka in the early days. Moka introduced the first Gaggia machine, a jet of hot water supposedly producing a more satisfying drink, so Frith Street briefly became Froth Street. Sadly the bar couldn't quite stand the pace and became a pawnbroker's.

The place to celebrate in Cambridge after a successful trip to Newmarket was the Turk's Head, opposite King's. With the choir sometimes practising in the background and a winner or two still fresh in the memory, it was the ideal watering hole. There was orange fluorescent lighting in my day, similar to the Hansom Cab in Earl's Court. They had something in common: striking up a conversation with complete strangers was perfectly straightforward; I think that's the best way of putting it.

Everyone thinks the Harbour Lights was named after the song but in fact the composer Wilhelm Grosz, an Austrian fleeing the Nazis, took his inspiration from the name in lights over the pub. They were good days. We used to drink something called a Mann's Boiler, which was Watney's bitter perked up with a bottle of Mann's Brown Ale. Stewardess was the best greyhound at the track and did us many favours.

I realised the other day how much I want to live in Micheldever. Not that there is anything wrong with Nailsea, far from it, indeed the accordionist has added 'Besame Mucho' to his repertoire and I was thinking what a coup it would be to get Andrea Bocelli over to sing it outside Waitrose.

But Micheldever! All those condemned carriages from my youth, line upon line of them with the fateful cross, never to see Berrylands or Woking again. Who could fail to be moved by that? I remember it as clearly as Galosh splashing through the mud at Newmarket. Just think: Newbury, Salisbury, Fontwell, Goodwood and St Mary's, all under an hour away and Frith Street no more than 90 minutes on a fast train to Waterloo.

I was pondering this when failing to make the Anglesey Arms at Halnaker before racing at Goodwood the other day. The A27 traffic can be unforgiving, which is a pity because the Anglesey is as important as Bar Italia or the Pope's Grotto. I need to sit in the garden and finish my deliberations. It's a long way from Bristol and a pint of Harvey's seems more attractive with every passing mile. Nothing ever changes at the Anglesey, which is probably why I love it.

DREAMING OF SOHO ... AND ALLY PALLY
Racing Post April 2013

I believe I backed only one winner in the Hill's shop on Cricklewood Broadway – Rose Dubarry in the Norfolk Stakes at Doncaster in 1971. She looked good for the 1000 Guineas the following year but finished third behind Waterloo. This came as a setback rather than a crushing blow, though the latter duly followed with Jacinth's defeat 12 months later.

"You were never very lucky in the Guineas," Pedro said, having tapped on the café window when he saw me ambling past, lost in thought. I used to live in Cricklewood and thought I might see if the old house was still there, which it was. That's more than we can say for Alexandra Park racecourse, my next intended port of call.

I don't know how many pubs Pedro was involved with over the years but he spent a lot of time in Soho in the old days and had an afternoon drinking club there. Peter Martin became Pedro Martinez and bore a passing resemblance to Burt Lancaster in *Valdez Is Coming*. There were many women.

He seemed to be working on a giant crossword and there were Lotto and EuroMillions tickets all over the table.

"New Year's resolution," he said. "I'm off the horses for a while, apart from Certify in the Guineas, but I'm entering every single competition that comes along and waiting for the miracle combination or the phone call that changes everything. What's a slang word for vigour, five letters?"

"Let me think about it," I said. "By the way, isn't Cricklewood a bit far north for you?"

"I had a place up near Hanger Lane but there was no atmosphere," he replied. "It's hard, when you've seen Soho regulars turn up at 11.30am, looking for their first glass of champagne. Francis Bacon used to go on to Wheeler's restaurant and ask the head chef, Mister Song, how he was getting on just to hear him say: 'Mustn't glumble.'

"I read the other day about a very big gambler called George Hanger. He was around in the late 1700s and befriended the Prince of Wales. He'd bet on anything, including a foot race between 20 turkeys and 20 geese. He lost £500 on the turkeys who gave up because they couldn't stand the noise. How are you, anyway?"

I said I was fair to middling and that I didn't bet odds-on any more but my dreams were rather strange. Last week I went to bed knowing that Morandi had been beaten at 8/11 at Longchamp but in the dream I was wandering down the Escalier de la rue Foyatier in Paris, intent upon placing a massive bet in some tabac or other. In the race itself, the line-up included old Operatic Society and they seemed to run down a hill before turning into the straight, meaning it could only be Brighton or Epsom. When they went past me, Morandi and Operatic Society were locked together but there was a long way to go and I had to wait for the result on BBC Radio.

"Who won?" Pedro said.

"I don't know because I woke up. It was probably Operatic Society, though, because he was more or less unbeatable at Brighton, as you know."

"Yes, he'd have defied the 50-year age gap," Pedro said. "I'm so old I remember Ken Gethin winning on him at Manchester before Scobie Breasley and Lester took over. Breasley against Soumillon would have been a fascinating duel. Have you ever told anyone else about these dreams?"

"No, of course not," I replied. "I never discuss gambling with non-gamblers because they always end up asking the same thing – how you stand, profit and loss wise over the years. No one needs a question like that."

"Are you writing about Ally Pally? I used to listen to journalists dictating copy in Soho before they touched a drop. They were so precise, so clipped. The mistake with Boris Godunov was just sheer bad luck, really. Doris was a much more popular name then than it is now, don't forget. The same chap – Philip Hope-Wallace, was it? – said that a *Tosca* he'd seen the previous night was 'like a tigress robbed of her whelps'. The copy-taker must have misheard because *Tosca* came out 'like a tiger robbed of his whelks'. It made all the papers."

"I'll be careful, Pedro," I said. "I'm off to the Flask for a pint of Young's if you fancy it. Don't just sit there all day thinking about the past, show a bit of oomph. That's five letters, isn't it?"

And so we said our goodbyes, promising we wouldn't leave it so long next time and agreeing that a Windsor night meeting by boat would be just about perfect, yet knowing in our hearts that the next hurrah might well take place a long way from Windsor, a long way from Ally Pally and probably a long way from Longchamp, as well.

ALL PAID UP – AND NOT BEFORE TIME
Racing Post June 2016

Well, I've paid off the mortgage. It's taken about 25 years longer than anticipated and we needn't go into all the reasons for the delay but I am available for consultation on risk management. Also the restorative powers of Underberg, horses trained by John Meacock in the 1960s and where to go in Solihull when you're lonely.

I had it in mind to finish the payments with a mega bet at Brighton, just for old times' sake, and Pour La Victoire certainly fitted the bill but the timing was awry.

Leaving aside the remote possibility of getting a moderate three-year-old into a race confined to slow two-year-olds, I stopped believing in certainties around the time Roberto beat Brigadier Gerard at York in 1972. However, backing the winner of an apprentices' handicap when it turns out again, unpenalised, with the same jockey (in this instance Georgia Cox) claiming against senior riders comes pretty close.

Unfortunately I was all paid up by then, so I put the money towards a new drive, completed in three days flat by Joe the Irishman who isn't really Irish, despite the accent; in fact he's never been there. His Irish-sounding brother isn't Irish, either, so I assume they are the sons of Irish parents who came over many years ago and have never truly mingled with anyone else. It's an Irish enclave in the south Bristol suburbs. Smashing drive, I must say.

There was clearly little point in talking to Joe about Phoenix Park or the casino in Merrion Square, which is unusual because it looks just like an ordinary house, albeit a handsomely appointed one. But they're all playing away inside, just a couple of tables and a pleasant if slightly subdued atmosphere in the wee small hours; the purest form of escapism in the room with no clocks.

I was lucky enough to visit Phoenix Park a few times before the racecourse closed in 1981. A consortium including Vincent O'Brien and Robert Sangster got it up and running again two years later and it lasted until 1990.

I took quite a caning there, though I suspect I'd have fared better in the 1950s. If you want to recapture a vanished Dublin – always damp, always misty, tea rooms wreathed in cigarette smoke, an all-powerful church – you should read the

Quirke novels by John Banville, written under the pseudonym Benjamin Black.

Quirke is a deeply troubled pathologist who tries, with limited success, to face another day without the warm glow of alcohol. He still retains enough savvy to be of considerable assistance to the Garda and was played to perfection by Gabriel Byrne in a mini TV series. However, it was Dublin itself, shot in muted greys and browns, which made the deepest impression.

It was interesting to see a reference to the dice game 'Shut the Box' in The Dikler column this week. I'm not saying my own involvement amounted to more than a patch of damp sand around the edge of the financial whirlpool but we played for high stakes in the Baker & Oven off Marylebone High Street.

It's a simple game. The slots are numbered one to 12 and you keep closing them while you can. If you throw a total of seven, you DON'T close the five and the two because, if you happen to roll 'snake eyes' – two ones – you're finished. The person with the lowest total wins, and shutting the box altogether pays double.

One night in the Baker I ended up with just the 'one' still open and a chap we'd never laid eyes on before, but who'd plonked his £20 note down, as good as gold, quietly and calmly shut the box. Time stands still, doesn't it? Moments later, 20/1 shot Ben Casey beat the warm favourite at a Wolverhampton night meeting. They still had grass in those days.

My mother doted on my father and never recovered when he passed on. Even so, I'm pretty sure Vince Edwards, who played the TV doctor Ben Casey, fanned a minor flame in her heart. Unforgivably, I forgot to tell her he was running.

The stranger, softly spoken and £140 richer, gave me a lift to the Victoria Sporting Club. I gained the distinct impression the night was still young for him, though I doubt he was going as far as Solihull.

TRIP TO THE BUSH JOGS THE MEMORY
Racing Post March 2018

We used to jog past the Scrubs, late at night. Up this grassy path, under the M40 when people still rambled on about it being the longest stretch of raised motorway in the world, back down the other side, past the Mail Coach and home.

That was before they demolished a whole section of Holland Road, forcing four of us to find another place to share. Cricklewood, if memory serves, George Ward and the Grunwick dispute, people all over the road, television cameras etc. Not really a trade union man, old George. We moved on in our different ways and I steered well clear of Grunwick when interviewing him for the crowd at Cheltenham, concentrating instead on Bonusprint, Tripleprint and all the other prints.

I still go back to Holland Road, of course, though the Kensington pub has gone and we eat in an Iranian restaurant with wine from the supermarket next door. It's a pity because there was music in the evenings at the Kensington, a decent jazz quartet and a female vocalist, Annie I think, who did a mean, sultry version of an old Shirley Bassey song called 'How Can You Tell?'

'How can you tell, when the right one comes along? How can you tell if he's Mr Right or Mr Wrong?' Search me, although Mr Right is probably a shade of odds against. Probably best to say nothing at all, I suppose. I used to shrug like some troubled yet philosophical man of the world when she got to that bit and she'd smile in her 'vodka and tonic later, petal' way.

Unfortunately, she had a boyfriend called Larry who'd done time just up the road. He'd kept himself pretty fit, and knowing when you're clear second favourite in certain situations has served me well over the years. Anyway, I turned the whole thing into a short story called 'Zarzuela'; the Kensington became the Talbot and Annie became a Scots chanteuse from Dundee, or 'jute city' as she called it.

Larry said all the crims were innocent, a view shared by many of the indisposed on my rare visits as part of a school initiative years and years ago. Not that you can do very much to help. I remember one inmate at Winchester asking for some solid advice and it was the year Nunshoney won the Wokingham at a big price but you can't pass on things like that, not at 16.

I was in Holland Road and Shepherd's Bush on Thursday of last week and bumped into an old cove from the Kensington days. I didn't know all that much about Zarzuela, to be honest, and had to ask John Reid whether they went left- or right-handed at the Madrid track. Fortunately, I knew rather more about the bullfighter Manolete, who was gored and died at Linares in 1947. He was also a decent handicapper with Ryan Jarvis when the world was young.

Anyway the old toper was outside the Iranian place and seemed to have a regular spot, the inevitable tin cup by his side. I remember what everyone drinks, especially in Shepherd's Bush, where I sold a strong (14%) Spanish rosé called Lagunilla which was helped on its way by halves of strong lager in a West Indian pub on the Green. But old Alfie was a neat brandy man in those days and I'm pretty sure he still is. By now he'll have forgotten that Altior paid for it but he was very grateful at the time.

I thought the horse was a near certainty in the Queen Mother Champion Chase. When lameness at the 11th hour became public knowledge, you either let it worry you or believed Nicky Henderson when he said Altior had recovered and was fine. I believed him and could hardly credit the SP.

I went from Holland Road to Hatton Garden, the Sir Christopher Hatton and Ye Old Mitre, where I met some 1970s wine trade friends. But the last port of call was a huge, deafening place in Farringdon where at least five giant screens were showing the Festival.

The Storyteller, King's Odyssey each-way (he often comes third), Laurina … everyone should experience a crowded London racing pub on days like these. I was so happy I even thought of a quick game of roulette after a brisk jog to the Betsey Trotwood not far away. Then my brain ruled out the first and my gammy hip the second. It's not the same without the Scrubs nearby.

TAKING A CHANCE AND MAKING IT PAY
Racing Post March 2017

No matter what the play-safers may say, you have to experiment sometimes. You have to say 'yes' against your better judgement and see how things turn out. It's hard to imagine a life without risk although, as an older, wiser (and indeed richer) friend recently pointed out, you don't need to embrace it every day.

Many years ago I was sitting in traffic, proper London traffic, on the Westway. We were just past Paddington, heading east.

My friend Tony Grafton was due at a wedding in sunny Donny, as Wogan used to say, at 2pm. It was about 10.30, the train due out of King's Cross at 11.00. There was a Tube strike and, when Tony rang me, worry was fast becoming panic. Normally I'd have quoted odds but, even if 100/8 had meant anything to him, it wouldn't have helped.

In those days the minor turn off the Westway down to the Edgware Road was still available. Down we went, hard left past the Victoria Casino and up to the only permissible right turn. Down a narrow street, sharp left and up to Lord's. Fairly quiet here and still all right to Regent's Park and the mosque. Stay north, Carnaby, stay north past the bandstand, as deserted as Jack Lemmon's in *The April Fools*, past the zoo and the Barque and Bite on Regent's Canal, over to the far side and the lovely Nash buildings, all well-heeled embassy staff and out through the gates to Camden Town.

About 11/8 now, I'd say. Traffic only a slight problem past the Young's pub on the right when Young's Special was still nectar, up the other side, under the Ferodo bridge and the bordello (great big black place, hardly as discreet as Proust's house of pleasure on the Rue Caumartin), up to the top where it levels out and the only 'iffy' bit, the illegal U-turn before the left where, fascinatingly, most of the parked cars were Citroen 2CVs for several years. 2/7 now, avoiding the trap for beginners and the St Pancras side, where the murderer had his lock-up garage in the very first *Prime Suspect*, approaching instead from the north-east. Join the queue of taxis and some predictable swearing. 10.54 and Tony has his return ticket to hand. 'But it was joye for to see him sweat. His forehead dropped as a stillatory.' Chaucer, I think. 'The Canon's Yeoman's Tale'.

"Go on, don't miss the bugger now," I said. "By the way, if you don't mind my saying, a change of shirt at some point before they walk down the aisle might be a good move."

To embrace risk is to embrace possible opprobrium as well, of course. Had the circumnavigation of Regent's Park and its dodgier environs not worked, Tony would have said we'd have made it by staying on Marylebone Road. As if.

Trying to reach Central London in a hurry from the west, the trick is to cross the Thames early and drive along the south side, though the speed bumps are horrendous (more opprobrium) and you sacrifice a panoramic view of Battersea Power Station, which looks like an upside-down billiard table – exactly what planner Giles Gilbert Scott intended.

None of this is likely to feature in Memory Lane conversations when as many old Raceform hands as Will Lefebre can muster meet at The Candlemaker pub on Battersea High Street, not far from their old headquarters at 2 York Road, on Wednesday week. This column is not noted for its exclusives but the star raffle prize is one of Sir Peter O'Sullevan's old trilbies.

I'm not married to Raceform but we've been living together for quite a long time. The late Shrewton trainer John (MJ) Bolton's wife Sally asked if I could trace all of his winners. Not many people have a full set of Raceform but old *Sporting Life* hand Howard Parker had most of them, as did Hilda Marshall, who worked with Peter O'Sullevan and Clive Graham when the world was yet young. Together, and working against the clock with John very ill, they came up with all bar two of the 152. So I went to the Newbury office, where politeness and a heart-warming desire to help recalled another era, and found them.

Sadly, John went on ahead just before I could deliver the list to him. Had it been possible to get there in time, I'd have taken a few risks. Even embraced them, probably.

A TESTING TIME IN LAMBOURN
Racing Post February 2014

Along with several other racing people, I queued up for a PSA test towards the end of my friend David Ashforth's prostate cancer awareness evening at the Pheasant in Lambourn on Tuesday. It must have been a very good dinner because I suggested to Jim Old that I might claim one out of a seller and send it to him with a view to winning the Grand National. It may take a while to sort out the first part but the second should follow as a matter of course. I would remind you that Red Rum started out in the lowest grade.

I made it to the pub after a sentimental visit to Bianchi's on Frith Street in Soho (only possible after a successful night at the tables), where a fading poster for J M Synge's *The Playboy of the Western World* graced the upstairs room long after the play had departed the West End. It's very close to the Bar Italia, a family-run place since 1949 occupying the premises where John Logie Baird demonstrated his television breakthrough 23 years earlier.

I interviewed professional poker player Barny Boatman in the Bar Italia about a dozen years ago. He'd done very well at the World Poker Championship but, with time to kill before the flight home, had fallen for the attractions of roulette and the blackjack table. This surprised me and I believe it surprised Barny, too, because he knew full well that the only chance a committed gambler has is to specialise. He was over this unlikely aberration, though, and in good form that fine bright morning on Frith Street.

How long it takes people to recover has always fascinated me. In affairs of the heart you can't always tell, of course, though it might be unwise to tell a rejected lover in thrall to Leonard Cohen's 'Hey, That's No Way to Say Goodbye' to snap out of it.

I took only a passing interest in the Winter Olympics but the Swedish skip looked completely wrecked by the mistake which gifted GB a place in the curling final and there will be a few 3am thoughts over the coming years. Also, President Putin said he prized the gold above all else before Russia's ice hockey team led but went down 3-1 to Finland. It could have been worse. Just imagine if the game had been played in Helsinki; the two nations have a bit of history and there'd have been flag-waving, chanting and a burst of Sibelius's 'Finlandia' – the Finnish way of saying "One nil, and you f … d it up."

That Barny Boatman piece appeared in a magazine called the *Sports Adviser*. I was thumbing through some old copies and came across one from May 2001 featuring Charlie Brooks, who was interviewed by Alice Plunkett and told her he'd been due to meet Sir Alex Ferguson one morning but woke up with such a hangover that he decided to charter a plane from Newmarket to Manchester. To pay for it he sold one of Henry Cecil's on the spreads, thinking it wouldn't stay.

"It didn't but still finished second and I lost more than the plane cost," he said. "I suppose under close inspection my whole life has been a gamble. I did my brains at Lloyds, bought Uplands for £1.2 million and now run a pub!"

Top marks for honesty and the pub just happens to be the Pheasant, where life must have seemed a good deal more straightforward (too straightforward, perhaps) back then. Charlie has gone now but racing personalities abound and one of them, Colin Brown, did a fine job as master of ceremonies the other night.

I associate Colin with Desert Orchid and some youthful experiences in Dorset. With me I suppose it's because of the occasional trip to Poole greyhounds and, before that, my aunt's caravan at Sandbanks – soggy tomato sandwiches, the gas ring, Snofrute ice lollies, Kia-Ora, the guest house inland with the frightening landlady, beach huts everywhere.

When did it become Millionaires' Row? Where is that bit exactly? I worry about finding anything now, including the old greyhound stadium at Hackney Wick.

The fact is I worry about everything, and I haven't even had my results yet.

RAINY DAYS AND BRIGHT TOMORROWS
Racing Post February 2019

It always rains on Sunday.

No it doesn't but sometimes, in our youth, things seem to be drifting that way. My old advertising friend Arthur Sears, 95 now, smiles and sips his manzanilla.

"These quiz questions are getting harder," he says. "A couple of years after the war, I should think. Bethnal Green just before the Krays started roaming the streets and causing trouble. It was quite a well-made film but all I remember is Jack Warner as the copper. There was a chase through the railway stockyards, yes? *It Always Rains on Sunday* and *The Blue Lamp* probably got him the role as Dixon of Dock Green but only your older readers will remember that."

"He's only GOT older readers," Marvel Mason says, rather cheekily, but the truth often hurts and I'm not about to argue with someone who tried his level best to introduce the Albanians to Radio Fun. They were very fond of Norman Wisdom, apparently.

Old Arthur chuckles. "1947 is my best guess," he murmurs.

He is spot on but I suppose, even though it costs a round of drinks, we want him to be.

I watched *It Always Rains on Sunday* the other day. A chap called Nicky Henderson claims damages from the police for wrongful arrest. And Googie Withers' husband is checking the back of the *News of the World* for the greyhound results, having backed one at Harringay the night before. All gone.

"They were tough times in Bethnal Green," Arthur continues. "We found it hard to market cheaper cigarettes because the wide boys and the gang bosses smoked Senior Service and people copied them. Everyone bet and met up in the barber's shop in the morning. Hackney, Dalston and Poplar were breeding grounds for betting offices but that didn't happen for another dozen years or so. Of course, there were bookies and street runners everywhere and I well remember '47 because they had a 'skinner' in the Grand National with Caughoo winning at 100/1 on a filthy day at Aintree. The placed horses didn't help much because they were outsiders as well. I think John Hislop as an amateur may have been on one of them."

We ramble through a few more dates and Seagram (1991) is easy because I worked with company boss Ivan Straker during my BBC days.

Lord Gyllene's 'rescheduled' year, 1997, is straightforward but the main reason I remember it is Dextra Dove's bold effort as far as the 20th. I backed all of the Doves in their Gordon and Richard Price days, although Dextra Dove was ridden and later trained by Simon Earle.

When he rode the horse for Philip Hobbs and Robert Alner, no one else got a look-in. He was on board 29 times out of 29 and returned victorious on 13 of them. He then won on him at Worcester after taking out a licence to train and landed five more handicap chases when looking on from the stands. A grizzled old hack is impressed. Simon has relocated to The Beeches near Warminster and it occurs to me that Arthur and Marvel might be interested in taking a share or two in a shrewd purchase.

"I don't know. Marvel has a new girlfriend, quite a bit younger," Arthur says. "The last one was a Fulham supporter and she took him along every fortnight. It worked out quite well, though, didn't it, Marvel?"

"What about the heart murmur?" I wonder.

"I'm hoping it'll turn into a roar," Marvel says, deadpan.

"We should eat," Arthur says. "Did I tell you what Kingsley Amis said when someone asked him what the worst thing anyone had ever said to him was? He said it was: 'Shall we go straight to the table?'"

"Can you imagine that, going straight in without a G and T, a Pernod or a drop of manzanilla?"

No.

RIDING THE TIGER TO ISLINGTON
Racing Post May 2013

Greyhound tracks, black horses, loose-leaf tea; we could outlive them all, you know, though I suppose it's odds against. With the tea it'll probably be close, because those little red packets in Tesco are lost amidst the serried ranks of glorified sweepings known as teabags.

Soon the world will be full of people who've never been to Park Royal on a Friday afternoon, never heard of Ruffian and never had a proper cup of tea. Born too late to have seen the Portsmouth inside-forward Albert McCann, they'll assume that Inspector Montalbano is the bandiest man to have walked the earth.

Ruffian wasn't just black, she was jet black and won all of her ten starts before taking part in a match against 1975 Kentucky Derby winner Foolish Pleasure. Sadly, she broke both sesamoid bones in a foreleg and surgery failed to save her. In fact, the vets did an excellent job but she was far too active, even frantic, after the operation and undid all the good work. They buried her at Belmont Park.

There are very few officially black horses in training in this country and today's Qipco 1000 Guineas field does not include a filly of that hue. It's a pity, because I'd have backed her for sentimental reasons. Many years ago, when Richmond Sturdy's Black Pirate won a Pontefract seller by seven lengths, I thought all my troubles were over and they probably were for a while. I was very fond of small black bitches with early pace running out of trap 4, as well, but all the tracks have gone now – Portsmouth, Park Royal and Bristol Eastville, not to mention Walthamstow and White City. Eastville Stadium, now an IKEA, was dominated by a giant Hofmeister bear, miles above the goal at the city end. Long-suffering Rovers supporters suspected the players had had a bet on who could hit the bear first.

I probably wouldn't have thought about any of it but *Six Black Horses* starring Audie Murphy came on the box the other day and then the master thief Peter Scott died. I always look forward to the funeral cortège headed by six black horses in the pouring rain, which is how the film ends (hope I'm not spoiling it for you). Both of the Kray twins favoured that sort of exit as well, though I believe they were luckier with the weather.

Peter Scott, born Peter Gulston in Belfast, was a notorious Mayfair cat burglar and claimed to have robbed the actresses Vivien Leigh, Zsa Zsa Gabor and Sophia Loren. What is definitely true is that he handled Picasso's *Tête de Femme*, stolen from a Mayfair gallery in 1997, and went down for another three and a half years, making 14 in all behind bars. There were four wives, a fondness for rum and a weakness for gambling. He made it to 82 and got through millions, ending up bankrupt, penniless and cheerful in a care home in Newham. The funeral was organised by his loyal friend, *Guardian* writer Duncan Campbell, who wrote a fine piece about him a few days ago.

The 1965 film *He Who Rides a Tiger* was loosely based on Scott's early exploits and ends with Tom Bell, who plays him (Judi Dench is the girlfriend) fleeing from a greyhound track as the law closes in. Many times I've tried to work out the venue and I just favour White City, though not for big money. The title is from a Chinese or Indian proverb, He Who Rides a Tiger Can Never Dismount, which I think is both clever and true – and probably applies equally to thieving and gambling.

Scott was a gentle, philosophical man. "I have a suspicion that I was sent by God to put back some of the wealth that the outrageously rich took from the rest of us," he wrote in his memoir. Well, I'm all for that, even if I find it a rather convenient justification for his choice of occupation.

He knew gangsters and even drove around in a battered Mercedes given to him by the law-abiding son of the legendary Billy Hill, who ran much of London's illegal gambling in the 1950s, but he was non-violent himself and would not have wanted the six black horses' treatment at the end. He said goodbye at Islington cemetery, where the sign at the entrance reads: "There are thieves operating in this area. Please keep your valuables out of sight."

Baroness Kennedy QC was one of the mourners and it was hardly a pauper's funeral, though it reminded me I did once attend one myself. There were only a few strangers, the reverend said some kind words in the makeshift chapel and it cheered me up a bit after a lean spell on the horses. There's nothing quite like a pauper's funeral to remind you we all force a draw in the end.

Anyway, I remember we had a nice cup of tea afterwards.

AIMEZ-VOUS COGNAC? MAIS OUI!
the-racehorse.com November 2014

I have just turned 66 as I write this.

Although Classic FM can be irritating, between 6.30 and 7am this morning they played the third movement from Brahms' Third Symphony, Tchaikovsky's 'Serenade For Strings' and the second movement from Dvorak's Ninth, 'From the New World'. If asked for my birthday choice, those three pieces might well have featured.

Regarding the Brahms, there are some fascinating angles. The third movement features in the 1961 film *Goodbye Again* from an original short story by Françoise Sagan called 'Aimez-Vous Brahms?' It's a low-key Parisian affair, Ingrid Bergman foolishly taking up with the feckless, irresolute and much younger Anthony Perkins because her husband, the philandering Yves Montand, has left her alone once too often.

There is a nightclub scene featuring the singer Diahann Carroll, who had a minor hit with 'Have I Changed'. This was the third movement set to words. She was going to marry David Frost at one stage but something went wrong and she ended up marrying several other people instead, a sort of compliment to him really, when you think about it.

When recalling 1961 the Berlin Wall looms large, as it must have done to everyone in the city, but I also think of *Goodbye Again*, Psidium and Mandarin, the Blind Beggar, the Krays and Hennessy Cognac. Psidium started at 66/1 in the Derby and wasn't even Harry Wragg's first string, but in he went in the hands of Frenchman Roger Poincelet.

It was also the year that the indomitable Mandarin won his second Hennessy Gold Cup under 11st 5lb, five pounds more than he'd carried in his first, the inaugural running (at Cheltenham, not Newbury) in 1957. Perhaps the De Pracomtal family fell in love with the race there and then. When I worked in the drinks business for Gilbey Vintners in the 1970s, as each year came around we thought they'd announce a change of plan for the marketing budget but they never wavered and the 2014 race is the 57th renewal.

Sponsorship is not truly about moving the product on the day, though Hennessy is in all the bars at Newbury. It's about maintaining contacts. In those early days, Hennessy was sold to smart hotels and restaurants by a firm called Morgan Furze, part of the Gilbey's organisation within Maxwell Joseph's Grand Metropolitan Hotels group. Down at 'foot soldier' level, it was sold in the East End by a remarkable old character called Stan Caulkett, who called on the Blind Beggar in the Mile End Road when the Krays were in residence.

"If you didn't have anything they wanted, the Krays could be quite charming," Stan once told me. "I used to go in on a Sunday lunchtime, when they'd be with their old mum. When she was in there, no one swore. If they did, Ronnie or Reggie would send one of the lads over and he'd say, quite gently, 'Excuse me, squire, Mrs Kray is in today, so if you could just mind the language, please.' You were nursing a sort of death wish if you forgot yourself again after that. When I walked in they'd say: 'Hello, it's Stan! All right, Stan?' and they'd tell the guv'nor I needed an order. It was like an instruction, really."

George Cornell, a member of the rival Richardson gang, was shot dead by Ronnie Kray in the Blind Beggar. It is part of Mile End Road legend that the Walker Brothers' 'The Sun Ain't Gonna Shine Any More' was playing on the jukebox at the time.

Yet it's such an ordinary, innocuous-looking pub all these years later that you wonder how many people know of its lurid past. The regulars are not cognac drinkers, favouring the inevitable pints of lager and occasional whisky chaser. It's probably fair to say that the great brandy days are over in this country, which is surprising when you think how many companies invested heavily in sponsorship – Martell, Courvoisier (which contained more vanilla) and Three Barrels, as well as the German brandy Hine and the very different Metaxa from Greece. An altogether sweeter concoction, Metaxa always put me in mind of very alcoholic dolly mixtures, if you remember those.

Happily, things have not changed in France and the day before the Arc, when I was hunting for a *Paris-Turf*, it was heartening to see how many locals started the day with a very strong coffee and a drop of Hennessy. I almost expected Diahann Carroll to appear and sing 'Have I Changed?' Then I could have reassured her that, *au contraire*, there was no discernible change at all. Charm is halfway round the world before the truth has got its boots on.

HOSTELRIES HAPPY TO LET THE PAST GO

Racing Post February 2015

On Sunday I repaired to The Old Duke in Bristol when Andy Murray went two sets to one down against Novak Djokovic in the Australian Open final. He was giving himself a hard time by then, Dr Jekyll giving way to Mister Hyde as his blameless team took its share of criticism.

The crowd turned against him, which was a bit rich, given Djokovic's predictable use of minor but highly effective gamesmanship. If Murray, a sublime player capable of exploiting impossible angles, cannot handle that by now there is little hope. I quietly accepted the loss of a hundred.

This followed Sam Twiston-Davies' swift exit via the side door from Atlantic Roller at Wincanton. He fairly hurtled to the ground, not your typical 'unseated' at all, and quite impressive when you consider how slowly everything else happened on a rain-sodden day.

I like Wincanton, though, because it restores my faith in certainties. There will certainly be many lorries there, like Scotsmen in Corby and bears doing their thing in the woods and one-legged ducks swimming in a circle and that other one about the Pope.

Anyway, the jazz band was playing a soulful version of 'Bei Mir Bist Du Schön' (you'd recognise it if you heard it; old Andrews Sisters song) in the Duke and I was nursing a pint of Bath Ales Gem and looking out of the window, wondering why the Llandoger Trow opposite doesn't make more of its impressive history. Quite apart from the fact that it was here Daniel Defoe is said to have met Alexander Selkirk, his model for Robinson Crusoe, the pub also became the Admiral Benbow in Robert Louis Stevenson's *Treasure Island*.

Of course, pubs don't always want to advertise their past. There are no pictures of the Kray twins in the Blind Beggar and no mention of master planner Bruce Reynolds in the Anglesea Arms off the Fulham Road.

When reporting Chelsea matches many years ago I favoured the Anglesea for a pre-match beer. The oldest profession seemed less tawdry in those days and the girls used to put cards in a local newsagent's window opposite Stamford Bridge – Ex-Air Hostess Seeks Ground Position, etc.

The other day I was studying the Schweppes, sorry the Betfair, in the Anglesea and thinking about the extraordinary sequence of events in 1963 – the assassination of John F Kennedy, the Profumo Affair, Martin Luther King's 'I Have a Dream' speech – but a good friend long retired from the Met insists it was a base in Nine Elms that was used by Reynolds and an associate when they were planning the Great Train Robbery. There is no doubt they originally considered the train transporting South African gold from Southampton docks to London, even carrying out a recce at Weybridge in the small hours. They changed their minds and Surrey's loss became Buckinghamshire's gain, so to speak.

I imagine the current proprietors of the Plumbers Arms in Belgravia seldom mention the arrival of a very distressed and bloodstained Lady Lucan in 1974, though the pub's history holds much fascination for tourists.

The late Charles Benson, formerly The Scout on the *Daily Express*, was a member of the Lucan/Clermont Club set, of course, as was Dominic Elwes, a playboy painter who fell foul of both John Aspinall and James Goldsmith when an incriminating painting appeared in the *Sunday Times* following Lucan's disappearance. This showed Goldsmith at a group 'plotters' lunch he had not attended. Elwes was ostracised and committed suicide. Aspinall may have thought of himself as the ultimate hard man but, when he spoke ill of Elwes at the funeral (who would even think of doing that?), he was felled by the latter's cousin.

They were all huge gamblers but I don't know whether Elwes was descended from the MP John Elwes (1714–89), who was a massive player, then became a miser with inherited money but remained very generous towards other punters. He ended up spending nothing on himself and walked around in rags but once rode from Berkshire to Newmarket with £7,000 in cash for Lord Abingdon to put on a horse. We all need friends like this.

His old stamping ground was Portman Square, home to the Jockey Club before the move to Shaftesbury Avenue and he knew Marylebone like the back of his hand, wandering down Wimpole Street, later the setting for *My Fair Lady*, where people would often mistake him for a beggar and offer coins, though he left the equivalent of £28m.

Sitting in The Old Duke, it occurred to me that Murray's sudden capitulation would not have bothered him very much.

THE ORGANIST ENTERTAINS
Racing Post New Year's Day 2012

I thought it was a very good Christmas. On television there was a brand new *Poirot* and, although the plot completely lost me, I've come to the conclusion that there is never any need for the miscreants to be apprehended. When the Belgian 'tec calls his meeting in the big room in the final half-hour, just don't go.

It seemed to me there were more carols this time, especially on the radio. You can't hear them without thinking of the lyrics added by mischievous schoolboys, just as you can't hear the 'William Tell Overture' without thinking of the Lone Ranger. If they stop teaching history in schools, some of the references will miss people entirely – 'Hark! The herald angels sing; Mrs Simpson's pinched our king,' for example.

The Coral Welsh National has always been one of my favourite races so it was disappointing to see so many horses toiling a long way from home on Tuesday. It is no exaggeration to say that, barring accidents, only Le Beau Bai or Giles Cross could win from the home turn. That was good news for those who relied purely on previous form in the race because both had given their all in the past, but the simple truth is that the test proved much too demanding for the others. The breed is not as durable as it was.

It was an enjoyable programme on the BBC and reference was made to Richard Pitman's admirable offer of a kidney to save a life early in the new year. As Richard Dunwoody pointed out, you have to be pretty fit before they take the kidney anyway, so some of us would be withdrawn at the start. Does the recipient remain a complete stranger? I'm not sure. If not, the correspondence afterwards would be very interesting, especially if more than one organ were involved.

"Dear Mr Entwhistle, I cannot tell you how grateful I am for the donation of your various organs, together with instructions; you are indeed a lifesaver. I hope you will not mind if I mention the fact that one or two of them have taken a while to, ah, bed in, as it were. A lifelong teetotaller and something of a worrier, I followed your recommendation regarding New Zealand Sauvignon Blanc and, to general astonishment, have become a 'glass half-full' sort of person. I have also taken your advice regarding the 'morning after livener' – a term hitherto unknown to me, I must say – and find I am taking more risks in the afternoons. Not all of these are successful but I have made many new friends.

I cannot thank you enough. I feel like a new man and my wife says exactly the same. Yours ever, etc."

One year I did actually fill out the authorisation slip in my diary but I was walking down Archer Street in Soho and a fleet-footed mugger snatched it from my hand, mistaking the diary for a wallet. It was mid-February and my up-to-date betting record had been faithfully recorded. What a sad night that must have been for him. Of course, had he known how speedy I was over 100 yards in those days he'd have been thanking his lucky stars I let him go. But then he'd have studied the list of bets and realised that a wallet wouldn't have been much use, either.

He stuffed it in what we used to call a pig bin behind the Raymond Revuebar and one of the kitchen staff kindly sent it back to me with a sympathetic note. It was damp and whiffed a bit and there were strips of carrot all over the February page where Bootlaces in the Schweppes Gold Trophy appeared as my only winner thus far in 1980. I gave up after that. I don't think I ever kept detailed records into March because the 'minus' sign used to get on my nerves.

Incidentally, I think this 'dry' spell that people opt for in January is ill-advised because it only confuses the system. I recommend opening a nice bottle of Barolo at lunchtime today and then giving the sportinglife.com Handicap Hurdle at Cheltenham your undivided attention. Win or lose, this is the year everything comes right. I open a little French bistro in Southampton with a chanteuse singing Edith Piaf songs, write a racing short story worthy of comparison with Hemingway's 'My Old Man' and claim one out of a seller, sending it to Jim Old with Aintree in mind.

I listen, scribble and dream. Everything is in place.

Part Four

Orient 3 Blackburn 1
28 January 1978

It rained and rained before the FA Cup 4th round* in late
January that year. Real Ikdam rain, if you know what that
means; real Galosh rain, Coppermill Lad rain, when things
can't go ahead but manage it somehow … and stay in your
mind for ever.

The sport was on BBC Radio 2 in those days and they wanted
a reporter at every match. We lived in Sawbridgeworth then
and West Ham, Orient, Millwall and Charlton were within
easy reach. Through the Peter Bills agency I must have
worked for half the local radio stations in the country, often
listening to *Sports Report* from other people's car radios
while waiting for the traffic to clear afterwards. To be honest
I thought some of the reporters were pretty ordinary and, as
someone who remembered the likes of Bill Bothwell from
another era entirely, it mattered to me. Professionally, I
wanted to be part of *Sports Report* more than I've ever wanted
anything. For that reason, I prefer to give it a miss now.

Anyway, the rain would not relent and I said to Jimmy Bloomfield, the old Arsenal inside-forward who managed Orient at the time, that the game was bound to be off, though I could see a small army of groundstaff and volunteers forking the pitch.

"We've let Blackburn travel," he said. "If we call it off now we have to pay their expenses. It'll be on."

And so it was, and Blackburn played Orient off this sodden pitch but somehow lost 3-1. Jimmy was a lovely man who died too young. "They played league football and we played cup football," he explained, with the hint of a smile.

So it was my Radio 2 debut and I must have done all right because – and I wish I still had the relevant diary – I was soon covering two games a week and going in to voice the sport on the *Today* programme on Radio 4, with Brian Redhead and John Timpson the main presenters. Given that I was also working for Exchange Telegraph in their Prestel department, it was a golden time. In Iain 'Jimmy' Thomas, radio sports editor in those days, I had a big supporter. He died a while back and I wish I'd thanked him properly.

Not to labour the point, the 'trick', if you like, was to remain a freelance and not become a member of staff. It's just that I couldn't see it at the time. Even if the Orient game had been called off, it's long odds-on that another opportunity would have presented itself, I'd have ended up applying for the next vacancy and things would have panned out in much the same way.

There is often a tendency to wrap everything up in the same bag marked 'failure'. That would be unfair; the happier memories also deserve their place in the overall picture. As a freelance, and before they knew I was a racing man, there was the day the line to the Curragh went down before Shergar's Irish Derby and I chatted away about him in the London studio to fill otherwise completely dead air time. Much later there was the piece with Omar Sharif at Goodwood, going out to interview Billy Connolly, Sugar Ray Leonard and Vitas Gerulaitis, to name but three, for *Sunday Sport* and sitting with Ken Dodd on the lawn at Epsom at the start of Derby day. There was the Hallo Dandy tip on *Today* the morning before the '84 National – quite a few of my BBC memories involve Aintree – and I loved days at the races with Peter Bromley, making Gloria Hunniford laugh by telling her the Queen Mary winner Night Of Wind was by Chili Bean out of Takeaway Blues. But most of all I enjoyed the pieces put together with talented producer Emily McMahon for the Saturday morning programme *Sport On 4*.

However, as time went on I tended to gild the lily, striving for effect when straightforward reporting would have done the job better. I was neither a commentator nor an official correspondent and, in those pre-5 Live days when sport had to fight 'easy listening' music for airtime, there was no way forward. One of my few saving graces – knowing when it's time to go (in this instance a feeling readily endorsed by the management) – came into play.

I knew at that stage, 1985, that writing would gradually take over from broadcasting when it came to making a living. A brief spell at HTV West in Bristol and a longer one at SIS did nothing to dispel that rather worrying prospect. It was a pity because I certainly found broadcasting much easier but you have to do your best with the hand you've chosen to play – or, more correctly, the hand you've left yourself with. I thought setting this down might provide some sort of background to the pieces which follow.

* That FA Cup 4th round was quite something. Quite apart from Jimmy Bloomfield and Orient effectively giving me my chance at BBC Radio, Blyth Spartans won 3-2 at Stoke. So my dad would have been very happy on two fronts. Like Jimmy, he went too soon.

ECHOES OF MA, YOSSER AND THE BOYS

Racing Post April 2015

When it comes to great Liverpool memories, Echo and the Bunnymen and John Oaksey are right up there, together with Alexei Sayle and Ma Egerton. I'm still rather fond of David Icke and Frank Windsor, as well.

Looking back now, it's hard to believe all that happened in 1982, Grittar's year. The night before the Grand National, animal rights protesters set fire to two of the fences and Margaret Thatcher sent the troops to the Falklands, thereby upstaging Ken Bates, who bought Chelsea for a pound.

It was a time when people who knew a little about these things would tell you the Bunnymen were the second-best band to emerge during Liverpool's extended golden era, though my own experience of them was limited to a 24-hour 'happening' a couple of years later entitled Crystal Day. The best part was when everyone crowded into Brian's Diner, the band's favourite café, though I must say service was slow.

During the BBC Radio years, by which I mean my time at the Corporation, we stayed at the Atlantic Towers. Nowadays, with few if any commitments, I'd head for Ma Egerton's on Pudsey Street or the place in Birkenhead where they used to run a Billy Fury competition. In 1984, if I'd chosen 'When Will You Say I Love You?' instead of 'Halfway to Paradise', I feel I might have nicked it. Obviously you'll say it hardly matters 30 years on, but for some of us regret is a lifelong thing.

Ma Egerton's is opposite the Empire Theatre, a famous old music hall venue. Dr Crippen's wife used to drop in; she sang under the name Belle Elmore, or at least she did until the doctor decided she was surplus to requirements in 1910.

Legend has it that he visited the pub before fleeing to America but Ma, no mean performer herself, incidentally, shopped him to the police and was therefore instrumental in his capture and execution.

I expect lots of other people saw John Oaksey dance but I'm probably the only person still alive to have witnessed it in the commentary box. He did well to make it in the first place, because in 1982 Aintree had a long, long way to go and there were still 'danger' signs here and there on the roof of the County Stand.

Anyway, the Noble Lord started bouncing up and down in sheer delight as soon as Grittar went clear. I suppose, as a very talented amateur rider himself, he was thrilled to see Mr Dick Saunders become the oldest winning rider at 48. Unfortunately the ancient commentary box had been constructed along Heath Robinson lines, there was a sloping floor and John's erratic progress carried him across Peter Bromley's line of vision.

"Most unprofessional thing I've ever seen and I shall be taking it to the highest level," the commentator said afterwards. It never happened. Peter was a lovely man and his bark was far worse than his non-existent bite, though when he threatened people it was generally with the name of someone quite close to Lord Reith. Happy enough with a winning favourite at 7/1, I nodded sympathetically. I can do the furrowed brow bit, no problem.

Frank Windsor ('it's time to think about those final expenses') was DS John Watt in *Z Cars* from 1962 but I liked him best as the harassed, well-intentioned paterfamilias in the film *Sunday Bloody Sunday*, which captures perfectly the easy-going liberalism, the elegant household clutter of Hampstead and its environs.

Frank was at Aintree in '82 and so was David Icke, the former goalie turned commentator and Green Party evangelist who predicted that Mount Rainier in the USA would explode, followed by the Channel Tunnel and Naples Cathedral. You may laugh but even today Icke's lectures and rallies are sold out. I am not making this up.

Grittar triumphed a few months before Alan Bleasdale's seminal television drama *Boys from the Blackstuff* underlined chronic unemployment on Merseyside, especially within the building industry. Yosser Hughes – 'Gizza job!' – and his gang became national heroes for a while.

Sensing that trendy Londoners would soon be taking the mickey, Alexei Sayle recorded 'Ullo John! Gotta New Motor?' which effectively debunked flash Essex boys long before Essex girls became famous.

I don't suppose he'll be there on Saturday and we can be pretty sure John and Peter will be absentees as well. It's a pity because, 33 years on, they'd marvel at the transformation.

LAY IT ON THE TABLE, JOHNNIE
Racing Post July 2018

Well, I knew all about Betty Shine but I must say one or two of Fanny Cradock's gifts had passed me by.

It seems they were both well acquainted with famous figures from the past. Betty, a Brighton medium who advised former goalie David Icke, told him he was here to heal the earth and would be world-famous. This much became clear from a phone conversation with Socrates (the Greek-Athenian philosopher, not the Brazilian midfield man) via an 800-year-old Chinese priest. To be fair, David is quite famous, though the first part may take a little longer.

Fanny, the daughter of a butterfly collector who was married to Bijou, an actress and singer, claimed to be on intimate terms with the court of Louis XIV. At the age of 17 she eloped with her first husband to Brighton (where else?) but he soon passed away and she met Johnnie, an old Harrovian. They were together for 50 years.

There are several famous stories from the BBC cookery years, the best one featuring Johnnie's carefully scripted 30-second piece at the end, when he invited viewers to send in for the recipe. This was always word-perfect and exactly 30 seconds in duration. Indeed, he was incapable of cutting it back, always a worry when a programme goes out live.

One day, forced to halve the length – and with an anxious floor manager hardly helping the situation – his hastily contrived precis began: "So there we are, ladies and gentlemen, if you want scones that taste like Fanny's …" Needless to say, people loved him even more after that.

They came into the radio sports department on one occasion and I remember it quite vividly because it was Ayr Gold Cup day, 1984.

There was a discreet afternoon drinking club near the Baker
& Oven, just off Marylebone High Street, in those days and
Benny, one of the regulars, a sprint handicap devotee and
a proper punter, had narrowed it down to Able Albert and
Alakh.

I recall gambling conversations more or less word for word
and I mentioned to him that all he needed was the 'A's to
come good at Ayr. Indeed, I thought the main danger was
Amarone, a superb Italian red when things are going well
and you can afford it. But he was deeply into horses trained
by Jeremy Tree and Alakh was the call. He had this mental
picture of Monica Sheriffe's horse going clear on the far side,
with Able Albert doing his best up the stands' rails.

Whether there can ever be justification for a £100 straight
forecast, with no saver at all, in a race like this is open to
question. However, I had a feeling he was on the 'end it or
mend it' road and I've travelled it a few times myself so I
wished him well.

I cannot maintain eye contact when an important horserace is
in progress so the Cradocks came and went as I fussed around
pretending to edit something while the television murmured
away, up on the wall behind my left shoulder.

When pressed for a tip these days, commentators will fudge
and dissemble like newcomers to a house of pleasure;
reputation and all that. Not so Graham Goode, who on this
famous day in '84 makes the point that Able Albert, drawn 29
of 29, is 'extremely well in'. When he repeats this, even I am
with him, though my main bet resembles Benny's. Anyway,
Alakh bursts clear on the far side and surely holds on for
Pat Eddery. Graham thinks so and so do I, even though I'm
pointing the wrong way because I cannot be seen to ignore
famous guests in favour of a sprint handicap.

As we know, Able Albert got up by an inch, costing Benny in

the region of £10,000. He went away for a while and managed not to emulate the hero in a short story by Balzac called 'The Last Napoleon', in which a young man takes his time before entering a gambling parlour in Paris, loses his last gold coin, then heads for the Pont Royal and the ultimate solution. It's not the dead of night, either, it's late afternoon.

Benny came back eventually and I bumped into him in Soho; the Mazurka, I think. It's a strange thing but Roger Charlton, who took over from Jeremy Tree, has Projection in the Stewards' Cup on Saturday. All we need is something trained by the Easterbys on the opposite wing, though there's no telling if we'll recoup, of course.

Not unless we bump into Betty Shine.

AINTREE – FROM PENNY LANE TO MILLIONAIRES' ROW
Racing Post February 2014

As the man said, it's funny the way things turn out.

John McCririck is dropped by Channel 4 and before long a mistake occurs that he would almost certainly have prevented. Maybe I overestimate his old scribbler's instincts, but I suspect he'd have perused the Saturday papers and noticed the *Sun*'s 'Sam Twiston-Davies for Big Buck's' exclusive, which would automatically have become the main topic of conversation when the jockey arrived as studio guest on *The Morning Line*.

Now that the horse has bolted, so to speak, someone has probably been instructed to read all the papers at first light. If you're going to do that, you might as well resurrect the review, which would be a step in the right direction entertainment-wise. Big Mac* was an old print journalist with a keen eye for a story. The thing was to get people talking; that was what mattered most. As a broadcaster, if he knew a fellow panellist held strong views on something, he'd adopt the opposite stance to get a heated debate going. It was fascinating to watch. During the Olympics I doubt he'd ever given the triple jump more than two seconds' thought, but referring to it as the 'hop, skip and jump' made it sound like a playground pastime and was certain to get up someone's nose. The man who infuriates half the audience and tickles the other half tends to see out the journey – which he very nearly did.

Thirty-two years ago he and I attended a press conference when the future of the Grand National was in grave doubt. The Liverpool property developer Bill Davies, a morose Scouser whose downbeat delivery and utterly impenetrable accent disguised a rapier-like business brain, was in a position to build a housing estate and shopping precinct on the famous Aintree turf. The National meant little to him but he eventually came to an arrangement with Ladbrokes, who took over the running of the course while Seagram boss Major Ivan Straker, whose role in saving the race has been undervalued, agreed to sponsor.

That day in the hotel McCririck took over, as he often does, and tried to get Davies to see that part of the nation's sporting fabric was about to be ripped apart. It was an honest attempt by a great traditionalist but it fell short. My interview on BBC Radio hardly helped. If you haven't heard Bill Davies, you haven't heard a truly raw, building site Liverpudlian, though listeners probably gathered that the race was on the edge.

Straker, originally a Glen Grant and Glenlivet man, sponsored the National under the Seagram banner but sensibly switched to Martell before the 1992 race. It helps if the public is familiar with the sponsor's product and most people know that Martell is cognac. Soon they will know that Crabbie's is an alcoholic ginger beer. John Crabbie had ginger wine in mind when he formed the company in Leith in 1801 but beer is the big seller now.

If someone had said to me in 1982 that a future sponsor would put up a million pounds and also back the weights luncheon at Abbey Road studios, I'd have advised him to take more water with it. But it happens on Tuesday and it will be a true Liverpool occasion, nearly 47 years after the Beatles laid down the LP *Sgt. Pepper's Lonely Hearts Club Band* at the same venue.

I overdo the nostalgia thing, of course. Asking someone in their late teens about the Beatles is akin to asking me in 1967 about Fred 'n' Ginger films of the thirties. (Not a problem for one mired so hopelessly in the past, but you take the point.)

Crabbie's already have a link with the great race because the distributors are Halewood International, who owned the 2004 winner Amberleigh House, trained by a man who just happened to be called Ginger. I sat next to John Halewood at the weights lunch that year and thought at one stage I'd persuaded him to be guest of honour at the Liverpool Lions' do the night before the race. He had about 50 other invitations and I wasn't that surprised when it didn't happen, though I was relieved not to have mentioned it to the organiser Peter Hart, an ex-copper liked and respected by everyone.

Sadly, they've all gone now. Ginger, of course; John Halewood, whose exuberant lifestyle made few concessions to a heart sending out occasional distress signals, and Peter, who rang me the day they told him he was too weak to undergo any more chemotherapy. His ashes are buried in the special room they have at Goodison Park, where Crabbie's have become official partners of his beloved Everton.

Yes, it's funny the way things turn out.

* John McCririck passed away on 5 July 2019

TAKING A SHINE TO DAVID
Racing Post April 2013

So, now you know who won the Grand National and I do too, but deadlines being the way they are I have no idea as I write this.

It would be quite something if I did, of course. Do you ever think about tomorrow's papers, today? How quickly would you react? You'd be in a position to warn people of their impending doom but how much time would you give to that, and how much to writing out your bets? No need to be greedy, because a £50 accumulator on seven straight winners at fancy prices would see you and yours safely through to, well, just safely through really.

I generally get as far as the apartment in Faubourg Saint Germain and the flight times from Paris to Southampton, but then a little voice insists that the last couple of winners couldn't possibly be the price they are in the paper, so I give up and think about something else instead – football, Greta Scacchi, a nice bottle of New Zealand Sauvignon Blanc; two out of three are within reach, a decent strike rate in anybody's language.

I have happy memories of Aintree, especially the fund-raising evening at the Liverpool Lions do, where the comedian once said he was taking Viagra eye drops because he wanted to look hard, but I missed a trick or two along the way. Knowing what we know now, I should have asked David Icke for a winner or two on the opening day a few years ago but I let the moment slip.

I was thinking about him because the first Brighton meeting is not far off. I read the other day that Betty Shine is no longer with us. Betty was a Brighton-based medium who convinced

David that he had a higher calling. You can smile and shake your head but that only puts you in the same camp as the Pharisees and Sadducees all of 2,000 years ago and they're not smiling now.

"I had to experience extreme ridicule so that I could emerge stronger and wiser. My predictions were meant to be wrong on a massive scale because I have always been scared of ridicule," David said. Fair enough. Anyone who's tried to go through the card in front of a roomful of Scousers at Haydock Park will identify with that.

We all suffer for our art. People laughed at Charles Wells when he invented the musical skipping rope but they weren't laughing when he broke the bank at Monte Carlo. That's because they were too busy chasing after him, having supplied the money he used in the casino. Eventually he was sentenced to eight years' hard labour, a small price to pay for lasting fame. You can read more about him in Willie Donaldson's entertaining book *Rogues, Villains and Eccentrics*.

I've never invented anything apart from the occasional roulette system. One of them worked perfectly. Employing a more sophisticated version of the potentially ruinous 'doubling up' strategy, a friend and I would wait for three reds or blacks to come up before backing the other colour, with funds to cover eight spins. In other words, 11 of one colour had to come up to deny us our modest profit and we played for exactly an hour. Although we never lost, there was one occasion when the sequence reached nine and the share-out in the Coach and Horses could not disguise the fact that the odds against a complete change of undergarments were no bigger than 100/30.

I did once think of a sort of buzzer that would go off in your trousers if an experienced claimer, having ridden the winner of an apprentices' race, then used his full allowance on the same horse, with no penalty, against senior jockeys a few days later. This happens only four or five times a season and I promise you'll be ahead, though there may be moments of social embarrassment.

I believe the idea came to me in Earl's Court, possibly because a dance teacher called Derek Imrie lived there and invented a small vibrating device, no bigger than a cricketer's box, which fitted inside the trousers and emitted a low humming noise if two gay men passed each other on the street. Obviously this made contact that much easier and amounted to a considerable breakthrough.

Unfortunately, extensive tests in the countryside showed that various animals, especially badgers, were also attracted by the hum. Production was suspended but the device later did well in Australia where, we must assume, the tests were less stringent or all badgers are straight.

Anyway, I hope you won yesterday. What a pity the big race isn't on a Sunday because I could have given you a topical tip. Morning Service at 10/1 would do, but that was in a Flat race on a mixed card 50 years ago. Part of a different world, really, though I believe David Icke remembers it very well.

PASSING OF A GENTLE MAN
Racing Post April 2016

A colleague's funeral which ends with 'All Blues' by Miles Davis is not to be missed.

Not that any of the old *Sporting Life* faces assembled in the Church of the Ascension, Burghclere would have missed John Santer's anyway. There would have been even more of them but the Grand National meeting was about to start and newspapers do not write themselves. Favourites went in like clockwork – Annie Power, Cue Card, On The Fringe – and John would have approved. There's not much point in giving a large chunk of your life to the form book if it lets you down on the final day.

He was a gentleman in every respect but most of all a gentle man, not given to mood swings or the raised voice. He seemed to regard much of life with wry amusement, chuckling quietly when friends pointed out that he was hanging on rather longer than the original cancer diagnosis threatened and was therefore costing Betfair and the spread firms a pretty penny. A devoted family man, he was determined to stick around for the birth of his latest grandchild and he made it.

Whether religious belief sustained him over the final months we don't really know. It would certainly have sustained his brother Mark, the former Bishop of Birmingham, who read Psalm 121 at the service.

The Santers might have been taken for twins. Since John, inevitably referred to as 'the Bish', changed hardly at all in the 30-odd years I knew him, we must assume the same was true of Mark. Slightly older than their years in early middle age, time decided to leave them alone after that and concentrated on other people. (I know, I know.)

So, what to say about the whisky and the smokes? Well, we could say John did well to make 71 and leave it at that but I think proper Scotch drinkers should be celebrated. He loved it the way a doctor does, loyally and unconditionally. Suggest a Campari and soda to John and you might as well have offered Churchill a Wills Whiff.

Steve Taylor's address was perfectly judged, covering the *Daily Express* years, the Racing Information Bureau, the *Life* and the spell as a freelance. What came across most tellingly was John's willingness to help younger journalists trying to get started – Steve himself being one of them.

Of course, it helped if you were prepared to work hard and play hard, which is where the Cartoonist came in. I found myself thinking about the *Express* in the old Fleet Street days, when John was assistant to racing correspondent Clive Graham. It was a broadsheet then and Peter O'Sullevan had a column which sometimes featured 'Bert at the garage'.

I never knew whether Bert actually existed but Peter was a very clever man and knew how to keep people interested. So he'd stop for petrol and Bert would be asking about this and that, the latest word from France and the rest of it.

I think we can safely assume that the Cartoonist shifted quite a bit of Scotch in those days, not all of it after work. It was reached via Gough Square with its warren of discreet alleyways. Gough Square will always be famous because Dr Johnson lived there but many of the other houses have gone including number three, where a surgeon once brought the body of a man hanged at Tyburn.

He had medical purposes in mind but curiosity can get the better of us, as the maid who could not resist a peek discovered. The man was far from dead and suddenly sat bolt upright, much to her consternation. The surgeon cleaned him up and arranged for him to go to America, where he made a fortune. History does not relate whether the good doctor relaxed with a stiff Scotch (odds on, obviously) but John delighted in the story.

Thirty years ago, during the BBC Radio days, I had one of my best-ever bets in his company. £1,300 to £200 about Ian Balding's Mailman in the Chesterfield Cup at Goodwood mended a few fences and he was pleased, whilst noting it was another bet to get out of trouble.

He loved racing, he loved its characters and its scribblers. He was shrewd and he noticed things. He'd have lamented the passing of the *Independent* and spotted that Chris McGrath tipped Rule The World in its humble replacement.

It was good to see him just before he died and good to see all the people who loved him. The Miles Davis wasn't bad, either.

LET'S ALL GO DOWN THE STRAND
Racing Post February 2013

The Chris Huhne affair made me think of his constituency, Eastleigh – an inoffensive borough of old engine sheds, the Pirelli factory, a thriving Celtic supporters club and the setting for Benny Hill's 1971 hit 'Ernie (The Fastest Milkman in the West)'.

Ernie was very fond of the widow Sue, who lived at 22, Liddley Lane. "They said she was too good for him, she was haughty, proud and chic; but Ernie got his cocoa there, three times every week." You don't hear lyrics like that these days.

Benny, who attended my old school Taunton's in Southampton, was asked to leave early and worked at Hanns Dairy in Eastleigh. His career has been extensively documented though there are very few references to gambling. He was actually a keen roulette player but took himself off to the south of France for the occasional spin because his fame precluded any chance of a quiet night at the tables in this country. For many years he had so much work that any losses were soon recovered.

How gamblers take defeat and (sometimes) fight back has always fascinated me. There was no fighting back for Harry Hastings, of course, because opposing Henry Chaplin's Hermit in the Derby of 1867 cost him £120,000 at a time when he was already struggling financially. It didn't help that he'd eloped with Chaplin's bride-to-be, Lady Florence Paget, which probably made the rivalry quite personal. Anyway, he ended up in the clutches of the evil moneylender Padwick and died in his twenties, a broken man. Still, you have to admire someone who said, very near the end: "Hermit's Derby broke my heart. But I didn't show it, did I?"

It wasn't Harry Hastings who made me think of Benny Hill, it was the thriller writer Edgar Wallace – and that was only because I was wondering where to go for a pint before Tuesday's Grand National weights lunch at the Savoy. Needless to say, I go there only once a year because I tend to stay on and have a glass of Sancerre in the piano bar, where the prices are imaginative, to say the least.

I've always been a sucker for piano bars – the Grand in Brighton, the Living Room in York and my favourite from years gone by, the Chesterfield Hotel just off Berkeley Square in London. The great Billy Milton used to play there, his welcome for gauche young men not quite as effusive as Frankie Howerd's, though I believe he nursed similar desires.

The obvious place for a glass of Chilean Sauvignon Blanc before the lunch is the Coal Hole, just along the Strand from the Savoy, though the Edgar Wallace on the corner of Devereux Court nearby is equally pleasant. For someone who was abandoned at birth by his actress mother, left school at 12 and became a building labourer, trawler cook and milkman just to get along, Wallace did remarkably well. He wrote songs for music hall and army concerts and reported on the Boer War for the *Daily Mail*. Unfortunately, he was also a gambler and whatever remained of his earnings he lost in a poker game on the return voyage to London.

Completely unfazed by this, he began writing again and built up a sizeable fortune, largely due to his thrillers, including the

Sanders of the River series, later turned into a film. He had something in common with Huhne as well as Hill because he stood as a Liberal candidate at Blackpool in 1931 but suffered a crushing defeat. Asked why he was standing for Parliament, he replied: "A writer of crook stories ought never to stop seeking new material."

With over 150 titles to his credit and a stint in Hollywood as a screenwriter on *King Kong* it was some performance to end up owing £140,000 on the day he died. The fact that he believed in living life to the full and had 21 racehorses in training at one stage may have had something to do with it.

Wallace could have walked from his office in Temple Chambers to the Savoy in five minutes flat and he'd have enjoyed the weights lunch. My favourite moment came a few years ago when Ted Walsh, interviewed on stage, dismissed the widely held view that Numbersixvalverde was named after the owner's holiday chalet and said it was, in fact, a brothel in Lahinch.

As for finding the winner, I generally ask Nigel Twiston-Davies and it works often enough to show a profit. If one of Nigel's is on 10st 6lb you can double the bet because that's the weight to look for in the original handicap. Or you can make some money on the side by challenging people to name the only mare in modern times to have produced two Aintree Grand National winners. (Miss Alligator, responsible for Red Alligator and Anglo.) Failing that, you can ask who penned these immortal words:

"She nearly swooned at his macaroon" and "when she seen the size of his hot meat pies, it very near turned her head."

(Be careful. This is quite a bit easier.)

THE SEVEN DWARFS – SIX ARE NOT HAPPY
the-racehorse.com February 2014

Pressed for my favourite gambling film, I'd go quite strongly for *California Split*, made in 1974 by Robert Altman and starring Elliott Gould and George Segal.

Altman's films, with their overlapping chatter, aren't for everyone and I've known people walk out of the private eye movie *The Long Goodbye*, which one critic regarded as 'a spit in the eye to a great writer' (Raymond Chandler). I wouldn't agree with that and in any case there's an affecting, bluesy soundtrack by John Williams and Johnny Mercer.

Altman was quite a gambler himself and there is one lovely story about him. With filming finished for the day and looking to end an appalling run of cards, he headed for the blackjack tables, instructing his secretary that on no account was he to be disturbed. In the mid-afternoon quiet with only the gentle murmur of the casino to calm him, he experienced further major setbacks and was suddenly aware of her at his elbow.

"What is it, Helen?" he said, a trifle tetchily. "I told you I was to be left alone."

"I'm sorry, Mr Altman," she said, "but your bookie is on the phone."

Gould and Segal are happy-go-lucky gamblers who come together by chance. Altman captures the way complete strangers talk to each other at the races, that sense of stolen time, an escape from reality. Then there are the edgy conversations around the card table, the growing realisation that things are drifting out of control, the refusal of credit at the casino, a long night coming on. In the end, Segal has enough (just) for a poker game and insists that Gould sits it out. Everything comes right and they emerge blearily into a brand new day, that wonderful dawn feeling when all of the money has come back with interest and new adventures lie ahead.

Except that it applies to only one of them. Gould lives like this the whole time and even Mexico does not seem too far but Segal knows that he will be going back to the office in his rumpled suit. There will be some odd glances, some muttering because he left early the previous day without saying anything but gradually it will die down. It's quite serious but the job is still there. It's the real world: dull, predictable and safe.

At one point in a bar where the waitresses appear to be bottomless rather than topless, they bet on the identity of the Seven Dwarfs. The world is divided into those who know the answer to this and those who don't. There is a third category, namely those who not only don't know but ask with some irritation why they should. They are not gamblers, of course. A gambler would memorise the names in case the topic came up again, earning him a few pounds. Then he might move on to *The Magnificent Seven* and tease his interlocutor by pausing, rubbing his chin and saying: "Let me see now, Brad Dexter, Horst Buchholz, Robert Vaughn …" When people start off with Steve McQueen and Yul Brynner (which nearly everyone does), you know they probably won't quite make it.

I was thinking about these things at the Grand National weights luncheon at Abbey Road Studios the other day. This was an inspired choice of venue, 47 years after the Beatles laid down the tracks on *Sgt. Pepper's Lonely Hearts Club Band*, Foinavon did his stuff and the Summer of Love was upon us. Of course, we were deep into autumn before some of us realised what was going on, but better late than never.

It was a splendid lunch and, never far from a little wager, I thought of challenging the guests alongside to name a dozen people on the *Sgt. Pepper* cover, excluding the Beatles themselves. If you decide on something similar yourself, I think you'll probably win. Of course, if someone produces a nifty (£50), pretends to think hard, strokes his chin and says, "Let me see now, H C Westermann, Sri Paramahansa Yogananda, Albert Stubbins …," you've almost certainly got a problem.

WAIT FOR ACOSTA IS MY ADVICE
Racing Post April 2017

I am seldom asked for advice and these days tend to limit myself to some routine recommendations. Never play poker with anyone called Doc, have a good look at runners from Kenya or Ethiopia in the marathon because they could all go round twice and then jog home, don't back anything penalised 6lb in a sprint handicap.

None of these sensible guidelines has boosted the bank balance of late but at least there's still Acosta, who improved a tiny bit to finish third in a long-distance hurdle at Newton Abbot last week. A ten-year-old plodder without a win for three years, he may be capable of one last hurrah. It would be good to see Dr Jeremy Naylor flying the flag at Shrewton, a famous old yard formerly run by John Bolton and Richmond Sturdy which goes all the way back to Bob Sievier, who saddled the legendary Sceptre to win four Classics, though not the Derby. Naylor, who ran the Bristol University Equine Research Centre as well as acting as Martin Pipe's vet, deserves better ammunition.

Acosta's third at 20/1 paid for a taxi and a drop of burgundy in the Italian restaurant in Notting Hill Gate. Since the television series ended in 1978 I don't think I've heard the theme from *Z Cars* outside Goodison Park (composer Johnny Keating is a big Everton fan) but the cabbie had it on. I believe the programme may have been paying tribute to the late Jimmy Ellis, who played desk sergeant Bert Lynch in the police series and never missed an episode.

"It's actually an old Liverpool folk song," I said, quite forgetting that a London cabbie *d'un certain age* would be pretty clued up.

"Johnny Todd came home from sailing, far across the ocean wide," he sang before glancing over his shoulder. "He was looking for his old sweetheart but she'd married another sailor. Same old story, guv'nor." At this point I thought Jimmy Ellis must have been in the cab at some point and I'd have had an even fifty on it but the cabbie just went on humming the song.

He was probably just as well acquainted with 'Don't Let the Sun Catch You Crying', which was playing softly in the background in Il Carretto. You know it must be Grand National week when two Liverpool songs turn up in the space of 15 minutes. My moneymaking ideas are sketchy but I do think the old Gerry and the Pacemakers hit would do well if rereleased because there's much more to it than your average pop song. Gerry Marsden still lives by the Mersey and is married to the girl who inspired the lyrics. An engaging character, he wasn't into the psychedelic phase embraced by the Beatles as the sixties wore on and went his own way. He even had a spell on the children's programme *The Sooty Show*, and not many of us can say that.

Frank Windsor was DS John Watt on *Z Cars* for the first three years and I remember seeing him at Aintree in 1984, Hallo Dandy's year. That was when clerk of the course John Hughes and I endcd up in a Birkenhead establishment where my version of 'Halfway to Paradise' came third in a Billy Fury sound-alike competition. All went well until the cabbie took advantage of our slightly confused state and we ended up halfway to Bootle.

Billy, a Scouser through and through, loved his racing and owned Anselmo, who was fourth in the 1964 Derby. I thought I knew much of his background and there were obviously regular business trips to London, though I was surprised to see him on Tottenham High Road one day after a match at White Hart Lane. Passers-by were quite unaware of his identity but fame can be a transient thing and I doubt he was all that bothered. Anyway, we put together a short interview and it went out on BBC Radio.

"You should rerelease 'Like I've Never Been Gone'; it was great, really atmospheric," I said. Palc, gaunt and not long for this world with a long history of heart trouble, he smiled sadly and shook his head. "Well, maybe you're right. I'll give it some thought," he murmured.

He didn't take my advice, though. Well, that's tradition for you.

PINK CHAMPAGNE AND A FUNNY GIRL
Racing Post July 2015

So, graduation day in Bristol; caps and gowns everywhere and some new faces in the Botanist, where the manager has already served several glasses of pink champagne to the proud parents and their beaming offspring. I interrupt my detailed analysis of the Catterick Placepot and raise a glass to the future; theirs, principally, though a winner or two at Goodwood would come in handy.

"Given my time again …" is a pointless conversational gambit, or so Marvel Mason says, though at college I do think I had the amount of time allotted to French author and philosopher François de La Rochefoucauld and the Guineas meeting at Newmarket the wrong way round.

I remember bits and pieces of my own graduation ceremony. Lester had already won the 2000 Guineas and the Derby on Nijinsky and much of the talk was about the St Leger, still several weeks away. The great man also won the Stewards' Cup that year on Harold Wallington's Jukebox and the Ebor on Richmond Sturdy's Tintagel II.

The first Stewards' Cup winner I remember fairly clearly is Ashurst Wonder, while Marvel won the school sweep in 1964 with Dunme. ("Highly appropriate. Three or four of them still haven't paid," he said this week.) Evens And Odds and Rex Imperator paid a few bills not so long ago.

I'm not sure how Al Trui ended up with Stan Mellor – from Willie Musson, I think – before winning in 1985, though I do remember Stan jumping up and down with excitement. I also recall BBC Radio commentator Peter Bromley jumping up and down at the Glorious meeting in 1983, though it had nothing to do with a blanket finish. With his usual grace and charm Omar Sharif, working on a documentary for Central Television, agreed to do an interview for Radio 2 as well. I was pleased with the way it went and Peter was quite ecstatic.

Unfortunately, the England v New Zealand Test match was entering a critical stage and, although ball by ball commentary was going out on *Test Match Special* on Radio 4, it was decided that Radio 2 would stay with it, as well. So the interview sat on the shelf for quite a while and Peter stormed off, which was a good thing, really, because I didn't want him jumping on the headphones.

I suppose Sharif, who passed away recently, and I were always going to be gamblers. My mother loved a game of bingo and his played cards with King Farouk of Egypt. In the end he hit the financial skids, much like Nicky Arnstein, the character he played in *Funny Girl*. As with so many of us, pride obliged him to try and make horseracing pay; paradise was lunch at Deauville followed by some substantial wagers. Had he simply played major bridge tournaments – he had a column in the *Observer* for many years – things would probably have been all right. Apart from the boredom, of course.

He lived by his own code and the fact that Egypt made him *persona non grata* when he filmed *Funny Girl* in the middle of the Six-Day War was hardly likely to stop him pursuing his off-screen affair with Barbra Streisand, a staunch supporter of Israel. "When I kiss a woman, I never ask her nationality or her religion," he once said. No wonder they were fond of him.

Although famous for *Lawrence of Arabia* – he got on very well with Peter O'Toole, whose father was a bookie – *Dr Zhivago* and *Funny Girl*, he later came out of self-imposed retirement to produce a charming French film called *M Ibrahim et les Fleurs du Coran*, which saw him playing a Turkish shop owner who befriends a Jewish teenager. Somehow, politics seemed to miss him altogether. He was simply a man of the world.

"I was rather hoping for the winner of the Stewards' Cup but I think I'll get you a glass of pink champagne," Marvel said. "I suspect you'll end up in the Paris suburbs, wandering around the art houses, looking for old Omar Sharif movies."

"Well, there are worse ways to go," I said.

Part Five

Hopping Around And Heading East

I tend to think of 1987 as the 'Finchley' year. Rather a lot happened. At a Wheeler's fish restaurant in Soho the late Valentine Lamb offered me the job as British correspondent for *The Irish Field* and I readily accepted. I also became racing correspondent for the ill-fated *London Daily News*, which Robert Maxwell said 'would blow the *Evening Standard* out of the water'. (Having interviewed Maxwell for the BBC when he told me Oxford United and Reading would unite and become Thames Valley Royals, I kept my own counsel on this.)

Early in November I met some old friends from Exchange Telegraph for a drink in Finchley. It was a memorable day, a blissful autumn day with Chris Thornton's Hopping Around and Pat Eddery clearing all debts in an Edinburgh claimer and Charlie Chester's in Archer Street adding a couple of thousand many hours later. I needed it with the *London Daily News*, where I was perfectly happy, lasting only a matter of months.

I don't know how Extel, with its long-established racing

background, missed out when it came to beaming live racing pictures to the shops (I'd have been the presenter), though over-confidence was almost certainly a factor. Quietly but most effectively, former BBC *Grandstand* producer Mike Murphy was setting up the operation in Corsham Street which later became SIS. When he interviewed me for the presenting role I turned it down the first time in favour of Maxwell's paper but circumstances changed, of course, and the second approach was successful.

Knowing as much as I did about betting shops, I never doubted that the pictures were all-important and it didn't matter very much who presented. This was early SIS, not the Racing Channel or ATR and, despite some notable coups – Chris Waddle and Gazza as studio guests one day, Lawrie McMenemy on several occasions and regular trips to interview Lester Piggott – the absence of any notably encouraging feedback merely emphasised that what really mattered to punters – and bookmakers, who funded the service – was the first race and the first bet.

I'm pleased that the arrival of racing pictures in the shops, in licensed premises and finally at home brought opportunities for many people, especially broadcasters, who might otherwise have followed a more mundane path for one of the big firms or failed to establish a lasting connection with the sport at all.

For my own part, I enjoyed presenting for the better part of three years but then it all became very routine and Saturdays, when I'd have been at Highbury or Stamford Bridge for the BBC, or watching Southampton on a rare day off, were sometimes hard to bear. Boredom for most people is merely a listlessness which passes but for some of us it carries more of a threat. Mind you, in its defence – and this applied particularly to me – it was certain to force a sharp change of direction. Put simply, I'd had enough.

PAT EDDERY

The Irish Field November 2015

The memories jostle each other, unwilling to be cast aside like a child's once-favourite toy. Pat coming fast and late on Dancing Brave in the Arc, Pat trying to nurse El Gran Senor home in the Epsom Derby, Pat talking the very Christian and ultra-correct Steve Cauthen into a game of poker on a flight back from Cyprus, then travelling the length and breadth of Britain, looking to deny him the title in 1987.

It all but burst the pair of them but captivated an audience well outside racing's sometimes narrow confines, like Piggott and Breasley all those years ago. And then there was Pat gradually coming to grips with the media, that endearing way he had of pronouncing 'they' as 'dey', maybe going all the way back to his Newbridge childhood.

Sometimes he'd come out with a deadpan one-liner, such as pointing out that he was always bang on time on the gallops, 'though you'd be first anyway if you were riding work for Neville Callaghan'. How we cherished those dry asides, normally reserved for his weigh-room colleagues. It wasn't that he disliked the press or the battery of cameras and microphones, it was just that, like Piggott, he simply and genuinely didn't understand what all the fuss was about. You went out and did your job; if you did it well you attracted the attention of the best trainers, and once you'd achieved that you were certain to ride the best horses, which he did for many years.

Now that he's gone, tragically early, the mental pictures are even more vivid. All of Dick Hern's meticulous planning, with two pacemakers to assist Bustino and thereby run the finish out of Grundy in the King George, came to nothing as Pat, with perfect timing, loomed up on his outer and delivered the killer thrust close home. It was a gentler time and Hern paid for Peter Walwyn's new suit, the bet having been struck in the days leading up to the race. It comes as a blow to the heart to realise that the jockey who made it all possible has departed the stage only a few short weeks after the legendary commentator who called him home.

Pat Eddery was a great jockey, of that there is no doubt. Like many outstanding talents, he was not only deeply respected in the weigh-room, he was copied. If Pat thought the ground at Salisbury was soft enough to come stands' side, everyone else thought so, too. Above all, he was a superb horseman – something the shrewdest judges notice very quickly. When he started attracting attention on Major Michael Pope's Alvaro, who set up a remarkable winning sequence in 1969, another trainer took a dim view of the young apprentice's effort in a minor race, claiming that he'd dropped his hands. "Well, you'd better get out there and pick them up, then, because they're the best pair you're ever likely to see," Pope replied.

Like Piggott, Pat wasn't all that interested in criticism, though it had nothing to do with arrogance. Many thought he should have rousted El Gran Senor at Epsom as Christy Roche gave a fair impression of a whirling dervish alongside him on Secreto. For a while he said nothing but later, in a rare moment of public candour, he said: "Dey don't understand. Epsom is a much stiffer course than people realise and this horse barely gets a mile and a half. He'll be happier at the Curragh." El Gran Senor went on to win easily, of course.

Pat was never going to make it as a trainer. These days the most important races are concentrated in relatively few hands and he was too good, too much of a perfectionist, to be training a series of syndicate horses for Chepstow and Brighton handicaps. There were family problems and then alcohol, a fickle, dangerous ally, began to compensate for having the guts kicked out of his raison d'être. If Pat couldn't work with top-class horses, the days must have seemed long indeed.

His passing has affected everyone, with no tribute more poignant than that of his friend Willie Carson, no longer the cheeky chappie of yore but a man with a keener sense of time's implacable arrow. A few years ago there was this wonderful picture of the pair of them, backs to camera, leaning on a paddock fence as a bunch of mares skittered around. Happy as sandboys, they looked for all the world like two schoolboy urchins on the threshold of a dream. Well, they both lived the dream for a long, long time and now one of them has gone. But Pat Eddery leaves us with a rich seam of memories; dare we say it, many, many more than most of those who go on to complete the proverbial good innings. Thanks for everything, Pat.

25 YEARS ON – THOUGHTS OF CURZON STREET AND CHARLIE
the-racehorse.com April 2014

Flicking through a copy of the *Daily Express* in Shepherd Market, Mayfair the other day, it was hard not to reflect on the way newspapers have changed, especially with regard to their racing coverage.

The market was named after Edward Shepherd, an architect who laid out the street pattern in 1735 on the site where the annual May Fair had taken place. He would have approved of Ye Grapes, a cosmopolitan pub featured in Arthur La Bern's novel *Goodbye Piccadilly, Farewell Leicester Square*, which Alfred Hitchcock turned into the film *Frenzy*.

Someone had left a copy of the *Express* lying on the bar in Ye Grapes. The paper used to be seen as a rival to the *Daily Mail* but that is no longer the case. Indeed, it seems to have fallen back exhausted and it is hard to believe that Clive Graham and Sir Peter O'Sullevan once graced the racing pages.

You can be around at the right time, of course. Graham and O'Sullevan also teamed up on BBC Television and were followed by Julian Wilson. All three would have despaired of the way things have gone, with the Corporation opting out of racing coverage altogether.

As The Scout on the *Express*, Clive was followed by raffish Old Etonian Charles Benson, a larger-than-life character who was a member of the Lord Lucan set and fraternised with Barry Hills and Robert Sangster. I came to know him around 25 years ago when his autobiography *No Regard For Money* ('No regard for the truth, either, old man', as O'Sullevan impishly remarked) came out and he arrived at Corsham Street to do an interview for SIS, then broadcasting exclusively to betting shops.

Whether he had ever ventured that far east of Mayfair is a moot point but he was excellent company and came up with some real gems. "People say I ponce off Robert (Sangster); well, I do!" was one memorable admission and when we came off air he confided that the *Express* had wanted him out *tout de suite*, and the line 'by mutual agreement' should be taken with a large pinch of salt. "I got a £100,000 pay-off, you know," he said. "The only trouble is, I owed £95,000 of it to one of the big four bookmakers!" He asked what I thought of that and I said it was a good job he didn't owe £105,000.

But what really made me smile was his request for a taxi to take him back to the Mirabelle in Curzon Street for lunch. Things like that make you realise how utterly ridiculous a term like 'classless society' is. The bookmakers let Charles run up a near six-figure bill because they knew he or his well-heeled friends would find the cash somehow. That day in

Corsham Street, it wouldn't have mattered how much Charles had lost, how much he owed or how much he needed to borrow; in the absence of a chauffeur-driven car, the only way to travel was by taxi. My guess is that it cost at least £30, even 25 years ago, but no doubt SIS paid.

I liked him, though, and I think you'd like the book, which must be very cheap on Amazon now. Yes, names are dropped here, there and everywhere – the Aga Khan and his wife Sally, bridge and backgammon with Omar Sharif, holidays with Bryan Ferry, games of tennis with the charming hedonist Vitas Gerulaitis, whose star burned brightly and all too briefly – but the friendships were real, not invented.

As often as not Sangster or Hills, or both, would come up with something to help fund the ongoing adventure and there in the background there was always Curzon Street, the Mirabelle and his elitist chums in the Clermont Club – Goldsmith, Aspinall, Elwes, the fearless Bill Shand Kydd, a talented amateur rider who died a month ago – and Lucan, of course. If Charlie looked soft – let's say 'well covered' – he proved pretty tough when heart trouble came to claim him. "Split me in two from here to here, you know," he told me a while later, indicating his groin to his chest after a major operation.

The book is very interesting on the subject of Lord Lucan's disappearance following the bludgeoning to death of the family nanny Sandra Rivett in 1974. The case needs no further analysis here, but Benson was quite certain his friend, increasingly worried about his children's future, had planned the murder of his wife Veronica and attempted to carry it out, only for Rivett to appear in the dark at the worst possible moment.

"Lord only knows why he was nicknamed 'Lucky'," Benson said. "He was the worst gambler I've ever known. But on that fateful day I believe he planned it, did it and killed himself."

Those requiring a fresh look at the whole affair should consult Laura Thompson's recently published *A Different Class of Murder – The Story of Lord Lucan* (Head of Zeus Ltd, £20) because it is meticulously researched and offers many new angles. For sure, Thompson believes the Curzon Street set was not particularly interested in helping the police in the immediate aftermath of the dreadful denouement, whereas Benson told me the officers were merely incompetent.

He was a snob, of course, as they all were to a greater or lesser degree. But to me he seemed capable of laughing at himself and there was certainly no denying his loyalty. At the end of the chapter on Lucan, he writes: 'I still think about him often and dream of meeting up with him. There is so much to tell him.'

Maybe it happened.

STILL HOPPING AROUND AFTER ALL THESE YEARS
Racing Post November 2014

I mention elsewhere that 1987 was a key year as regards employment in this quarter. Quite apart from the unfortunate demise of the *London Daily News* and the renewed approach from SIS, there was also the Soho lunch with Valentine Lamb, leading to 32 years as British correspondent for *The Irish Field*.

And, of course, there was Hopping Around winning the Edinburgh claimer when Steve Cauthen and Pat Eddery were travelling far and wide in pursuit of the jockeys' championship. Pat won on Hopping Around, who must have been in the nature of a certainty because he finished just behind the leaders in the November Handicap a few days later.

It's fair to say the horse sorted out a few problems for me at 7/2 but the interesting thing is that Steve's agent John Hanmer had asked for the ride, only to be told by trainer Chris Thornton that Pat had first refusal. Steve started the day one ahead and ended it one behind, with John's ante-post bet on his man (this would not have been for a couple of gin and tonics) looking very rocky. Everything came right the following day when Cauthen rode a double at Hamilton and established a narrow lead which he held to the end.

"Yes, Edinburgh was a black day for me," John admitted in a recent email, though the main reason for getting in touch was to say he was the Raceform reporter responsible for the purple passage, recalled in the *Racing Post* the other day, when an old rascal finally consented to put his head in front. "He would happily have gone down any convenient rabbit hole but no such orifice presented itself," it read. Apparently the horse in question was Kabuki, trained by Guy Harwood and ridden by David Mould, and it happened at Wye. Happy days.

Anyway, on Hopping Around day I walked from Finchley to Swiss Cottage and across the park to Marylebone, ending up in the Strand. Only those of a certain vintage will remember 'You're never alone with a Strand', which was a brilliant cigarette advertisement in the sixties, with a real Sinatra-type loner in a white mac, down on his luck, walking in the rain and ducking into a shop doorway to light up – cue music, etc.

"It was wonderful, right up there with the best Guinness ads, Hovis and Martini with Leonard Rossiter," my friend Arthur Sears said. "It won awards. Terence Brook was perfect as the lonely man and the music made the charts. The cigarettes were all right, too, but Wills were soon forced to take them off the market because no one wanted to be as lonely as that!" He laughed softly. "There you have the power of advertising in reverse, I suppose. It's a funny thing, but even when I was in the business I never knew anyone who remembered the exact shop they used, though it seemed to be on the Strand towards the Fleet Street end."

"Did you back Elm Park at Doncaster?" I asked. (Arthur backs horses purely on names and breeding and does rather well.)

"Not at 13/8," he said. "I know nothing of football, but someone told me the other day that Reading used to play there. H & G Simonds were Reading-based when they had Mackeson and I worked on the account later on. They were good ads, you know. Eleven Mackeson bottles dressed as footballers or whatever and one of them would miss a sitter, whereupon the crowd (who were all Mackeson bottles in hats and scarves) would go: "Oh, Mackeson!" so he'd take a swig of the old milk stout and run rings around the opposition. The race has had a few sponsors, but none of them has come up with anything quite like that.

"Of course it was only the price that put me off at Doncaster, because you'll know that Elm Park Lane in Chelsea is where the late Brian Jones lived in 1965. Keith Richards was a regular visitor just before the Rolling Stones became world-famous."

Ah yes, of course. Sometimes I take heart from the fact that Arthur is 90 and I still have 25 years to catch up.

Hearing from John Hanmer and bumping into Arthur Sears was a pretty good win double. I continued on my walk and found the little park at the top of Marylebone High Street much the same as in 1970, when I was thinking about a change of occupation but had Chatham's Mackeson to look forward to. The old boys were still there – a different group, it's true, but with remarkably similar tastes.

AN OLDIE STRIKES AT CRAYFORD

Racing Post January 2013

I backed a winner at Crayford on Tuesday: Venture Free at 4/1 in the 4.27. I don't know what came over me, really, but I've always liked 4/1 on the dogs, especially when it's the only one that can start at that price.

This is hardly a scientific approach but I was never any good at science. Air is necessary for burning, that's the only thing I remember. You had these little wood chips in a sort of crucible thing and put the flame underneath and they made a merry blaze but then, when you covered another batch with sand, they were as safe as houses. Not that houses themselves would be entirely safe if you kept experimenting, of course.

Anyway, that's all I know of science and I also struggle with mobile phones. Trying to text my daughter in Australia from a freezing St Mary's the other night, the closest I got to nil-nil was mij mij with no hyphen. Given the time difference, she was probably up and about. You wouldn't want the beeper going and a spot of mij mij at three in the morning, no matter how much you loved the Saints.

The greyhound expert broadcasting for Ladbrokes was in fine form and Venture Free gave him a hat-trick. To be honest, I don't think people in the shops pay much attention and I think that was also the case when I started out with SIS all those years ago. One day I went to pick up a trifling sum when someone else was presenting and all the customers were pointing the other way. As with many things in life, the trick is not minding that it hurts. Anyway, the fact that the bookies arc in competition with each other means more jobs for broadcasters and I'm all for that. Also, with numbers down in the shops, you're being ignored by far fewer people.

The other day I discovered that the ten pence per minute malarkey if you ring a bookmaker's commentary service doesn't apply to mobiles. Therefore, if you're well in contention in a three-mile handicap chase run on heavy ground, it's as well to check that the potential profit covers the cost of the call. When you ring the William Hill one, you sometimes hear John Budden analysing the way things have turned out. John speaks in slow, measured tones and you will soon be absolutely skint but that, in my view, is a small price to pay for the kind of precision broadcasting which might have brought news of war casualties on the old Home Service.

We can't all be around at the right time. For instance, I should have been a crooner in one of the smarter London hotels. A crooner by night and a Marcel Proust lecturer by day, with no thought of the 4.27 at Crayford and every chance of denting my father's assumption that I'd never have any money.

I see now that he was pretty shrewd. As time goes on, most of us take a nose or a short-head defeat quite calmly. But when we start out as gamblers even a neck comes as a hammer blow. When I fancied one of John Meacock's – Qarazan, perhaps – it was beaten a neck at Warwick at 33/1 and I agonised at length over the margin. "Yes," murmured my dad, no longer surprised by anything. "Mind you, horses have quite long necks, don't they?"

I thought of these things at a lunch given by *The Oldie* magazine this week. One of the speakers was Charlie Mortimer, son of the late Roger Mortimer, who was racing correspondent for the *Sunday Times* for 30 years and whose collection of letters to his wayward son was recently published as *Dear Lupin*.

The book will divide opinion. Mortimer senior had a dry, engaging sense of humour and *Dear Lupin* is very amusing, especially where his wife's fondness for a tipple is concerned, but there are reservations on the political correctness front. Maybe the cosy assumptions and privileged background helped push Charlie in the opposite direction. He failed to see things through at Eton, found employment an unnecessary complication in life and experimented with various substances before starting the long climb back.

He spoke very well, like a man who has peered over the edge and has no reason to fear anything. I can confirm it's a most agreeable feeling, even if the days sometimes seem rather long.

FRIENDS BY DAY, STRANGERS IN THE NIGHT
Racing Post October 2014

The James Joyce Pub in Paris could use a lick of paint.

The establishment at 71 Boulevard Gouvion St Cyr attracts plenty of British and Irish visitors during Arc weekend and, if it were mine, I'd offer Victor Chandler a sizeable sum for that wonderful black-and-white portrait of Lester Piggott – lined, obsessive, implacable – that sits in his office. Then I'd have bits and pieces of Joyce's *Ulysses* photographed and framed around the walls.

"Unless you're in the know, there's no straight sport now. Lenehan gets some good ones. He's giving Sceptre today. Zinfandel's the favourite, Lord Howard de Walden's. Won at Epsom."

That is from *Ulysses*, as Leopold Bloom continues his lonely journey across Dublin with a visit to Davy Byrne's bar. A year later, Zinfandel won the 1905 Ascot Gold Cup (by which time Sceptre had retired) when the late Lord Howard's father, happily ensconced beneath a tree in the paddock, is said to have contemplated the score for an opera. He wrote the libretto for at least three successful productions. If I ran the James Joyce I'd arrange a special promotion of White Zinfandel which, curiously enough, is not white but rosé.

Zinfandel and the incomparable mare Sceptre, owned and trained by Bob Sievier, were great rivals. Sievier was unquestionably a rascal (not as harmless a term then as it is now) but the general consensus is that he always ran Sceptre on her merits; she rewarded him with four Classics, though not the Derby.

Of the many fascinating stories about him, one that stands out concerns his reaction when police officers arrived at his Shrewton yard to charge him with perjury – an alleged offence going back at least six years. Giving them the slip, Sievier went to Swindon station, where he must have dossed down before catching the first train to London the following morning. There, he met his solicitor, Mr Blanchard Wontner, instructing him to prepare his defence and brief counsel before – and this is the bit I love – repairing to Romano's, a favourite haunt, for lunch. Suitably refreshed, he then strolled round to Scotland Yard to answer all charges. If you want to know more, you should order a copy of John Welcome's *Neck or Nothing – The Extraordinary Life & Times of Bob Sievier*, without delay.

Romano's must have been quite a place, more Italian red than White Zinfandel, I should think, and perfect for Sievier's post-race celebrations or heart-searching analysis. No doubt it had racing prints around the walls and was quite expensive. I was thinking about it in La Barca this week, La Barca being the Romano's *de nos jours*, an excellent but very pricey Italian restaurant behind Waterloo Station and just opposite the Old Vic.

Skaters Waltz helped pay for this, the ex-Paul Cole-trained grey having lobbed up in the closing handicap at Longchamp on Arc day. He used to be ridden by Luke Morris but a Frenchman called Prat does the honours these days and I, for one, was very grateful at 22/1.

They're kind and loyal enough at La Barca to have kept the picture of my friend John Watt dining with Brian Clough in the old Bell's Manager of the Month days. John would have liked Tuesday's companion Bill Chapman, a close friend of mine from the old wine trade days, a world-class authority on Frank Sinatra and the head of accounts at J & B when the whisky was regularly picking up the Queen's Award for Exports.

Justerini was an impoverished Italian count who fell in love with a touring English opera singer and followed her back home. No joy, apparently, but at least he had some family recipes that he sold to Alfred Brooks. The latter diversified and you can work it out from there.

Bill has been a Chelsea supporter through thick and thin for 60 years or more and remembers the title triumph in 1955. I told him that when the Blues signed Peter Sillett from Southampton, his mum insisted they take John, as well. John is a lovely, larger-than-life character but the arthritis is troubling him now and he can't look after Graham Bradbury's one-time Cesarewitch hope Black Or Red, so it would be nice to find a loving home for the old horse. He canters but galloping is beyond him. I know how he feels.

It was a long, rewarding day. Taking in the George, Great Portland Street, and returning home via Reading station, I met a woman who asked if I spoke English. 'Un poquito, si!' I replied, thinking this would get me out of it, but she told a very strange, rambling story about lost car keys, unhelpful police and needing to get to the far side of Swindon. Henleyon-Thames came into it somewhere, as well, and it was clearly a fabrication, but I suppose I was in a very good mood. Lunch with Bill tends to have that effect.

My wife says there's a big difference between easy-going and gullible but I like to think of a cheque fluttering through the letter box, restoring my faith in human nature. You will have your own thoughts on the likelihood of this.

THINKING IT THROUGH WITH ARTHUR
Racing Post December 2016

I think you'll see why this idea didn't quite work.

I'd invented a football match between artists – painters, writers, sculptors – and politicians. The artists, much more imaginative, 2-1 up and with little thought of running the clock down, are about to celebrate when Auguste Rodin's back-pass falls woefully short. Beethoven is quickly off his line but to no avail as Benjamin Disraeli rounds him and makes it 2-2 with seconds left.

Well, it happens. Dickens and Chaucer write it all down and the artists accept their fate graciously with the exception of J S Bach, who stares at Rodin and shouts: "Rodin! What were you thinking?"

I told Arthur Sears the story and he chuckled, which was gratifying, but even at 92 the old advertising man is more acute and analytical than most. "Hmm. Entirely dependent upon people knowing that Rodin sculpted *The Thinker*," he said.

This is true and I suppose you end up playing the percentages, which involves risk. I don't want to live without risk. Recalling a match at the Dell in 1953, when Northampton

Town survived a second-half onslaught and won 3-2, the sub-editor on 'The Pink 'Un' came up with the headline: Cobblers Hold On in Battle of the Hamptons. Now, I think this is wonderful but a more cautious person might wonder whether enough people would know what Northampton is famous for, or whether they'd have a passing knowledge of Cockney rhyming slang.

I'm pretty sure Neal Wilkins would have liked it. His picture came up at the HWPA Awards lunch on Monday, when they went through the list of sadly departed figures, human and equine, in 2016.

Considering how many thousands of people were around, I saw Neal surprisingly often before Arsenal and Southampton matches, though most recently we shouted greetings across the tracks at Paddington underground station. The smoking ban had left him temporarily without his trademark cigar but he was immaculately turned out, as always.

He worked for the Press Association and Victor Chandler and had a fund of stories. With Neal, I never had the slightest doubt that he knew which side of the fence a sensible man needed to be, though I did once mention that, without the greater or lesser weakness that most of us display on a regular basis, he'd have been seeking alternative employment. He smiled.

He could tell a story quite beautifully, with a burst of laughter at the end. Many years ago the radio and television performer Leslie Welch, universally known as 'The Memory Man' (try saying his name to anyone over 65) made a handsome living from answering questions, many of them sporting, sent in by members of the public.

I think it not overly cynical to suggest that there may have been a little tinkering here and there, and Neal agreed.

"He was a very keen punter, you know," he said. "One day at Kempton when it was very busy he really had it away, the only problem being that he lost his ticket and couldn't remember who'd taken the bet. He went to the course office and they went through the bookmakers one by one until finally it was uncovered. But the funniest thing was, Leslie couldn't see why people were falling about laughing."

I shall miss Neal, his suits and cigars, and I shall miss Hennessy, though the suggestion that the name might survive on the racecourse, apart from in the bars, misses me altogether. When things end, they end, after six years or 60 and I say this as someone who is biased towards the product, having sold enough bottles in my time.

The late Arthur Hopkins, 'Scoop' to everyone and PRO for Hennessy when the brand was in its pomp, was an old sweat. Like a hotel doorman, he didn't ask how you were getting on, he just glanced at your shoes. One year I helped him contact all the surviving owners, trainers and jockeys associated with Hennessy winners since 1957 and all bar three came to a special lunch at Newbury. Arthur missed the big day, though, because he used to moonlight for the *Sunday Mirror* and was covering a game at Tottenham.

"That sounds like Scoop, all right," Arthur Sears said. "The Rodin piece never saw the light of day, then?"

"No, it was spiked. I even had Proust and Francis Bacon creating chances for Franz Schubert, but he couldn't finish them off."

Arthur took another sip of manzanilla, his wrinkled face a picture of health and happiness in the weak December sun.

"Maybe it's for the best," he said.

CAPTAIN ZARCO – MY SORT OF MAN
Racing Post December 2013

I once passed an exam on the subject of Madeira, the island and its wine. Always one for the shortcut, I memorised the four main grape varieties and concentrated on Captain Zarco, who is one of my heroes. When the Portuguese came across the island centuries ago it was completely covered in forest so Captain Zarco simply set fire to it and came back later; about five years later, I seem to recall.

Well, everything was quite badly singed but the soil proved ideal for the cultivation of vines. Madeira, a fortified wine not dissimilar to port, has a 'burnt' quality to it but was very popular in this country 50 years ago and more. It even had its own music hall song: 'Have some Madeira, m'dear! You really have nothing to fear. I'm not trying to tempt you, that wouldn't be right; you shouldn't drink spirits at this time of night'.

Someone asked for a glass of Madeira the other day, which was a 50/1 shot. The last place I remember seeing it on the shelf was in the Pope's Grotto in Twickenham which was a very handy stopping-off place for Kempton on Boxing Day. In 1978 we shared a bottle of Sercial, which is the driest Madeira, and Gay Spartan did us proud, but most places were closed after racing. That is still true today, though Earl's Court carries on much the same as usual.

The King George has been kind to me, and indeed to my mother, who was a big Gordon W Richards fan and would not hear of defeat for Titus Oates in 1969. I'm not saying I've come to rely on one particular week but Kempton and Chepstow in late December have been known to balance the books to a degree, Supreme Glory's victory in the Coral Welsh National in 2001 leading to prolonged celebrations.

(Of course, when I say 'balance the books' I mean in a vague, notional sort of way. I don't really do profit and loss, I do 'feel good' and 'not so good'. That's always worked for me and I recommend it.)

Now that I've been told to take a long walk every day it's important to decide on some new routes. Kempton to Sandown makes some appeal, past that great big reservoir in Sunbury and on through Hampton, where there used to be a nightclub called Alexander's. Perhaps there still is. I sold them quite a lot of Smirnoff 40 years ago but no Madeira. You'd think a place with a name like that would have a ragtime band but it was all the Doors and Lou Reed mumbling away in the background.

Salisbury to Wincanton should be possible, up the old A303; so too Lingfield to Gatwick and the ghosts of Bill Wightman's ponies at the old racetrack all those years ago; and Brighton to Lewes, or the other way round, I suppose, because we might as well end up in the Regency Tavern. I've got it all worked out.

Brighton was wonderful this year: Eric Wheeler's Even Bolder at 20/1, Mark Tompkins getting another race out of Judi Dench's Smokey Oakey with Sutton Sid keeping on for the forecast. At one stage I even thought I might be getting the hang of the whole thing, but that can't be right.

Incidentally, I mentioned a few weeks ago that Dench played the master thief Peter Scott's girlfriend in the film *He Who Rides a Tiger*. Reading Scott's autobiography the other evening, I was struck by the size of bets he had with Victor Chandler as long ago as 1957 – £8,000 profit at Ascot, all given back, with interest, at Newmarket a few days later.

It's probably time for a book about the Chandler dynasty. Obviously those bets were with Victor's father but I recently came across some even more fascinating information concerning the late Lucian Freud. Sometimes his gambling debts reached the sort of level where he'd paint the present Victor, the debonair actor manqué we all know and love, to bring them down a bit. I believe Victor managed to keep his clothes on, which was quite unusual with Freud.

I was thinking about this at Sutton Scotney Services the other night while pondering a walk from Stockbridge to Littleton. Stockbridge racecourse played host to the future King Edward VII and his mistress Lillie Langtry, whose saucy lyrics he clearly found irresistible, while deeply troubled war poet Wilfred Owen wandered close to Littleton just under a century ago. More recently, local trainer Les Hall landed any number of canny gambles, including a memorable four-timer at York. He lost his licence over a filly called Littleton Queen, not that she did anything afterwards.

Or there's Stockbridge to Boston, even if December sees the turnpike covered with snow, according to James Taylor in 'Sweet Baby James'. Still, upon arrival in Boston we could raise a glass to the Stars and Stripes. The Declaration of Independence was toasted in Madeira, of course. Captain Zarco must be proud.

SOUTH AMERICAN GETAWAY – BUT NOT FOR LONG
Racing Post October 2015

During the long afternoons at SIS in Corsham Street I sometimes thought back to the days when I was selling this and that in South America.

It often occurred to me that Paraguay was the ideal place for a man to disappear, should the need arise. I'm not saying I seriously considered it – Import in the Wokingham and Mailman in the Chesterfield Cup eased the situation at different times – but I don't think too many questions would be asked in Paraguay.

I liked it there, even if I was selling the wrong product. I couldn't shift much Underberg, an 80% proof pick-me-up, in Hounslow and Twickenham but it came in these special bandolero belts and would have gone down a storm in Asunción. It's just a pity I was selling graphic arts materials.

I went racing in Brazil, losing money in a claimer, and made little impression in a casino in Quito, Ecuador. As for Abidjan in the Ivory Coast, where I was lucky to get the last plane out before Christmas, the least said the better, though I was sensible enough to avoid a game of Find the Lady in a Chinese bar. The decor was redder than anything in the film *Mean Streets*. It looked a good place to lose quickly and politely.

It's harder to disappear than you might think. For a start, you still have to find work of some kind. All right, that wouldn't have applied to Jay Gatsby, but he was always bound to come back to Daisy in the end, even if things didn't work out. Anyway, real though he may seem to us, he was a fictitious character, like Jack Nicholson, who takes a dead man's identity in *The Passenger*, and Terry Lennox, who decamps for Mexico and returns as Senor Maioranos in Chandler's *The Long Goodbye*, though without fooling Philip Marlowe.

I've known people go away for a while after a bad run on the horses, and I've known people stay on the first train the morning after the night before, just to see where it ended up. That can be tricky for gamblers, of course, who may not have the wherewithal for a drink when they get there or the fare back.

Many years ago there was an afternoon drinking club just off the Marylebone Road where they played really good jazz – 'Waltz for Debby' and 'On Green Dolphin Street' by the wonderfully gifted pianist Bill Evans, for example. Bill wrote 'Waltz for Debby' after watching his three-year-old niece playing on the beach – a peaceful moment in a deeply troubled life.

Like outstanding saxophonist Stan Getz, who was almost impossible to get along with, Bill hadn't actually done anything wrong or broken any laws. (I'm leaving out 'recreational activities' here.) Therefore they differed from the disgraced politician and fraudster John Stonehouse, an old boy of my school, who faked a drowning suicide in Florida. If he'd asked me, I'd have tried to talk him out of it. Once that failed, I'd have advised against leaving a pile of clothes on the beach. If you walk out to sea in the general direction of Cuba, being eaten by a shark is a pretty short price and it's not a method many of us would choose.

I thought it was a bit of a giveaway but he disappeared for a while and was probably a bit unlucky when arrested in Australia, because the police there thought the 'mysterious Englishman' might well be Lord Lucan. He had to drop his strides but there was no telltale blemish high up on his thigh, which disappointed them. Stonehouse, who died in 1988, was extradited and sentenced to seven years.

You have to be very careful what you say about things like this at the school reunion dinner on the eve of Remembrance Day. These occasions are a reminder of how many people stay close to home for their natural span, whereas I might have ended up in Paraguay and I certainly had a funny turn in Bolivia. Or there's Salford, of course, if I'd stayed at the BBC.

Salford! The 'Dirty Old Town' referred to by the Spinners is suddenly famous; Albert Finney's birthplace, Fred Done's very first shop before he made it big, Shelagh Delaney's *A Taste of Honey*, Rita Tushingham's puckish, gamine face, cheeky and sad at the same time.

The song doesn't feature in the film but the nursery rhyme 'The big ship sails on the ally ally oh/On the last day of September' does and is quite moving in its own way. The Salford girl is left with something of a problem and the young sailor who brightened the dirty old town for her, well, he disappears.

HOW INSENSITIVE – THAT'S WHAT CLIFF THINKS, ANYWAY
Racing Post September 2015

Sitting in the Botanist, listening to Paul McCartney's 'And I Love Her' and wondering whether to back both of Tom Segal's in the Guinness Kerry National, I was startled to read about Cliftonmill Olympus II.

Not a camera shop in the trendier part of Bristol, Cliftonmill was a bull called upon to service a cow named Celia. This was theoretically a most enjoyable assignment but they were many miles apart and his sperm, millions of them, had to be frozen and driven across country in a white Volkswagen to the barn where Celia waited patiently. Whether she or Cliftonmill suffered the greater indignity is a close call.

A handful of television reviewers might have mentioned this in passing, but only the great Clive James (it's from one of his *Observer* pieces in 1975) would have gone on to wonder whether Cliff availed himself of a copy of *Penthouse* to help with an encore.

Soft porn can take you a long way, of course, even as far as West Ham. But it had me thinking about how we all differ when it comes to developing a thick skin. I am hopeless in that respect and can remember every slight, real or imagined, over half a century or more. If I were chairman of Southampton – a very big 'if', I grant you – with a 'top shelf' background, there would be the best white wine in the boardroom, recalling the days of the wonderfully hospitable Cobbold brothers at Ipswich Town. But in the back of my mind would be the nagging worry that the visitors' chairman, smiling but smarting from a late Saints' winner, might politely enquire whether I had any old copies of *Readers' Wives*.

Charles II must have been quite thick-skinned because he didn't mind Nell Gwyn calling him Charles the Third, her first two lovers having also been called Charles. I avoided a yellow card for staying too long in the wine bar (you can't leave when Diana Krall is singing 'How Insensitive'; thank you to the lady who texted me) by telling my wife she was born exactly 300 years after the orange girl on 2 February. Women are strange, though. I once mentioned the great tenor saxophonist Stan Getz, another to share that date, but she was unimpressed.

The temptation upon leaving the Botanist is to go next door to the University and Literary Club. They have a two-year-old filly called Unilit, who did them proud by finishing third in the Group 3 Dick Poole Stakes at Salisbury. She'd already run ten times but Mick Channon typically spotted a likely opportunity for some black type and it worked. The owners are more than happy.

Mick Channon

The trainer and Chris Scott, who is arguably the driving force behind the club, go back many years – all the way to Piccolo and beyond. Mick has spoken at the club's sportsmen's lunches but most recently the guest was Bristolian Ed Morrison, who refereed the 1995 Rugby World Cup Final between South Africa and New Zealand. He was introduced to Nelson Mandela the night before – not a bad picture to have on the back of a menu card – and managed to play a dead bat when the great man asked him who would win.

Morrison thought New Zealand would win comfortably but the host nation famously prevailed 15-12 in the first major post-apartheid sporting event held in the country.

A story went the rounds that the All Blacks had been poisoned at a function beforehand. It was probably tabloid nonsense but Morrison merely commented that, in all his years as a referee, he had never seen players being sick by the side of the pitch before. In lighter vein and having grown up in Hartcliffe, which is not quite Versailles, he said that, should anyone return and find the wheels of their car gone, he could at least furnish the name of the pub where they might be recovered. A small handling fee is involved.

Late in the day on Wednesday I checked Tom's tips and my investments. Incredibly, Lots Of Memories and Owega Star had both come to grief at the twelfth and been put down. I needed Radio 3 but it's all Bach at present. I once remarked to a posh woman that you never knew when Bach had finished, not a criticism anyone ever levelled at Jimmy Shand and his Band, and she said I was the biggest philistine she'd ever met. It didn't matter much because I was an even bigger price than old Cliftonmill Olympus II.

It still hurts a bit, though.

Part Six

Boyst And Dougie And The Other Boleyn Girl

I may run out of space, writing about Brighton. Early teenage visits with my girlfriend Eileen, Albert Neaves winning a decent sprint with All Promise when everyone thought he only trained jumpers like Certain Justice, Boyst turning up at 8/1 for Tom Waugh, Phil Bell persuading David Ashforth and me to sponsor a race.

We came down from Cambridge in early June. Raceform still produced a daily ratings booklet with a yellow cover in those days. There was nothing 'glossy' or pretentious about it; a 'minus' by the horse's name was good news because it meant it was carrying 2lb less than Raceform's assessment. Boyst was -2 and won an apprentices' handicap quite tidily. I was hooked anyway but down there by the furlong pole, where I still stand today, the moment would have seduced me without coming off the bridle.

That was 50 years ago. It's now all of 25 since Phil, who gave up local radio to become clerk of the course and has since gone on to Chepstow, had his little chat. David, the best racing journalist of the modern era, was so busy with the *Racing Post* that I eventually took over and am now, in 2020, up there with the late Doug Marks, who sponsored the Flanagan And Allen Handicap, named after two of the most famous Crazy Gang members, and used to present the winning owner with a smart wooden chess set.

I followed his horses with almost religious zeal. I believe he was the last man in Britain to run a horse twice on the same day, winning a seller at Newmarket before retaining it at the subsequent auction and then sending it out to finish third in a non-seller an hour and a half later.

Selling races fascinate me – everything from the slow, steady plod around the parade ring to the hard-fought battle out on the track and the auctioneer's glowing account of the winner's prowess. "You've seen him win today!" he barks, as if we've already forgotten this dazzling triumph. And all the while the winner ambles round in a circle, waiting for his loving lad or lass to take him home and wondering what to do if a horse matching the auctioneer's assessment suddenly turns up.

I'm pleased to sponsor in September (though Covid-19 ruled out the 25th running) because interesting things happen in this particular month. In 1990 a mare called Ann Boleyn unseated her rider and galloped all the way to Roedean Girls' School, where she was captured by the headmistress and the chaplain. The better-known Anne, beheaded in 1536, would have welcomed such a sanctuary. The equine one – rather cleverly named, by Tower Walk out of Femme Fatale – also failed to produce any male progeny, not that there were many opportunities.

I've tried to give a flavour of Brighton, the racecourse and the town (where anything goes, in the nicest way) in the next few pages, though you should also read – in addition to Greene's *Brighton Rock*, obviously – *The Brighton Races*, which is a fine history by Jim Beavis, and Nigel Richardson's *Breakfast in Brighton*. Once here, your return home may well be delayed …

3rd of August 1960 - Barbary Pirate deposits Lester Piggott near the winning post at Brighton as Colin Moss on Bob Barker goes on to win the race.

CRUISE TO THE SEASIDE
Racing Post June 2012

"We're all coming back," Mrs Rocking Billy says. "We'll be sitting here, having another drink. I'm psychic, darling."

At first I think she means in September, when an intriguing apprentices' selling handicap (mine) graces an exceptional card, but then I realise more of a Buddhist slant is intended.

"Well, I hope you're right, Pam," I say, despite nursing a few doubts.

The pub opposite Brighton racecourse used to be called The Winner but now it's the Fox on the Downs. We sit outside in the sunshine before racing and it's good to see Billy, the legendary local DJ, looking so well because he nearly lost a foot not so long ago. Apparently hospital staff were concerned about the volume on his radio but the operation was a success and he's back in action later this month. "Keep rocking!" he says to well-wishers on their way to the course. No one knows how old he is but he can remember the odd dust-up on the front when most of the participants looked like the Fonz. Billy still does, of course.

"Can you do me a favour, darling?" Pam says. "I've got a feeling about these." I thought being psychic gave you more of an edge than that but I study the piece of paper and the two £3.50 reversed forecasts with great interest. Should they come up I shall not have to worry about carrying the cash for too long because Pam has kindly written the number of a Santander account on the back.

There are two ladies *d'un certain age*, which means my sort of age really, at the next table who want a tip. The only horse I fancy is Cruise Tothelimit in the 9.05 at Newbury but they need something for now so I go for the safest option,

Stonecrabstomorrow in the first at Brighton. He falls out of
the stalls and finishes last. Stone last, I should say. By this
time I am at the furlong pole, waiting for David Ashforth, his
friend Mart and Mart's son Dan, who is in a rich vein of form,
especially here.

Mart will ask many quiz questions over the next few hours
and I do quite well with one or two of them – the 17 players
capped by England while playing for Southampton and the
two horses which, with two letters reversed, have won an
Ascot Gold Cup and a Royal Hunt Cup. Yeats and Yeast.
Ashforth is very impressed; also clearly relieved that he
doesn't have to think about it any more.

We miss a couple of winning favourites but manage to back
Ooi Long, who takes the romantically named Pipe Center
Handicap under a good ride from Toby Atkinson. Ooi Long
is trained by Mark Rimmer, whose picture was on my wall at
home for ages because he won a little race at Nottingham on
Mrs Leadbetter (25/1) 30-odd years ago. I had a share in Mrs
Leadbetter, as I mention elsewhere.

Colin Brown of Desert Orchid fame is on the microphone,
doing the announcements and conducting excellent post-race
interviews. We need Mick Quinn to win with Royal Defence
so that Colin can interview him and set the crowd a quiz
question. Which three managers did Mick play for who were
World Cup finalists – two winners, one loser – as players?
Alan Ball, Ossie Ardiles and Arie Haan (PAOK Thessaloniki).
Colin writes it all down but Royal Defence comes sixth. This
is something of a setback and has not done Pam any favours,
either. I'm glad I bought her a ham sandwich.

Dan bumps into the in-form Eddie Fremantle, who says that Paperetto (14/1) will nearly win the last but jockey Daniel Cremin (7) has yet to get off the mark. Well, that's the last time we'll be able to say that. We repair to the Regency Tavern.

"Dirty rifle," Mart says.

"Pardon?"

"Which pop singer reminds you of a dirty rifle?"

You have to stay sharp but after an eight-race marathon I miss the fact that a Dusty Springfield tape is playing in the background. Then my dad's watch stops in the Casalingo Italian across the road. Actually it's my watch now because he's been gone for 42 years but you know what I mean. Mercifully the others remind me that it's nearly five past nine, so I run to the William Hill around the corner and back Cruise Tothelimit, who wins at 100/30.

It's a perfect day, even with a three-hour drive home. The radio in this Volvo estate I've borrowed seems to be stuck on Radio 2. There can't be any other station in the world that would follow Leonard Cohen's wonderful 'Suzanne' (total bliss between Brighton and Hove) with 'The Organist Entertains'. They do have something in common, though. Rocking Billy has never played either of them.

WHAT'S IN A NAME? QUITE A LOT, ACTUALLY
Brighton Racecard Piece 24 August 2015

Good afternoon and welcome to Brighton for the latest renewal of the Ian Carnaby Selling Handicap. I think this is the 20th running of my race, scheduled to take place between York and Doncaster, though I must say an initial glance at the participants indicates that very few of them venture that far north.

I thought we'd found the winner last year, a charming filly of Peter Makin's called Just Isla, who took it up for Richard Hughes approaching the furlong pole but was caught and beaten by Bookmaker. Not the first time we've been beaten by a bookie, of course, and certainly not the last. Mind you, it seems a strange name to give a horse and there was no clue in the breeding because he's by Byron out of Cankara.

My friend Arthur Sears backs only cleverly named horses and his favourite was one of Gary Moore's. By Seeking The Gold out of You'd Be Surprised, the owners called it Wait For The Will. As we know, where there's a will, there's an unknown relative. He was a good old boy, Wait For The Will, and won 16 of his 98 races, finishing up in a seller at Lingfield, where he dead-heated for first at the ripe old age of 12. Funnily enough, Gary never raced him here, though he tried Epsom, Goodwood and even Plumpton.

I once had shares in a hurdler by Master Willie out of Limelight, a mare we owned. Asked to name him, I came up with Afterglow. If you think hard about that, it's quite clever. It must be, because even my wife thought so, but there'd been an Afterglow in the previous ten years so Weatherbys couldn't register him. Truth be told, I haven't had much luck with names. I entered a competition to name something by Trumpet

Major out of Flibbertigibbet and thought Strumpet Voluntary wasn't bad but never heard any more.

The first horse I part-owned was called Bianca after Bianca Jagger. She made her debut here many years ago and finished third but the unluckiest story concerns Mrs Leadbetter. She ran here and trainer Gavin Pritchard-Gordon quite fancied her but she fell down the hill and George Duffield sensibly eased her right down. A week or so later, at Nottingham, she went in at 25/1 in the hands of Mark Rimmer, unbacked by me.

She was nicely named because the head of the syndicate, Margot Stewart, was a big fan of *The Good Life* and especially of Penelope Keith, who played Margot Leadbetter. When Mrs Leadbetter (the horse) went to the sales and was led round, we thought she'd fetch a pretty penny but she had a boil on her bottom, which was rank bad luck and could happen to anyone. You, me, anyone.

I've tried hard over the years to convey how much Brighton means to me. I once interviewed Lester Piggott, hoping he'd come up with some glowing appraisal, which was possibly a tad naïve of me. "It's a funny sort of place," he said. "You have to pull up a bit sharpish or you end up in an allotment."

I go back as far as course specialist Operatic Society, of course, though more recently I was very fond of a slow old miler called Stimler, trained by a lovely man, John Bolton. John has something in common with celebrated local DJ Rocking Billy, because I said a few words at both funerals, though I should have turned up at the second one, a few months ago, in drainpipes and winkle-pickers.

I digress. Have a great day, make sure you find the winner and come back and see us again. After all, there's nowhere quite like Brighton.

YOU'RE HIRED, CHARLIE

Racing Post August 2016

Goodwood Cup day was more or less perfect. Any day starting with a winner owned by George Materna and ending with the Sarah Harrison Band at the Platform in Southampton has to be a bit special. People wandering past (not something I've ever managed) might have thought Cher was in full flow; Harrison is very, very good indeed.

It's fair to say You're Hired was strongly fancied at Amanda Perrett's and if ever a man deserved a 9/1 winner at a course he has supported for 30 years it was George. Typically, quite apart from his own bets, he had £100 on for charity and if You're Fired, which he doesn't own, had won on Friday, the £100 double would have added considerably to all the recent talk about major gambles landed.

It was an excellent meeting this year and the executive, together with clerk of the course Seamus Buckley, should feel proud. Buckley manages to look amiable and utterly focused at the same time, which is a neat trick. "You can have a drink on Saturday evening," I said. "Or maybe two," he smiled.

There was dancing to a live band at the end of the afternoon and I saw no hint of trouble. With respect, some recent correspondents have misjudged the root cause of racecourse conflagration. The problem has little to do with young people arriving for musical entertainment; it revolves around the consumption of alcohol long before racing starts.

On summer Saturdays especially, pubs close by are open at 11am on the dot and that is often three hours before the first race. Lager is the preferred drink – overwhelmingly so – and, to take a particularly popular brand as an example, Stella Artois is 5.2 per cent ABV.

The brewers acknowledge the problem and at Chester last month there was a Stella Artois 4 per cent Handicap to mark the launch of a lower strength product. It should be made widely available on draught and will mark a step in the right direction. But racecourses will never be able to control intake away from the track and to criticise them – 'time racing got its house in order' – is as unreasonable as asking 'football' to stop West Ham and Millwall supporters meeting near the most convenient Tube station before the match.

I was pondering this in the Platform but future expenses occupy a permanent place in the gambler's mind and I was thinking of letting Franklin D pay for the catering expenses at Brighton tomorrow fortnight. In the last decade I doubt there has been a horse that ticked every single box in a red-hot handicap the way Franklin D did in the Betfred Mile and yet, as we all know, backing 7/4 favourites in 19-runner races of this type is hardly the way forward.

Still, he was a bigger price early on and sorting out lunch for 24 thirsty guests would have left me with an inner glow. Speaking of which, even if Hennessy called it a day now, I'd have to live to 107 to become the country's longest-running sponsor. Odds against, probably. It's my own fault; I shouldn't have sold so much of their VSOP around Hounslow and Isleworth in the 1970s. Kept them going, no doubt about it.

Brighton should have more races named after local characters. There used to be a George Robey Handicap, of course, commemorating the great music-hall entertainer, who was greatly admired by Noel Coward. And for many years Doug Marks put on the Flanagan And Allen Handicap. Just before he died, Bud Flanagan recorded the theme to *Dad's Army*. Many suppose this was composed during the war but it was penned much later, in 1968.

Flanagan and his great friend Chesney Allen loved their racing and Brighton might almost have been designed for them. The only thing that went wrong was their decision to put another Brighton aficionado, top jockey Charlie Smirke, on the stage at the Talk of the Town in London. Unfortunately, although Charlie was brilliant with punters in a natural setting – 'What did I Tulyar?' after winning the Derby, for example – he 'froze' under the lights.

When he was warned off (probably unfairly) by the Jockey Club, Charlie slept under a tarpaulin on Brighton beach. Circumstances and, indeed, life generally never got him down. All these years later he'd have given Franklin D the same no-nonsense, flat-out, inches to spare ride Ryan Moore conjured up on Friday. And I dare say he'd have agreed to go through the card for the guests before my seller, as well. They don't make them like that any more.

BRIGHTON ROCKS FOR SOOTY
Racing Post September 2016

I take heart from racing material turning up in non-racing books – everything from Throwaway winning the 1904 Ascot Gold Cup in James Joyce's *Ulysses* to dear old Sooty Tern landing the Eric Simms Memorial at Brighton 93 years later. A sprightly ten-year-old then, he features in *Breakfast in Brighton* by Nigel Richardson.

Joyce must have researched tirelessly, bearing in mind that *Ulysses* was not published until 1922. Leopold Bloom, filling out the day in his lonely sojourn across Dublin, is the wandering Jew, accepted but hardly made welcome. He unwittingly tips Throwaway to Bantam Lyons, who is in turn dissuaded by Lenehan, no great friend of Bloom's.

Throwaway started at 20/1 in a four-runner field because one of his rivals was the mighty Sceptre. Sadly, she was deteriorating at five and, following defeat in the Gold Cup, was retired. Blameless throughout, Bloom fails to back the winner himself but the others persuade themselves he is a sly individual who has put them away.

Richardson tells us that Graham Greene visited the track only once before *Brighton Rock* was published in 1938. As for his own tilt at the ring, never has a £2 winning bet been recounted in such loving detail. Apparently Sam Trumpton of Eastleigh – 'the one with the whisky bottle in his pocket' – felt the lash as Royston Ffrench came fast and late, getting up to beat Victory Team by a length at 9/2.

Celebrations took place in the Racecourse Inn and if the jockey hasn't read the piece someone should show it to him. 'Royston's colours were bright as a maharajah's in the afternoon gloom'. Incidentally, there have only ever been two Sooty Terns and the American one was foaled in the same year, 1987, as Milton Bradley's grand old stager, still with us at 29.

I was pondering this while listening to Petroc Trelawny on Radio 3 the other morning. He was playing Hubert Giraud's 'Sous Le Toit de Paris' (1951), which sounds to me a dead ringer for 'Out of my Dreams (and into your arms)' from *Oklahoma!* but Petroc is one of the younger people. Working on Classic FM before Radio 3 must have tested him – all those adverts – and it had me thinking of Rishi Persad.

If you do enough graveyard shifts on the snooker and the bowls, you deserve a lasting shot at your first love and it's good to know that certain conversations with leading personalities will endure. "Ah, listen now, Rishi, listen, this horse …" Actually, that's quite possibly the only thing Aidan O'Brien and Harry Redknapp have in common; they both unfailingly remember your Christian name.

So, ITV has got one right and I happen to be a Matt Chapman supporter as well, though it's a pity there is no room for Tanya Stevenson, who not only knows the betting ring inside out but is one of those people you instinctively like without knowing particularly well. My mother would have approved of her hats, as well, and I thought we were trying to appeal to all age groups. Well, not my mother's group, obviously, which would be around the hundred mark, but you know what I mean.

I think there should be a slot for authors with a passing interest in racing. Hackney historian Iain Sinclair might be persuaded to comment on Alexander Baron's Jewish gambling tale *The Lowlife* from 1963, while David Szalay would surely be happy to talk about the perfectly researched (though fictional) coup at Huntingdon – tipping lines, the *Racing Post*, Betfair – which features in his bitter-sweet novel *Spring* (2011).

We don't care quite as much about the slightly mismatched lovers in *Spring* as we do about Bendrix and Sarah in *The End of the Affair*, arguably Greene's finest book. It's a strange thing, but 'Haunted Heart' by Jo Stafford is played all the way through at the end of both *The End of the Affair* and Jack Nicholson's *The Two Jakes*.

Needless to say, when this happens I'm all over the place; a bit like Leopold Bloom, you might say.

FINDING A LADY – OR A FUNNY GIRL
Racing Post October 2017

And so to Brighthelmstone and the sports. A spot of pricking the garter, the three-card trick in the company of tatterdemalions, fortune tellers and lewd musical girls with shrewd advice from David Ashforth, Dan Matthews, Simon

Holt and Rocking Billy's widow Pam. How could anyone lose?

I've seen Find the Lady practised on the front at Blackpool, at the bottom of the hill leading straight down from Notre Dame and in the car park at Windsor races, where an upturned *London Evening Standard* box served as a table. But Pricking the Garter was new to me until I studied William Powell Frith's painting *The Derby Day*, which he completed in Blink Bonny's year, 1857.

The leather garters that men wore to hold up their stockings would be made into two identical loops, the unsuspecting 'mark' being invited to choose which one would hold a stick firmly. Fast (as in tight) and Loose was the other name for the scam, with a skilled practitioner able to loosen either of the loops and let the stick fall. Shakespeare mentions fast and loose in at least three of his plays, including *Antony and Cleopatra*.

Nothing much changes with the passing of the years. When I saw an American tourist fleeced at Windsor, the dealer was so good you wondered why he didn't go straight and become a magician. Belleville in Paris was similar in that the queen was never the card you thought – that's the enviable skill – so you could play at even money by backing one of the other two. (They aren't going to pay out anyway, of course, and your chances of a beautiful friendship are seriously diminished.)

There was probably a time when the former Brighthelmstone might have come closer than anywhere else to emulating Frith's Epsom vision but it was Brighton by then and there will be no such shenanigans a century and a half on, except in my rambling imagination.

The last Brighton meeting, all done and dusted by the time you read this, means the onset of winter. The first short story I ever had published ends with the words: 'There's a definite chill in the air now and the lights are shimmering through a hint of sea fret on the front. I turn up my collar and set off down the hill.' Blimey. I must have been a sad old bugger even then.

When I was much younger a magazine asked for a feature on the crooner Frankie Vaughan. I only thought of it because the sprinter Green Door is running quite well at the moment. Sorry, you'll have to ask your dad. (I realise this may be tricky.)

Anyway, Doug Marks trained Water Rat for him when Frankie was president of the show-business charity of that name. In foal she was more or less unbeatable and won by miles at Salisbury one day. Doug said that Frankie was happiest at the races or sitting on the pier at Brighton with a stick, a bit of string, a pin and some bait. They were both lovely people.

I don't know why people say you should avoid meeting your heroes. I've met Bill Wightman, Omar Sharif and Vitas Gerulaitis, to name but three, and they were charming, helpful and unassuming. Interestingly, they were all gamblers, though Bill was more of an ultra-shrewd investor and only backed his own horses. Omar Sharif lost thousands at the track and should have concentrated on bridge and backgammon, while Gerulaitis lost more tennis matches from a winning position than any other top player, possibly because he was still playing the tables a few hours before.

They all had a wry, self-deprecatory sense of humour. Bill had placed The Goldstone to advantage at most southern tracks and finally found a winnable race for him at Brighton. Not a close follower of football, he affected a puzzled expression and remarked that "rather a lot of people seem very pleased".

In 1980 Gerulaitis finally mastered Jimmy Connors and told the press: "Nobody beats Vitas Gerulaitis 17 times in a row," while Sharif, asked whether he was in love with risk, observed that conducting an affair with Barbra Streisand during the Arab-Israeli Six-Day War was a pretty big clue.

Most of them have gone now and I was very sorry to miss the late Robert Altman when he was over here filming *Gosford Park*. What a gambler he was, with $10,000 bets on big American football games. There's still Barbra, I suppose, though it's hard to imagine playing 'fast and loose' with her. As for 'pricking the garter', well, only in your dreams.

ON DAYS LIKE THESE ...
Racing Post September 2018

It's hard to know what to do next.

Actually that's not quite true because my little grandson needs some Thomas the Tank Engine trousers and Sainsbury's are selling out fast. Leo will grow up in the 'post Sodor' era, political correctness obliging Thomas to leave the island and visit Russia, where a female engine will prove just too good for him in a race. If you missed the story I can pass on the good news that the Fat Controller has survived.

This comes as a welcome relief to those of us who regret the departure of Mr Golly from Toy Town. Frankly, that made no sense at all because he was a successful, kind-hearted businessman, a garage proprietor who made a meaningful contribution to Toy Town society – more of a contribution than Big-Ears, for a start.

Back To Mine, Solveig's Song and Princess Power will pay for the trousers but the days will seem long. Of course, the seller at Brighton on Monday was a minor event but, as always, it meant a lot to me. Needless to say, I'm biased; then again, I've never met anyone who isn't biased about something or other.

If you think the BBC isn't biased, try listening to Radio 3 early in the morning, where 'Bach before seven' has been running for the better part of a year. Not Tchaikovsky, Beethoven or Mozart, always Bach. It's a way of saying: 'This man is the absolute master and we're going our own way no matter what.'

As it happens, there's not much of Bach I like. He composed well over 1,000 pieces (which means Radio 3 can continue with this for at least another three years) but went to jail for a month at one stage.

When I read about this I had a mental picture of the Leipzig constabulary going round his place, banging on the door and saying: "One more cantata exactly like all the rest and you're nicked, Bach!" but he'd merely refused to compose for a local nobleman, a duke I believe.

When I tipped and backed Solveig's Song it was mainly because I thought she might keep on for a place at around 16/1; she tends to run better at Brighton than anywhere else. In the event she fairly bolted up at 10/1 and it's gratifying when cleverly named horses win. Solveig's Song is from the Norwegian Edvard Grieg's 'Peer Gynt Suite' and is by Norse Dancer. The crowd around the unsaddling enclosure will have noted this and passed it on. Even so, it seems highly unlikely there will ever be a 'Grieg before seven'.

Being interviewed by Colin Brown is a most agreeable experience because we have quite a few shared memories from his time as a jockey. However, nothing quite matches No Camping in a Southwell selling hurdle soon after the horse had failed to trouble the judge, or indeed anyone else, in a better race at Newbury.

The late Richmond Sturdy, suffering with a nasty head cold, had forgotten to organise a horsebox but Colin and David Elsworth managed to get hold of a bread van. No Camping won all right, at around 11/2 if memory serves, and from that day on – it was over 40 years ago – I became even more interested in sellers and ended up sponsoring one.

It's hard, working out what to do next. At one point after racing my friend Howard Dawson was playing Matt Monro songs – 'On Days Like These' particularly apt – on his phone outside the Regency Tavern, an almost surreal experience.

Still, the real world awaits and passing Swindon on the way home acts as a reminder. The Nailsea Betfred is not quite the same with the passing of Mel Wood, who bet small every single day and only took time out to act as jockey Fergus Sweeney's driver. The manager Steve is a good man, as well, and went close in the Betting Office Manager of the Year competition 12 months ago.

If he'd told me he was in for it I'd have given him a plug here, but some people push themselves and some don't. It's a pity, really, because I'm as biased as they come.

Part Seven

Modest Hopes, Fading Dreams

Several of the Ashforth-Carnaby sellers produced interesting stories but there is nothing to match the 1998 race, won by Sue Lamyman's 11-year-old Modest Hope, who travelled down from Lincolnshire and was led up by Basil Richmond.

The *Sporting Life* had just closed down after 139 years and there was much sadness in the camp. I was 'ghosting' Martin Pipe's column at that stage – he never considered anyone other than David or yours truly and we got along very well. Anyway, he said Highbury Legend should win our race and I was able to pass this on to Robert Cooper, a friend and former SIS colleague, when he broadcast the racing bulletin on 5 Live.

But as Highbury legends go, this one was more a Perry Groves than a Thierry Henry. Starting at 9/4 favourite, he was in front passing me a furlong out but then Country Thatch plodded past, only for Modest Hope, rated 28, and young Antonio Polli to nail him on the line. Antonio, an Italian apprentice, spoke little English but still wondered aloud if there was always champagne after a race as moderate as this. We don't know what he made of his stick of rock.

It was great fun but I was soon reminded of Pipe's ability. Within weeks he won two novices' claiming hurdles, at Wincanton and Taunton, with Highbury Legend – something you'd have found hard to believe if you'd seen the Brighton race close up. It was a salutary reminder of the contrasting pace under the two codes and it took me back to a conversation in his kitchen, where we put pieces together. "We like to think good horses can become top-class, those with a certain amount of ability can win decent races, and even the very poor ones can win SOMETHING. We improve them, that's what we do." Quite so.

I wasn't betting heavily by then, the thousand I had on Zoman when he was short-headed by Opera House in the Tattersalls Rogers Gold Cup at the Curragh in 1992 having forced a general rethink. The *Life*'s closure came as quite a setback, especially as it was another ten years before the *Racing Post*, or more specifically editor Bruce Millington, whom I'd known at the *Life* and the *London Daily News*, offered me something similar.

Of course, there were still some substantial wagers and some long nights along the Edgware Road. Before the *Life* departed the scene I used to buy the next day's edition at Marble Arch soon after midnight and read it in the casino.

I wasn't a good enough poker player to make an impression but I listened to people and watched them and used the name of one of the regulars, Lennie Miles, in my short story 'Zarzuela', which closes *Not Minding That It Hurts*. I went to the Old Duke, a famous jazz pub in Bristol, and looked for any excuse to spend time in the Platform (folk and blues) or La Regata Spanish restaurant in Southampton, especially if my great friend Brian Truscott, an excellent secretary at the football club over many years, was free from his duties at the stadium.

I suppose I was gradually storing up enough material in the hope that it might come in useful one day. I had bits and pieces written down just about everywhere and the discipline involved gradually made its presence felt where gambling was concerned. It never occurred to me to give up altogether because, leaving family matters aside, there is something about a short-head winner or the ball nestling contentedly in 16 red that is hard to replicate anywhere else. Well, anywhere apart from St Mary's, of course.

IN SEARCH OF LOST TIME
Racing Post May 2017

At long last I've seen Worcester Shrub Hill.

In the old days – the old *Sporting Life* days, I should say – I'd play the tables and, depending upon how well things had gone, consider the early-morning rattler from Paddington to Shrub Hill, just to see what it was like. I thought of it as a romantic journey; a view not universally shared, perhaps.

Nailsea to York and back by train seldom passes without incident. Last year on the return journey we were held up at Gloucester, where someone had appropriated a tractor and driven it into a bridge, dislodging the brickwork and blocking the line. One assumes that alcohol played a part and the story made the local press. Anyway, we all received free coffee and a Kit-Kat before trundling back up to Birmingham New Street, there to await a fleet of taxis and make all the necessary phone calls to our loved ones or study the following day's runners in the Lockinge.

This year there was a problem at Bromsgrove on the outward journey and we were redirected (without stopping) through Kidderminster, a fine town, and Worcester Shrub Hill – many shrubs, a forlorn industrial estate and an old boxer dog on the platform, his master gone for a jimmy, but no hill. I have every reason to return and investigate.

The passengers remain philosophical, even cheerful, as the delay reaches the hour mark and a refund of 50 per cent comes into play. In my case this is about £85, which is the sort of bet I'm thinking of having on Muntadab in the sprint handicap. I am perfectly relaxed. There could even be a mechanical failure of some sort but nothing serious enough to deny me a close-up view of the Musidora fillies as they surge past the furlong pole. Time is on my side and there have not been many days when I could say that.

I'm fond of Musidora, who was probably named after the celebrated French actress Jeanne Roques. The main reason concerns the way she calmly scooped up the 1000 Guineas and the Oaks in 1949 when her previous record hardly promised dual Classic glory. Trained locally by Charles Elsey, she became a Yorkshire heroine and no one should underestimate her Epsom triumph, which came at the expense of French challenger Coronation, who went on to win the Arc.

Also, it was on Musidora day in 1998 that *Sporting Life* stalwarts gathered in the Venice restaurant on Great Titchfield Street to mark the passing of the famous old paper. The only people missing were those working on the Knavesmire. In thrall to old haunts, old conversations and various cognac-inspired wagers, I kept going back to the Venice after my *Sporting Life* and BBC Radio days until it gave up the ghost and became a curry house. I thought they might have rung me up before it happened but both Proust and I learned to accept these disappointments long ago.

At York station the rain falls steadily, making Muntadab a near certainty, though the 'near' bit can be quite irritating sometimes. Mark 'Couch' Winstanley will not hear of defeat for Brando in the Duke of York and I tell him he could have been a contender, thereby prompting a stream of *On the Waterfront* jokes.

We're both better off than Prince Frederick, Duke of York and second son of George III. Unlike the grand old duke, Prince Frederick never had 10,000 men to march up and down the hill but almost certainly had £10,000 now and again, especially after winning the Derby with Prince Leopold and Moses. In love with the good life, he was a hopeless card player and died deep in debt.

I wonder what they played at his funeral. Frank wasn't around so it wouldn't have been 'My Way'. Just as well, really, because that bit where he goes: 'Yes there were times, I'm sure you knew, when I bit off more than I could chew,' would have brought ribald confirmation from the cheap seats.

A pity he just missed Brahms, too. Third movement, Third Symphony, a little gentle regret, the horn solo, some losing hands in the dead of night, the women who finally gave up. Maybe he was around at the wrong time. Two hundred years later he'd have been gazing wistfully out of a rain-streaked window at Shrub Hill, wondering if there was any action there.

TRAINS OF THOUGHT – FROM SLOUGH TO DIDCOT AND BEYOND
Racing Post July 2013

Sometimes you wonder what your own headline might be.

Well, not so much a headline – obviously we're not talking about the recently departed Bert Trautmann or Mel Smith here – what we're looking for is a gentle aside, a single happy memory, a fond reminder on a page otherwise replete with tips and running plans. 'Rambling scribbler who backed Patient Constable in the Stewards' Cup', perhaps. It came to me when the train stopped at Didcot Parkway, probably because Mel had horses with the Johnson Houghtons, not far away at Blewbury.

In my salad days, when I was green in judgement, I still managed to back Patient Constable at 33/1, so I probably have the edge on Cleopatra, who regretted her earlier dalliance with Caesar when she met Antony. Well, you never know what's around the corner. At least the mistake occurred early in life. There should be a corresponding phrase for the latter stages of our brief sojourn – plum duff days, something like that.

What do you suppose a 'parkway' is? Why isn't it Slough Parkway? Because you can't park there after a certain time, not unless you turn left and drive about half a mile, right by the side of the railway tracks, observing the train you'd quite like to be on coming towards you. 'Station stop', as in 'your next station stop' is a bit strange, as well. Then again, originality can prove a risky alternative. A few years ago I boarded a District Line Tube and the driver said: "Right then, ladies and gents, here we go, all the way to sunny Plaistow." He was stood down for a while.

Sir John Betjeman seemed rather hard on Slough – 'Come, friendly bombs and fall on Slough' etc. – and later explained the sentiments expressed in his 1937 poem, which sought to highlight the way certain places were used as a dump for war surplus materials. One night after a rather inauspicious spell at the tables I managed to get back as far as Slough and explained all of this to a Hindu carpet salesman moonlighting as a taxi driver but I don't think he was deeply into Betjeman; more of a Kipling man as I recall. There was a nice musky smell in the taxi, though, possibly from the carpet.

It was good to see Jimmy 'Marvel' Mason getting on at Didcot. "Give me a Patient Constable, an Ashurst Wonder, a Sky Diver," he said, by way of greeting.

"I'm not sure I can. Evens And Odds was my last winner. But what you need in the nursery afterwards is something that's been winning sellers or claimers in the north by a wide margin and gets in off a low weight. Dandy Nicholls always wins it but last year Jamesbo's Girl was claimed by Richard Fahey at Catterick. She still won the Goodwood race, of course. By the way, did you know a horse called Marvel won the Stewards' Cup twice? It was before our time, which is quite unusual."

"Jamesbo's Girl was 16/1 and that put me off," Marvel said, mysteriously. "Incidentally, do you remember Alf Tupper?"

"The Tough of the Track? Used to work nights, a couple of hours' sleep, coal dust still in his eyes but catches the bus and turns up with his spikes in a brown paper bag, just in time to take on the cream of the local athletics club? Outpaced most of the way but sheer guts and determination get him there in the end, blood pounding in his ears? Eschews the presentation because he has to get back to work? That Alf Tupper? Yes, I think so."

"I've got a full set of the *Rover*, the *Hotspur*, the *Wizard* and the *Adventure*," Marvel said. "In your opinion, would the collected stories of Alf Tupper sell in book form?"

I pondered this. It's not as potentially ruinous as his plan to open a nightclub called No Regrets. "All these people with no regrets, they should have a place where they can get together," he said about a year ago. "I ask you. No failed business ventures? No loss of temper with their loved ones? No unfortunate liaisons?" He stared at me intently. "No bedroom disasters?"

"I don't know, Marvel. They've probably experienced all of these things; it's just that they don't regret them. I can't see it working. You'd have to have Edith Piaf and early Scott Walker on the whole time and the bar staff and doormen would have to be super-optimists. To be honest, I'm not entirely sure about Didcot, either."

We said goodbye at Swindon and I was sorry to see him go. Maybe I'm missing something. Sigmund Freud said there's an underlying sexual pleasure in riding trains but I must say I'm not aware of it between Paddington and Bristol. I don't know about you but I suspect the good doctor thought of little else. Trains, trains, trains.

FROM BLYTH TO LA SERENISSIMA
Racing Post October 2018

Like many people I make lists, then come across them months, or even years, later. Time having moved on, some of the items have become rather mysterious.

Pay Wilson's. Signor Baxter. Royal Blue and the Spartans. Where Frank Saul? Mister Baileys/David Dand. Quinny and Lingfield.

This is from several years ago on the inside back page of a Chepstow racecard. The first one is pretty obvious and crops up in several other lists, as well. A statement from Wilson's reminds me, or I remind myself, that I start with small bets and end up with larger ones. In a nutshell, all of my major investments are designed to force a draw and feel better. This is poor strategy.

I just wish the cheques didn't have to be made out to Wilsonbet, which is a bit of a giveaway. In the old days, when you could write a couple of cheques in a casino, the identity of the recipient was rather vague. Distinctive Services Limited, I seem to recall, probably from Charlie Chester's in Archer Street, Soho. It's gone now, replaced by a smart Italian restaurant called Bocca di Lupo.

Signor Baxter had me puzzled for a while but then I remembered I once thought of checking whether you could fly from Newcastle to Venice, where I'd retrace all the steps taken by Donald Sutherland (John Baxter) in the superb Nicolas Roeg film *Don't Look Now*. It must have been a 3am fantasy because I think Hexham and Blyth were in there somewhere as well.

There is this wonderful scene where Julie Christie, Baxter's wife, leaves on a vaporetto for the airport. Tragically, she will never see him again and he cuts a forlorn figure on the shore, with Venice bathed in brilliant winter light. I used to watch it when I'd been cleaned out; it made me feel better in a perverse sort of way. (In the film *Blume in Love*, George Segal asks a friend why a mutual acquaintance never watches anything other than *Gone with the Wind*. "Because he knows it's good," he replies.)

When I was a child we used to go on a Royal Blue coach to visit my father's family in Blyth. I suppose the coach went up the old A1. It took all night and it was pretty cold when you got there, with the wind howling in off the North Sea. A giant slag heap has stayed in my mind for 60 years. A giant slag heap, a blind uncle, Mandarin winning the Hennessy.

I've never been able to find Frank Saul. When Southampton sold Martin Chivers to Spurs for a record fee we got Frank as part of the deal. He was all right but he wasn't Martin. Anyway, a few years ago I was writing features for the match-day programme and tried to locate him. There was a Frank Saul – Bespoke Tailor on Tottenham High Road or possibly Stamford Hill, so I left a message.

I had this charming phone call back and he was thrilled that I'd got in touch. Unfortunately, he'd never played football and knew very little about it but could do me a lovely suit with an extra pair of trousers at no extra cost. I should drop in at any time and I sounded a nice man. The other Frank seemed to have vanished, though the most persistent rumour had him working in the motor trade somewhere in the Essex hinterland.

When Mister Baileys won the 2000 Guineas in 1994 I knew it was owned by a horse-feed company but managed to work Baileys Irish Cream into a *Sporting Life* piece. I conducted all the test markets on Baileys in this country, though it was always going to be a Gilbeys of Ireland product. The managing director at Naas Road was David Dand, who backed Mister Baileys and invited me over for a celebratory lunch. Sadly, he died before we could organise it.

I thought 'Quinny' had to be Richard Quinn, who was my favourite jockey, but then I realised I must have been thinking about racing correspondent Quintin Gilbey, who was never involved in the wine trade himself but whose grandfather, Alfred, set up W & A Gilbey with Quinny's great-uncle Walter.

The very last original W & A Gilbey sign I saw was outside a corner shop on the main road as you turned left towards Lingfield when it was still leafy. I probably thought I should check whether it was still there, but then forgot all about it.

I expect it's gone. Royal Blue coaches, Quinny and David Dand certainly have. But Croft Park in Blyth is definitely still there, and so is Venice. For a while, anyway.

SHERRY WITH ARTHUR, LUNCH ON CHARLIE
Racing Post June 2014

Arthur Sears, nearly 90 and immaculately attired in pinstripe suit as the sun attracts some early beach-dwellers, will beat me at this game, as he always does. He'd beat me on Mahler and Dizzy Gillespie and, like most educated gay men, on Hollywood divas, as well. Still, you have to try.

"The Atlantic Ocean was really something in those days," I murmur optimistically.

"Ha ha. Very good," Arthur says. "Burt Lancaster in the film *Atlantic City*, I think. A rather seedy, down-at-heel Atlantic City as I recall. Just goes to show people could take the mickey out of nostalgia, even then. I've ordered two glasses of manzanilla, by the way. The girl has gone to ask."

I could point out that we're in Weston-super-Mare, not Sanlúcar de Barrameda, and he'll have to make do with Tio Pepe like everybody else, or like no one else, really, because you seldom hear sherry asked for these days. But I stay silent. Borodin can be heard faintly in the background, a string quartet in the hotel time forgot.

Arthur arches an eyebrow. "You know the show, of course?"

"*Kismet*. 'And This is My Beloved'." One-all; there may be someone looking after me.

"Mm. Did you go to Chepstow on Monday and back Johnson Houghton's Charlie Wells?"

At first I think this is part of the game but then I remember Arthur reads *The Times* and the *Racing Post* every day before doing anything else. He is hooked on names and breeding rather than form, an endearing trait that nets a handsome profit now and again, if not overall. I shake my head.

"I thought you'd be there," he says, a little disappointed. "Charles Wells was the man who broke the bank at Monte Carlo and Charlie must be named after him because he's out of a mare called Numbers Game. Beat a horse called Go For Broke at 16/1. Isn't it wonderful? Lunch is on me, by the way."

The girl arrives with a bottle of manzanilla on a tray with a cooler and two sherry glasses. "Bottle of manzo whatever you said, darling," she says in a deep Bristolian accent, flashing Arthur the sort of smile that might attract younger men from Taunton and Burnham-on-Sea. "Antonio says you might want more than a glass, just let him know."

"New Spanish manager," Arthur explains. "Nice chap and knows his Rioja, too. Charles Wells was a terrible man, you know. Broke the bank with money people had invested in his dodgy inventions. They caught up with him and he did eight years' hard labour but I suppose we never really change. First thing he did afterwards was invent a lifebelt."

The sherry butts are placed on the front at Sanlúcar and the sea breeze passes over them. When Arthur tilts his glass towards the light, closes his eyes and sniffs approvingly, a hundred wrinkles take their turn in the sun. The manzanilla does indeed smell of the sea, though I dare say being in Weston has left it on a very fair handicap mark in that respect.

"I don't know Eve Johnson Houghton but I like her," he smiles. "I always back What About Carlo because the name means a lot to me. Eve seems quite feisty, like Fulke. He told all the top owners where they stood – Charlie Engelhard, Sheikh Mohammed, the Aga Khan – even if it meant goodbye. You have to admire that, don't you? (Yes.) I can't remember where I read it now."

"I think it was one of mine, actually. Anyway, my shout. 'One instinctively knows when something is right'."

"Oh, dear heart. That was the slogan for Croft Original, a pale cream sherry you sold in Holland and Belgium about 40 years ago. Good of you to offer a lifelong advertising man a gift."

The 'Adagietto' from Mahler's 5th emanates from the kitchen area.

"I don't know how many times I've seen *Death in Venice*," Arthur says. "Poor old Dirk Bogarde with the dye trickling down his face and little Björn Andrésen leading him on in his sailor suit. Warner Brothers were going to withdraw it, you know, but the Queen attended a gala premiere and they changed their minds. She's obviously happiest at the races and the pictures. Shall we go through?"

SING THE SONG, BACK THE WINNER

the-racehorse.com May 2012

In a frivolous moment I suppose you might wonder which of Michael Tabor, Derrick Smith and Mrs Susan Magnier is the karaoke fan.

Perhaps they all are. It's hard to see how you'd name a filly Homecoming Queen unless you knew the lyrics to 'Daydream Believer' – 'cheer up sleepy Jean, oh what can it mean, to a daydream believer or a homecoming queen' etc. Someone on Channel 4 should have suggested an impromptu performance – Mrs M on vocals, Michael on vibes – when she bolted in by nine lengths in the 1000 Guineas but it's a serious world we live in these days and it came as a surprise when Aidan exclaimed: "Stone me! Strike a light! I didn't see that coming, did you?" (I made that up.)

Successful in a Leopardstown nursery off 72 (at the eighth attempt) as a youngster, Homecoming Queen was a shock winner and left at least one prominent pundit wondering whether detailed study of the form book is worth the effort. Well, of course it is. You just have to let the old Earth make a couple of whirls ('September Song', Kurt Weill), wait for the wet spring to run its course and bask in the glory of Epsom and Royal Ascot, when all of your other calculations will bear fruit.

What is the alternative? Backing horses purely on their names? 'Now you know how happy I can be', as one joyful punter in the Tote queue sang soon after the Guineas, though you had the impression it was a one-off. It was still good to hear, for the very good reason that there will come a time when the link between horseracing and popular songs disappears altogether as lyrics are forgotten.

People of my age still hum tunes as they wait to place their bet. The earliest example I can remember is 'Only You' – 'Only you can make this change in me, for it's true, you are my destiny' – who finished third in a Goodwood nursery the better part of 50 years ago.

Crowded Avenue – 'I don't know if we're in a garden, or on some crowded avenue' was very popular, as well, though you had to sing it through to get to the title, which is 'I Only Have Eyes For You', of course. Crowded Avenue was a good sprinter for Peter Makin but ended up in tricky Sandown claimers, though I never lost faith in him. Money gone, faith intact. He was by Sizzling Melody and a warm glow comes on when you realise someone must have taken the trouble to put it all together.

Of course, not everyone thinks things through. Some people were mildly irritated when commentators referred to Kris, the great miler, as Chris, the reason being that a kris (crease) is a Malayan dagger and the horse was by Sharpen Up. I sometimes wonder if the Chris thing bothered his owner Lord

Howard de Walden, though I imagine, if you owned half of Marylebone, you'd probably get other people to name your horses for you.

Sometimes, you're in a position to help out younger people and in my case the time has come when that means just about everybody. The ever-youthful commentator Simon Holt was struggling with Googoobarabajagal one day; the trick is to emphasise the 'raba' bit in the middle, but he was in full flow and it was a long way to the Brighton commentary box. 'Goo Goo Barabajagal' was a hit for Donovan in the late 1960s. Some have suggested that the lyrics owed plenty to a substance affectionately known as Bolivian marching powder. Be that as it may, Googoobarabajagal the horse remains a maiden.

Catch The Wind, on the other hand, made perfect sense and won twice. For a long time I thought Donovan had included a chap called Albert Almeers in this. 'To feel you all around me, and to take your hand, along the sand; Albert Almeers, well try and catch the wind.' Clearly this was a grand passion thwarted and Albert had missed out. I was never entirely happy with it, though, and one night, in a blinding flash, I realised it was actually: 'And to take your hand, along the sand, ah but I may as well try and catch the wind.'

Catch The Wind is by Bahamian Bounty, sea breezes no doubt, out of a mare by Music Boy. It all fits if you try hard enough. Sandy Lane in the Bahamas would be a good place for a karaoke, come to think of it. 'If I Were a Rich Man', 'The Best Things in Life Are Free', some of the old songs ... I expect they're setting it up, even as we speak.

EASY COME, EASY GO
Racing Post May 2016

I never hold on to money for very long. It stays a while and then drifts off, like a disenchanted lover. I'm not complaining; in the old days it used to storm off in a huff, leaving me to contemplate the future in the company of Miles Davis or Johannes Brahms.

Every now and then I build up a stash of £50 notes between the Julian Barnes books by the side of the bed. *Nothing to be Frightened Of*, that's my favourite. Then my wife spots them and they head off in the direction of Nailsea High Street, where rigid checks are carried out. I expect you know that rubbing a £50 note against a piece of white paper is meant to leave a mark and it's only when they leave no trace at all that someone has been busy in the attic or the garden shed.

By way of conversation I once told the girl on the Tesco checkout that any problem would be of great concern to the Victoria Casino but, let's face it, there are worlds and worlds and she probably wasn't deeply into 16 red or 33 black, not to mention the neighbours.

Most casinos pay out in cellophane packets of £1,000, all in fifties. The celebrated barrister George Carman QC used to enjoy a game after getting some household name off the hook – he hardly ever failed – but must have frequented posher places because his biography touches on the deep satisfaction brought on by handling 'those cellophane packets of £2,500'. I don't know where he went afterwards, though I never saw him in The Hope pub opposite Smithfield Market, where you could enjoy a pint at dawn in good company.

Anyway, I am holding folding, as we used to say, thanks to the great Jim Old winning with 14/1 chance Aldeburgh at

Nottingham last Saturday. Aldeburgh is one of the Wally Sturt-owned horses Jim took with him to Nigel Twiston-Davies' yard and I believe he is particularly happy with the lad who rides work on him.

So, lunch is on me if there is anything left after the train ride to York and a few optimistic punts in the sprint handicaps. It's £163.70 return from Nailsea if you have an old boy's, sorry senior citizen's card. (And if you're reading this, you probably have.)

I couldn't face a four-hour drive and in any case I wanted to look out of the window after a detailed appraisal of the form. I think the dream of an alternative lifestyle is precisely that although, given the hours I keep, I've often thought a late-night piano bar would fit the bill. I doubt the regulars would resemble Rick's clientele in *Casablanca*, although several of my friends have very similar suits.

I made a dent in the Aldeburgh winnings by going to see Harold Pinter's *The Caretaker* at the Old Vic. It was superb, though I had to glance down at the programme to reassure myself it was Daniel Mays and not my former colleague, racecourse commentator Ian Bartlett, playing Aston. The likeness was quite unnerving.

Tottenham v Southampton also cost a few bob, though an unlikely away win made financial considerations irrelevant. It was many years since I'd walked the length of Tottenham High Road and I found myself trying to work out whether there are more betting offices or barbers' shops. A high-scoring draw, perhaps.

On another day, and without my pregnant daughter for company, I might have walked all the way to Hackney Wick and tried to find the old greyhound stadium and the barber's shop, long gone no doubt, where old Sidney Kirsh did so well with leather purses he'd made himself that he was able to open the first betting shop in Poplar.

Barbers' shops and bookmakers are similar, aren't they? They can learn from each other. Just think, if you asked for a number two on top and a number three at the sides, and got it the wrong way round, you could be offered your money back as a free haircut.

I must go now. There is the Hambleton Stakes, dinner in Gilling East to follow and then Brahms. And while there is Brahms, there is always tomorrow.

A GREAT OLD CHARACTER CALLS IT A DAY
the-racehorse.com July 2014

Racing is not so richly blessed with characters that it can afford to lose one of the best. Sadly – and one still hopes there will be a late reprieve – trainer Jim Old has quietly retired.

A rumpled, amiable, phlegmatic horseman of the old school, with the driest of wits, he deserved a few more paragraphs in the racing press, more about Collier Bay and Cima and Mole Board and the rest but the world moves on apace. Jim always cared more about personal friendships than anything else and has dealt with far too many setbacks to worry overmuch about the latest one. This sudden retirement failed even to disturb his annual golfing day in aid of the Injured Jockeys Fund.

Over the years, in response to various rambling pieces in the *Sporting Life*, *Racing Post* and elsewhere, Old has sent me cards and tapes on the subject of Ella Fitzgerald, Kurt Weill, old-style crooner Al Bowlly and, more recently, Hampshire's middle-order batsman Peter Sainsbury, who died not so long ago. We share a love of old entertainers, the pair of us born a little too late for the vintage days of music hall. Old is a brilliant mimic himself, his David Gandolfo and Wally Sturt well-nigh perfect.

"If I'd gone on the stage I'd have been rich and insufferable," he told me many years ago. "Now I'm just insufferable." The last part is untrue but Dick Francis' wife Mary, who had trodden the boards herself, did indeed suggest that the young man might have plenty to offer the world of show business.

However, Dick introduced him to trainer Neville Dent in the New Forest and from there he went on to work for both Fred Rimell and Toby Balding, riding a handful of winners as an amateur. With no racing background, what actually attracted him in the first place was a Snaffles print which, until recently, graced the wall at the yard near Barbury Castle which he has been obliged to vacate. Sturt's patronage could not go on for ever.

"My grandfather, who was mayor of Bournemouth for two terms, owned a gents' outfitters. This chap couldn't pay his bill one day and offered him a Snaffles print instead. I loved it and from then on I knew I wanted to work with horses. At 13 I was absolutely hooked on the title battle between Lester Piggott and Scobie Breasley, and the writings of John Lawrence, later Lord Oaksey."

A man comes towards the end of his working life and, inevitably, there will be 'if onlys'. I have never heard Old dwell on these, though he was at Ditcheat immediately before Paul Nicholls and might have stayed longer, except that he was already training for Sturt, who did not get on with millionaire landlord Paul Barber.

He has had stables ravaged by fire and beset by the virus, the latter all but crippling his yard at Dundry, just outside Bristol, which he had in partnership with Norman Waterman, the boss of Faberge. After Ditcheat the final move to Wroughton, near Barbury Castle, was perfect for him but it was there that he nursed his wife Anne-Marie through a long, brave, unavailing battle with cancer. It may fairly be said that the gathering after the funeral, not quite joyous, perhaps, but not maudlin, either, showed exactly what the racing world thought of the Olds.

And, by golly, he can train horses, everything from classy stayers like Al Mutahm (Sagaro Stakes) on the Flat to Champion Hurdle winner Collier Bay, who beat hot favourite Alderbrook on that memorable afternoon in 1996, repaying all of Sturt's faith and part of his considerable investment in the process.

As for his handling of older horses, there has been no one to match him since the halcyon days of George Todd at Manton. That same year, 1996, Cheltenham regular Mole Board had reached the ripe old age of 14 when winning the Levy Board Hurdle at Ascot. Horses could be absent for two or three years with aching, dodgy pins but Old would nurse them back with the utmost sympathy and win races with them, even daring to land the occasional gamble. When Thedreamstillalive, also aged 14, won by a nose at Leicester in March this year, it was almost as if the trainer was demonstrating something for one final time – something that is very hard for some of us to bear.

It's gratifying when good people find each other. Old has long admired Jason Maguire as a jockey and if he sends you a card commenting on some aspect of 'September Song' by Walter Huston, or whatever, it will be a special postcard with Maguire coaxing a tremendous leap from old Attorney General in the Wally Sturt colours on the other side.

As things wound down slowly but inexorably at Wroughton there were still a few horses around the place and Maguire, recovering from the horrendous fall which might have claimed his life, never mind his career, agreed to look after them at his place.

Jim is up at Admington in Warwickshire, wondering what to do with himself. The romantic in me believes he will return, that there will be more racecards with the name J A B Old writ large in the staying handicap hurdle; the realist, on the other hand, acknowledges it will take a Lotto win to make it possible. And the optimist? Well, the optimist is busily filling out the numbers just in case. Like I say, we cannot afford to lose people like Jim Old. Good trainer, great bloke.

Jim Old

KEMPTON OPTIMISTS A LITTLE SUBDUED NOW
Racing Post January 2017

It was probably *The Optimists of Nine Elms* turning up in the post which finally brought me round to Kempton and its possible demise. Tell me that something won't be happening before 2021 at the earliest and I'm inclined to switch off. I add four years to my current age and think to myself well, you know.

I leave all the financial implications to those far better-equipped to give you chapter and verse. I'm stronger on pubs and clubs and Sunbury-on-Thames itself, a land of quiet reservoirs and sailing clubs, the annual regatta, walled gardens and swan-upping.

I like to think the marking of all swans on the upper reaches of the Thames is connected in some way to The Swan Checker, Cyril Mitchell's mile handicapper who was a regular here in the 1960s. Evening meetings used to kick off at around 6pm, so if you were turfed out of the betting shop right on time – no evening opening in those days – you had to loiter outside, trying to catch the commentary and find out how he was getting on. He was always there or thereabouts.

Kempton supplied some of my earliest and most vivid racing memories. There was Bill Wightman's Halloween, virtually unbeatable over three miles on a flat track with Fred Winter up, winning his two King Georges in the days of bookies' runners, scruffy bits of paper and results on the radio. I always thought his owner, the Contessa di Sant'Elia, was a genuine Italian countess – from the pages of Evelyn Waugh's 'Sword of Honour' trilogy, perhaps – but in fact she was a Liverpool lass, the daughter of a successful Liverpool businessman and married her Italian beau in Genoa.

Then there was Mackenna's Gold, named after a Gregory Peck film of 1969, who had to be backed first time up, like quite a few of trainer Peter Dawson's inmates. Therefore, the Kempton Easter meeting was perfect and I waited all year for him, only to be denied in a tight finish at 10/1.

I miss all the old greyhound tracks but Portsmouth and Park Royal were special. I loved that big old stadium tucked away a mile or two from the North Circular Road, the free coach ride from the Tube station and the optimism of early afternoon while everyone else was working. Interestingly, the greyhounds were kennclled at Sunbury, a fair old step from the NCR and the A40.

Celebrating after a good night at Kempton was easy because there was a lively nightclub in Hampton called Alexander's – soul a clear winner over ragtime, but never mind. Driving the other way to an afternoon meeting you could look between the trees and bushes on your right and follow the running rail from about three furlongs out. You were riding a finish, sort of.

Now and again we set off for the races from Nine Elms. In the film, largely forgotten but quite charming, Peter Sellers plays a busker befriended by two young children. The old Covent Garden market moved there many years ago and Nine Elms enjoyed brief notoriety in 1963 when the Great Train Robbers staged a full-scale dress rehearsal of their famous crime at Stewarts Lane railway depot by Battersea Power Station off Nine Elms Lane. We were more intrigued by the possibility of David East or Sammy Millbanks, both 7st 7lb specialists, getting up on one of Herbert Blagrave's in a valuable handicap.

All changed, all gone except the memories. 'Far too many Kempton programmes have produced totally unimaginative, bread-and-butter racing, and the modern racegoer tends to be selective. Whether Kempton holds any great future as a racecourse is a matter of opinion; the land it occupies must possess immense development value.'

You're probably thinking: 'Which recent in-depth article lampooning the Jockey Club does that come from?' But it's actually from the *Biographical Encyclopaedia of British Flat Racing* by Roger Mortimer, Richard Onslow and Peter Willett, published in 1978.

Personally, I shall be sad if the bulldozers move in. And glancing down at old Bill, in his trilby, overcoat and muffler, wrapped up warm against the winter chill as he looks out from the cover of Alan Yuill Walker's fine biography *Months of Misery, Moments of Bliss*, I reckon he'd be sad too.

THE GREAT ZARKAVA
Racing Post October 2015

For a filly who achieved so much, Zarkava is mentioned only rarely. Seven outings, seven victories including the Prix de Diane, the Vermeille – a truly unforgettable performance where she gave the entire field, including Dar Re Mi, three lengths and more rounding the home turn – and, of course, the Arc. She worked harder that day, Soumillon producing her with split-second timing.

The Aga's gimlet eye had caught a hint of temperament and Zarkava was promptly retired. There was never a realistic possibility of contesting the following year's King George so she inspired respect rather than genuine warmth, except among those of us who likened her to the girls at 'Le 122' on the Rue de Provence, who preferred to do their entertaining at home.

Whatever happens this afternoon, Treve will live longer in the collective memory. Yet she shares something with her illustrious compatriot in that countless observers will be willing her on, praying for the great and glorious result irrespective of financial reward – which, if we're really honest about it, is rare among horse players. Briefly we are children again, Hemingway's Joe, looking for a happy ending, one to see us through the stream of traffic in a dusky Bois de Boulogne. If Treve wins, we can handle a setback or two elsewhere. It's the sort of bargain we've struck a few times (a few hundred?) in life.

'I went around to the paddock to see the horses with my old man and you never saw such horses. This War Cloud is a great big yellow horse that looks like just nothing but run. I never saw such a horse.'

Several prominent critics disagreed at the time, but 'My Old Man' is surely one of the best short stories ever written, observing Joe's rite of passage via the racecourses of Milan and Paris and the gallops at Maisons with his father, an ageing journeyman jockey. It's about the way men are together, the gradual erosion of innocence, the casual cruelty, even in death. And if that sounds rather bleak, there's the odd wry smile, as well. Joe certainly finds it easier to pick up a racing paper than anyone looking for a *Paris-Turf* will today.

Hemingway wrote 'My Old Man' around 1922. The fictitious War Cloud, beaten inches in this Saint-Cloud race, was originally Kzar, which was probably a little too close to the real-life Ksar, winner of the Arc in 1921 and 1922. Much later, in *A Moveable Feast*, which was published in 1964 three years after his death and was compiled from notes and papers by his fourth wife Mary, the author looks back on the Paris years with deep, possibly rose-tinted, affection. All the boys and girls are there, of course – Ezra Pound, Ford Madox Ford, James Joyce, an extremely gauche (according to Ernie)

F Scott Fitzgerald, Gertrude Stein and Alice B Toklas – but I recommend reading it for the racing.

Hemingway loved his first wife, Hadley Richardson, and one of the saddest parts of his life story concerns their parting. They went racing when he'd finished writing for the day and would picnic at Auteuil, a winner here and there making the difference between a bottle of wine or going without. (In *A Moveable Feast* they seldom go without. Gamblers have selective memories, but we already knew that.)

Five years ago, Virago published Paula McLain's *The Paris Wife*, a labour of love which sees things through Richardson's eyes. One can only admire the research which went into this and there is no reason to doubt the veracity of a story concerning the jumper Chevre d'Or, an outsider who falls fatally at the last at Auteuil when 20 lengths clear. "He was sticks and string; a child's toy breaking with a crack. It was so terrible, I buried my face in Ernest's shoulder."

Auteuil, scene of the ultimate sadness in 'My Old Man', clearly appealed to American writers because it also features in Irwin Shaw's 'Tip on a Dead Jockey', a New Yorker short story from 1954. By contrast Longchamp is seldom mentioned, even in French literature, apart from fleeting references in Proust's *Remembrance of Things Past*. Arguably the most interesting character is the Jockey Club member Charles Swann, an elegant, well-educated *homme du monde* who falls for the charms of the ex-courtesan Odette de Crecy. Obsession is not too strong a word.

Poor old Swann. It's a pity he's not around today because at least Treve would have had him thinking about something else for a few minutes. Sometimes I don't know what we'd do without horses.

NOT SO WOBBLY ON LANSDOWN HILL

Racing Post September 2014

So, the week starts with a bookmaker and ends in Vermont. I'm talking about a three-day week, of course, from Brighton to Bath with Goodwood in the middle; from Bookmaker winning my humble seller to See Vermont getting up in the dying strides in the second division of the apprentices' handicap on Lansdown Hill.

It was paradise and I was even thinking about a fourth day at Salisbury but started listening to some sad old songs and couldn't get myself organised in time. Also, I'd promised to take my friend Brian out for a drink. There is no intelligible speech since his stroke so we write things down.

I try not to be biased but I wrote about Just Isla in the Brighton racecard and wanted her to win. It would be gratifying to see a rock-solid favourite land the spoils – it hasn't happened very often – but, hard though Richard Hughes tried, she was still a head adrift at the line.

Bookmaker's improvement attracted the attention of the stewards but he is a good-looking horse and probably responded to first-time blinkers. John Bridger picked him up for 4,000 guineas at the auction and will almost certainly turn him into a Brighton regular in low-grade handicaps with the option of returning to selling company. The thought occurs that I shall be seeing quite a lot of him.

For some reason I failed to have enough on 100/30 winner Bayleyf in the last, possibly because word came through from Sir Eric Parker's funeral, or just after it I should say, that Freddy With A Y (second) was the business. I was also strangely muted in the Genting Casino on Preston Street as Monday gave way to Tuesday and I fancied very little at Goodwood, where Hughes gave the impression on Last Minute Lisa that riding winners is like shelling peas, which to him it probably is.

Brian holds up a piece of paper which says: 'Channon 20/1'. Obviously he has monitored the results and knows that Emef Rock won the Brighton nursery.

The other day I had to tell him about Yogi, who couldn't see and couldn't hear, so we had to let him go at 15 plus, which is not bad for a bearded collie. He was a lovely old boy who listened to quite a few of my 'morning after' self-recriminations without passing comment. Brian took so long to respond that I thought a sonnet must be coming but when he held up the paper it just said: 'Sorry'. Sometimes you have to turn away and let the moment pass.

On Wednesday I went to Bath and did a talk for the University and Literary Club, which is next to the Botanist on Berkeley Square in Bristol. Mercifully I tipped the winner of the race they sponsored, young Chris Meehan never letting anything get near him on Glens Wobbly, whose three wins have all come over a mile and five at Bath.

We should never underestimate interviewing techniques around the so-called gaffs. Colin Brown was excellent at Brighton and on Wednesday Tim Peters wondered mischievously if the University and Literary Club was actually a 'gentlemen's' club. I suppose it is, really, not that I know many women who want to discuss the fortunes of Bristol RFC or Rovers' chances of winning the Conference.

Incidentally, I have no idea where we stand on the political correctness front when it comes to 'ladies' and 'women'. I assume someone called Audrey Braithwaite would be a lady – sensible shoes, Middle England, Radio 4, etc. – whereas Stella Dallas would be, well, I think you can see where we're heading. (I have just invented both of those names, so if there's an Audrey Braithwaite running a house of pleasure in Solihull I apologise unreservedly and the same goes for Stella of the WI.)

I won over the three days so I'm not sure why I ended up playing 'My Haunted Heart' by Jo Stafford on my return. It comes on at the end of *The Two Jakes* starring Jack Nicholson and is exactly the sort of thing you hear during lost afternoons in the Botanist. The only version of 'Moonlight in Vermont' I have is by Johnny Mathis and I couldn't find it.

Backing See Vermont was a determined effort to recapture the past. Still a maiden after 22 tries, he met exactly the right bunch, all of them practically blood brothers and sisters of mine. Down by the furlong pole on a quiet Wednesday I touch the kind of happiness that is hard to describe. He can't quite win passing me, but gets there in the end.

I take Brian to the George in Backwell. In the gents there is a truly wonderful photograph of a showgirl, I suppose, or a dancer preparing for a stint in a gentlemen's club. I ask him if he is impressed.

He sips his rosé and holds up the paper. 'Too old now,' it says.

Well, yes. There is that.

Part Eight

Coming Home ... And The Trouble With Harry

It's fair to say I missed broadcasting for its own sake and it was galling (though quite amusing) to be turned down for a job at Radio Devon because I was so over-qualified – or so the man said and I must say I warmed to him.

It takes a lot of freelance work to match a monthly salary so it was just as well the closure of the *Sporting Life* in 1998 was followed, a couple of years later, by a most agreeable stint interviewing gamblers for a magazine called the *Sports Adviser*, edited by Ed Chamberlin.

I also wrote for the Southampton match-day programme, interviewing former players and often spending more time and money tracking them down than any reasonable person would consider although, where the Saints are concerned, reason disappeared over the horizon many moons ago. I'd have done it for nothing.

I ghosted Harry Redknapp's programme notes – not difficult, given the way he is and the fact that I already knew him through racing – at a rather worrying time for the club.

Rupert Lowe started fairly well (some would say) as chairman after a reverse takeover in 1996–97 – I confess my ignorance of such things – and I think he loved the club but arrogance produced a series of mistakes as time went on. He should not have recruited Harry because they were poles apart, not least in the little matter of football knowledge, and the line about 'the public school boy and the barrow boy' was crass rather than cute. Harry Redknapp may have been many things (and even more now, as we see every day) but he certainly wasn't a barrow boy, not that there is anything wrong with earning a crust like that.

With time running out in 2005 he improved Saints' home form, his son Jamie – bandaged like the Invisible Man – and Peter Crouch making a big difference, but we were wretched away from St Mary's and went down, losing 4-1 at Portsmouth near the end.

I always felt his heart remained at Fratton Park and I fielded one or two enquiries from serious backers regarding a possible return there. It's not something he'd ever have told me but I wasn't surprised when it happened. We joked at the races a few years later and I said we should have lunch, maybe a few miles away from Southampton. "They say Aberystwyth is very nice," I murmured, but he was already thinking about something else.

He left Pompey with a mountain of debt but believed strongly in the players he had there and won the FA Cup with them in 2008, some very fancy odds appearing when they were drawn away to Manchester United in the quarter-finals, where they won 1-0. He is almost certainly the only manager to have beaten United with three different clubs – West Ham and Bournemouth the other two – but things were never going to work out at Southampton.

So we were relegated and relegated again before coming back up, thanks largely to the huge financial backing of Swiss businessman Markus Liebherr. My younger daughter and I followed the team everywhere, including Blackpool, where an off-licence had one of those faux china sherry barrels up on the top shelf and I was pretty sure I'd put it in there for Gilbey's way back in 1975. "Aye, it's done well," the manager said.

None of it would have been possible had I still held down a permanent job. I might not have seen the unforgettable 6-3 win against United (5-2 when I left because it was Breeders' Cup day and I was working with Jeff Stelling on Sky), Franny Benali's one and only goal and Le Tissier's sublime *coup de grâce* against Arsenal before the Dell gave way to Barratt Homes. All in all, I was more than happy with the way things turned out.

MINTRAM A HERO IN THE END
Racing Post October 2015

The White Star in Oxford Street, Southampton, seemed an appropriate place to back Deeds Not Words at Windsor, given that he is trained by Mick Channon and owned by my friend George Materna, who has extensive business interests not far away.

Now that the New Zealand Sauvignon Blanc has crept up to £29 a bottle it's just as well he won. The feeling of euphoria lasted until 20/1 chance Waseem Faris, formerly with Mick but now trained by his old mentor Ken Cunningham-Brown, followed up at Nottingham 48 hours later. (No, but thank you for asking.) That's three wins from his last four outings so it must be the air around Stockbridge. Well, let's face it, the future King Edward VII and Lillie Langtry had no complaints either. Maybe we should give it a try.

Old Arthur Sears was familiar with several of the music halls in London where Langtry performed. They included the Eagle on City Road, which features in the nursery rhyme 'Pop Goes the Weasel' and makes more sense than some of its bedfellows. To 'pop' was to pawn something and a 'weasel' may well have been a mishearing of 'whistle and flute' or suit. So, drinking and hanging around the Eagle left you short of cash and the next morning you needed to 'pop out and see Uncle', who was the pawnbroker.

"Yes, and the Eagle pub is still there, just a few doors up from a pawn shop. Some things never change," Arthur smiled. "Anthony Newley had a minor hit with 'Pop Goes the Weasel' and we were hoping to use him on a lemonade advert but it never quite worked out. He was an odd cove but you have to respect someone who could write 'What Kind of Fool Am I?'"

Arthur was born in 1922, ten years after the *Titanic* went down and his parents kept several newspaper cuttings. The pub/restaurant in Southampton has little in the way of photographs or memorabilia around the walls, although the vessel was one of the White Star Line's three luxury liners. Of course, a picture of chairman and managing director Joseph Bruce Ismay would only lead to further discussion about his actions when the ship sank, some reports suggesting that he was in a lifeboat while women and children were still in acute danger on board.

"There was never any proof of that but it's the kind of thing that gathers strength with the passing of the years," Arthur said. "Presumably some of the survivors must have known the truth. It's funny the way things work out because it was only the tragedy which prevented his brother, whose name I've forgotten, from being more famous. He owned a Derby winner, yes?"

Arthur's knowledge puts me to shame but the brother was Charles Bower Ismay, who owned Craganour – second in the 2000 Guineas when many thought the judge had called it wrongly, and victorious in perhaps the most infamous Derby of all, that of 1913 when the militant suffragette Emily Davison brought down the King's horse Anmer. Craganour prevailed by a head from Aboyeur but there was any amount of argy-bargy and at the subsequent enquiry – the result not of an objection lodged by connections of the second but brought by the stewards themselves – the 100/1 chance Aboyeur was awarded the race with Craganour thrown out altogether.

The newspapers had a high old time of it. Apart from anything else, the 'All Right' signal had been given and had to be reversed. It was thought that Major Eustace Loder was the prime mover in the enquiry and by common agreement he was never quite the same man again. As for Bower Ismay, a non-gambler in a gambling yard, he had a disqualification to go with two runners-up in the Grand National – Bloodstone and Jacobus. The former, a 40/1 shot, ran his heart out only a month or so before the *Titanic* went down.

I wandered down Chapel Road the other day. The convicted killer William Mintram lived there but still worked on the *Titanic* as a fireman/stoker, having signed on with Walter Hurst, the husband of his daughter Rosina. The two men met amid chaotic scenes, Mintram handing over his life jacket and saving his son-in-law's life before becoming one of the 549 crew from Southampton to perish.

Tried for murder in 1902, Mintram served only three years for manslaughter after stabbing his wife in a fit of rage when she nagged at him (so he said) for complaining when she pawned their little boy's boots to buy drink.

As I recall from a childhood spent in Southampton in the 1950s, she'd have found a pawnbroker's much closer than the City Road.

NELSON NEVER FORGOTTEN HERE
Racing Post July 2016

The Jolly Sailor at Bursledon is not a bad place to contemplate one or two major Goodwood investments, Secret Asset's chances of winning one more race at the age of 11 and the state of Hampshire cricket.

Of course, to look out over the River Hamble is to gaze upon immense wealth and to be reminded of my old French teacher R C Williams. 'Never forget, Carnaby, one half doesn't know how the other half lives.' Well over 50 years later, I see no reason to doubt his perspicacity.

Not that living quietly and sensibly would necessarily have brought any of the magnificent blue-and-white craft I see before me that much closer. You may feel the same way. If you'd never gambled, it doesn't mean that all the money saved would be sitting there on the hearth, a massive pile of ready-to-go wonga. You'd have had a Maserati, a lover in Maida Vale, a homburg.

I am reluctant to leave the Jolly Sailor, the pub used in the 1980s soap opera *Howard's Way* and right next door to the Elephant Boatyard, where HMS *Elephant*, the ship which took Nelson to the battle of Copenhagen, was launched in 1786.

Even so, it's time to return to Hampshire's rearguard action against Surrey at the Rose Bowl. Not many four-day County Championship matches go the distance but this one will as Hampshire, following on and still well adrift, must survive the last two sessions. At 198 for 6 time is starting to run out for Surrey but, once the stand between Smith and McLaren is broken, the last three wickets fall almost as a matter of course. Hampshire are bottom of Division One and need a miracle.

I have no real interest in T20 cricket, which strikes me as a bish-bash bastardisation of the proper game, though I appreciate the players have had to learn new techniques and the grounds are often full. There are only a couple of hundred traditionalists at the Rose Bowl, their pink knees confirming summer's belated arrival.

They are nearly all my age and shuffle off, muttering to themselves, but in the lounge I pause to look at the picture of Colin Ingleby-Mackenzie's 1961 Championship-winning team. In a couple of days' time, but 55 years ago, he and Ted Dexter managed to catch Peggy Lee at the Pigalle before driving back in the small hours for the final day of Sussex v Hampshire at Hove.

With the game effectively won, 'Lord Edward' managed to get himself out just before I Claudius ran at Glorious Goodwood. Both skippers were on in spades but the winner was 33/1 chance Writ Of Error, whose prospects had been summarily dismissed by owner Stanhope Joel at the Pigalle.

Dexter was a wonderful batsman and a gregarious character in those days, deeply into motorbikes and greyhounds and anything with risk attached. But later on he typified that Fleetwood Mac lyric from 'Dreams': 'Players only love you when they're playing.' By the time he became England's chairman of selectors he was the proverbial blood from a stone as an interviewee, though when SIS went to see him at home in Ealing his pet greyhounds had accepted retirement rather more readily and made us feel welcome.

Defeat for Hampshire is not quite the same thing as defeat for the Saints but there is a similar desire to feel better as soon as possible. Sometimes, after losing a job, I'd have a really big bet – Amigo Loco, I seem to remember, just before William Muir took over from Kim Brassey. The reasoning is perfectly sound; being removed from the payroll leaves you a bit down and you're unlikely to feel any worse. This was soon put to the test as Amigo Loco finished second.

Anyway, I devote my attention to the last at Sandown, a modest sprint handicap where Sir Domino will not like firm ground (he is taken out) and Mick Channon's Jaywalker has been rather busy of late. So, old Secret Asset will have his moment with the Esher course bathed in late-evening sunshine.

Sipping a decent Rioja Reserva in El Puerto in Bristol, I listen to him win by quite a long way. I am in funds. If I wore a hat I'd buy a homburg. One out of three's not bad.

IN THOUGHTS OF YOU – AND YOU, AND YOU ...
Racing Post December 2014

Mandy Rice-Davies, who died recently, must have been a lot of fun, I think. Very expensive fun, of course, but attractive, worldly-wise, amusing and a good-time girl rather than a prostitute, which was how the government, the courts and some (though not all) newspapers chose to portray her at the time of the Profumo Affair in 1963.

She joins a long line of famous people to have departed the scene in 2014. Some years affect us more than others but, in no particular order, Philip Seymour Hoffman, Robin Williams, Sir Richard Attenborough, Lauren Bacall and James Garner make up a pretty formidable quintet.

Needless to say, I did not know any of these stars personally but I was on very good terms with Toby Balding, Alistair

Haggis and Brighton DJ Rocking Billy. It's a strange thing, because I'm not superstitious in any way, but I thought Southampton would be drawn against Blyth Spartans in the FA Cup, my Uncle Tom having played for both when Hitler was galvanising his own youth team. I imagined a draw, a replay and the sort of sentimental journey a man might make at this relatively late stage.

Well, we were drawn against Ipswich, the mighty Spartans go to Birmingham and the sentimental journey will have to be Chelsea today followed by Billy's funeral tomorrow. Happily, I know his ten favourite rock tracks and, if asked to sing, can offer a passable version of 'In Thoughts of You' by Billy Fury. Whether this is suitable at a cremation I'm not quite sure but Brighton is different and Billy was a one-off, as his Teddy boy jacket hanging alongside Bryan Ferry's in Brighton Museum suggests.

Toby, who used to bet with a Brighton bookie in the old days, would have loved him. The fascinating thing with obituaries and tributes concerns the bits and pieces left out. Toby was quite a punter but, however badly things were going, he always had an idea, a scheme, something to get him out. And he adored the Saints; the link between Mick Channon and the late Bill Wightman is well known but Toby trained a horse called Scaramander for Terry Paine, bought with the £1,000 Terry received for being in the 1966 World Cup squad, and both Jimmy Gabriel and John McGrath were regular visitors to the yard. McGrath, Gabriel and Joe Kirkup would link arms and wander down Southampton High Street before footballers lived in gated communities.

I was in urgent need of a winner one day – nothing new in that – and asked Toby for a few ideas. He never hesitated, though results were on the patchy side.

"I'm getting Dickie Deadeye ready for the apprentices' race when the Flat starts at Doncaster," he said. "I can pass that on because the owner, Bridget Swire, never has a pound on anything and won't know anything about it!"

As I recall, Dickie Deadeye didn't make the party so no damage was done, but Toby had done his best. I hardly ever ask trainers for information but he'd move the odd mountain to help you because he was a gambler himself. In that respect he differed from Gavin Pritchard-Gordon and J A B Old but I'd back anything they told me with my last shilling, always supposing I could find it.

Years ago I knew people at the International Racing Bureau quite well. There were some high rollers there but I doubt that any of them quite matched Alistair, who was probably in love with risk. He'd moved on to Ascot when we had our last serious telephone conversation at a time when I suspect both of us were having a few 3am thoughts. I remember advising a final chat with the bank manager and a major remortgaging job.

There was a long pause. "Actually, Ian, I think things have gone a bit beyond that," he said.

He was softly spoken, well-mannered and charming, like Terry Lennox in Chandler's *The Long Goodbye* and with a similar self-destructive streak. Yet, from everything I've read, he must have pulled himself out, to a degree anyway, only to be struck down by motor neurone disease. He was such an amiable gambler, such a nice man and I liked him immensely. If you wanted the living, walking embodiment of Hemingway's grace under pressure, in Alistair Haggis you had it.

My bearded collie Yogi died, as well. With limited enthusiasm I consider the rescue home and a possible replacement. At the end of *The Urban District Lover*, the last in Jack Trevor

Story's wonderful Albert Argyle trilogy, tally-boy Albert dies and his long-suffering girlfriend Treasure is consoled on the way to the funeral by Mr Granger, who lays a sympathetic hand on her knee.

'Treasure didn't mind. If it couldn't be Albert then it didn't matter who it was.'

Happy New Year.

41 YEARS ON – AND STILL DREAMING
Racing Post February 2017

Jim McCalliog, a man of flicks and touches who does not find football especially difficult, pauses briefly then lifts the ball beyond United's central defenders. They are slow to react and this is all Bobby Stokes needs.

A man who finds football quite hard work by comparison, his shot is neither scuffed nor properly hit but, crucially, it drifts wide of Alex Stepney to rest, almost apologetically, in the corner of the net. In those few seconds 41 years ago, Southampton produce the greatest moment in their long and largely undistinguished history.

This unlikely FA Cup success will make a television star of Lawrie McMenemy, who builds two more outstanding Saints teams, and eventually prove all too much for Stokes, the much-loved journeyman who finally returns to his native Portsmouth and tragically fades away through self-neglect, dying in 1995. Some can handle Andy Warhol's '15 minutes of fame' and some can't.

Bobby Stokes

They were a fascinating bunch, though it goes without
saying that I'm biased and some might substitute 'rum' for
'fascinating'. Mick Channon was soon back on the racecourse,
thinking about his future career. The following month in
1976 Bill Wightman's Import won the Wokingham and
later on Mick sent Cathy Jane to the old sprinter, the happy
result being Jamesmead, winner of the Tote Gold Trophy,

universally known as the Schweppes, for David Elsworth in 1988.

The last time I spoke to McCalliog he was running a pub, the Hare & Hounds, near Riccall in York, while centre-back Jim Steele had the Black Bear at Moreton-in-Marsh. I'm not sure what the regulars made of the FA Cup pictures around the walls but 'Steely' is great company, if inclined to do things his own way.

He ran the Mizzymead Recreation Centre in Nailsea for a while and soon rounded out all drinks prices to the nearest 10p as well as ordering a giant screen for the old boys to watch the cricket on Sky early in the morning. It was pointed out to him that, in social clubs, all these things are supposed to go before the committee. Jim wasn't there for very long.

At Wembley I sat next to my friend Mark, from the wine trade. Five of us still get together now and again but 41 years is a long time and we've all had bits and pieces added or taken away.

Mark's stroke a while back means his left side is a bit iffy and any hostelry or restaurant has to be no more than a 20-minute walk away. From the Cheshire Cheese in Fleet Street to the Mar I Terra tapas off Blackfriars Road is about right; he was a bit lopsided over Blackfriars Bridge but not in any real danger of falling in. The restaurant is worth the effort and the Spanish boss is a proper racing man who even remembers the early SIS days.

We also use the Anglesea Arms off Fulham Road – handy enough for the Caraffini restaurant and the Victoria & Albert Museum. It's good to know that gallows humour is alive and well. Prior to the Grand National weights announcement at the famous old venue there was speculation in the Anglesea that, after sampling Martell and Crabbie's at every opportunity, the arrival of Randox Health as sponsors might prove too little, too late for one or two of the scribblers in attendance.

The champagne was excellent and so too the white wine, while any time spent in Jonjo O'Neill's company is a handsome bonus. It was a bit noisy, though, and Laura Wright would have done well to call it a day after two songs. She passed quite close to me on the way out and the last time I saw a diva look as angry as that was when Shirley Bassey's microphone cable got caught under my chair leg at a Gilbey's sales conference in 1974. 'Hey, Big Spender' still brings on a hot flush of embarrassment.

Anyway, nearly time for another Southampton v Man Utd Cup final, three children, five grandchildren and a few bits of tin in my chest since the last one. If you're having a bet I suspect the absence of Virgil van Dijk from the Saints' defence will be the key factor.

Or, of course, it may be 0-0 with seven minutes left when Shane Long sticks out a leg and sends 30,000 of us wild with delight. You'd probably get a big price about that and should therefore allow for a small financial setback.

On the other hand, dreams are free.

PATIENCE A VIRTUE FOR DUSAN AND JACK
Racing Post June 2017

Monday was a long day but an agreeable one, even though Hampshire were pinned down by Somerset off-spinner Jack Leach at the Rose Bowl. The Platform in Southampton was rather quiet but the Rioja very good. My daughter's cat Dusan was awaiting a midnight feast in Bristol and I am not one to disappoint my feline friends.

She named him after Southampton's Serbian number 11 Dusan Tadic, which I thought a nice touch. In the Platform there is a sign which says: 'Not All Who Wander Are Lost'. This is from J R R Tolkien, I think, and pleases flâneurs everywhere, especially this one.

Still, 'not all' suggests there are still a few wanderers around capable of endorsing public opinion. Having watched Dusan Tadic* on the right, the left, and lately in a sort of deep-lying role in the middle – a latter-day Don Revie, someone kindly suggested – the thought crossed my mind that he may indeed have lost his bearings.

Leach is a joy to watch and one of the reasons that followers of the four-day game have little interest in T20.

Watching him closely, I even forgot to back Pat Murphy's Catalina's Diamond at Chepstow, which was just as well. Leach bowled like someone who bets each-way at 11/2 with a quarter the odds a bonus. To everything pitched fractionally short, Hampshire's batsmen came down the wicket to smother the spin; anything pitched up, they leaned back and tried to force him away but the field placings defeated them. In 24 overs he conceded only 54 runs and hardly any boundaries. Finally, of course, two 11/2 shots came in as he dismissed Vince and Ervine. He is the ultimate percentage player.

Live long enough and names come around again. Jack Leach the jockey won the 1927 2000 Guineas on Adam's Apple and trained successfully for a short time, when one of his supporters was Fred Astaire. Later he became an amusing and forthright racing journalist with the *Observer*, as well as writing the very entertaining *A Rider on the Stand* and *Sods I Have Cut on the Turf*.

I like the Platform for several reasons, not least the music and the subdued lighting. As a post-racing or football pub it's perfect, though a few years ago I often mulled things over in the Oliver Goldsmith nearby. It used to be called the Bitter End (no, really), then it gave way to trendier wine bars and finally a convenience store, whatever that is.

The pub sign in Southampton was faithful to Goldsmith's smallpox-ravaged visage. He was a lifelong gambler, though he held on to the proceeds from *She Stoops to Conquer* for a while. The £60 for *The Vicar of Wakefield* went straight to his landlady, who'd had him put away for failing to pay the rent.

It's hard not to admire him, because in between drinking bouts in the Crown Tavern in Islington and betting stints day and night, he wrote fine articles for the *Monthly Review*. When he died at 45 he owed £2,000; not a bad effort under the circumstances. They honoured him with a monument within Westminster Abbey and a statue at Trinity College, Dublin.

I once sold Hennessy to a Hounslow publican called Ollie Goldsmith but I must say I never thought I'd see another ginger cat starring in a film after *Breakfast at Tiffany's*. Quite wrong, as you'll know if you've seen the Coen Brothers' *Inside Llewyn Davis*.

I mentioned this, among other things, to Dusan in the small hours but he was well into the generous chunks of tuna I found in the fridge. I told him that Elliott Gould's cat preferred curry bran in *The Long Goodbye*.

Sometimes I wish my memory was worth a lot of money. There's no sign of it so far.

*Tadic, who may have found Southampton training sessions unrewarding, possibly even naive, later joined Ajax. Playing further forward and with no 'tracking back' responsibilities, he scored THIRTY goals in a season and looked world-class. I have yet to meet a Saints fan who has come to terms with this.

A PERFECT WINE FOR PERFECT HEROES
Racing Post July 2014

To paraphrase the peerless Oscar, to lose one hero may be regarded as a misfortune, to lose two seems like carelessness. Yet both James Garner and P J Sainsbury have gone, within a week of each other, followed by Dora Bryan. '*Jamais deux sans trois,*' as the French say, or '*jamais trois sans quatre,*' if you include the old QPR and West Brom winger Clive Clark – which I have, obviously.

"I can stand most things at funerals," Jimmy 'Marvel' Mason says, "until some bright spark says: 'Of course, we've got to expect more of these at our age.' It's always someone who's never taken a risk, have you noticed that? The rest of us, the gamblers, are just happy and relieved to have got this far. A drop more Barolo? What do you know about 32Red, by the way?"

Marvel, who made a fortune from vintage comics and briefly found women with big hair calling him 'darling' and 'petal' and smoothing his pullover while he was still wearing it, is deeply into things Italian at present. It crosses my mind that the Barolo, open for three hours and the deepest, most beautiful red you've ever seen, is the result of his hottest streak for several years.

"It's next to zero on the roulette wheel, isn't it?"

"Very good. Very droll. Dostoyevsky once got out of trouble on zero, you know. There's that great line in *The Gambler*: 'In such moments one forgets all one's previous failures,' which is spot on, but you know full well I meant 32Red the bookies."

Well, I don't know very much about them at all, apart from the Stewards' Cup business, which bothers me less than it bothers some people because punters will refer to the great cavalry charge in the usual way for years and years. No one will be going into the Anglesey Arms in Halnaker on Saturday and asking: 'What's going to win the 32Red?' but I imagine the firm will do plenty of business on course and these days it seems to be all about getting clients 'signed up', which I happen to think is rather dangerous, and I should know.

The thing is not to show the strain and Garner was wonderful at that. From the moment I saw him in *Maverick* I wanted to be like him – "You had us pretty convinced at school," Marvel says – and I've never changed. Even now, if I heard the theme from *The Rockford Files* in another part of the building I'd excuse myself from a meeting and go and watch it.

It's a pity Peter Sainsbury couldn't hang on for a few more days because a Test match taking place at the Rose Bowl – England v India, starting today – would have delighted him. He was Hampshire's number five in A C D Ingleby-Mackenzie's championship-winning team in 1961 and once dismissed the great Len Hutton twice in a single day at Bradford with his left-arm spinners. The world was a very different place in those days and he also delivered paraffin around our way during the winter.

He served Hampshire as player and coach for 40 years and was unlucky not to play for England, though he was often 12th man. On one occasion he thought Ted Dexter was signalling for a hat and ran out to the middle with one, only for the great man to say: "What are you doing out here? I don't want a bloody hat. Get off!"

I am greatly relieved to see the Test going ahead because, at a recent four-day game against Derbyshire, the hotel at the Rose Bowl still needed plenty of work. The contractors used by Tesco or Betfred would have had it up and running in no time.

"Excuse me, I'd quite like the winner of the Stewards' Cup,"

Marvel says. "It's pretty straightforward, I think. Channel 4 interviews Richard Fahey in his dark glasses, he shuffles around a bit and looks shrewd, tells you nothing is certain, then wanders off and supervises the winner. Alben Star was fifth two years ago, you know." Marvel has done more research, so I go along with his choice.

I liked Dora Bryan best in *A Taste Of Honey*, as the gamine Rita Tushingham's blousy mother, clutching at a few scraps of pleasure late in life. Whenever I think of Salford now, though, I always think of Fred Done's single shop and the empire he's built up.

"Yes, but at the end of the game, the king and the pawn go back in the same box," Marvel says.

I am deeply impressed by this. "Did you think of that yourself, Marvel?"

"No, of course not, it's an Italian saying," he says. "More Barolo?"

SALISBURY PERFECT FOR STRIKER
Racing Post June 2017

My biggest bet so far this Flat season, humble enough when set alongside bets from the past, was on Richard Fahey's Noah Amor in a seller at Thirsk on 22 April.

There are no certainties in racing but it wasn't a handicap, Conor Murtagh claimed 7lb and the horse used to be with Dandy Nicholls. I'd have felt exactly the same if it had travelled the other way.

He won all right and has now picked up three sellers in recent weeks, prompting Gallop Racing and David O'Meara to step in after the last of them and buy him for £9,000. Raised to a non-selling handicap at Hamilton on Thursday, and starting 2/1 favourite, he finished fourth of six. He's a smashing horse and I wish I had him but he'll prove expensive to follow from now on.

That Thirsk contest was on a Saturday, which is unusual for selling races, though they turned up often enough in the past. My good friend Nigel Davies won a Stratford selling hurdle with Extremely So on a Saturday five years ago and those of a certain vintage will remember that the old ITV Seven often included a seller (generally at Catterick), just to set punters a proper test.

Ken 'Window' Payne often had three or four runners in them and the only clue to the stable selected, as we used to say, concerned the riding arrangements. How John Curant coaxed his mounts over the line ahead of the others need not trouble us here, though I think it fair to say the current whip guidelines would have dented his strike rate. Indeed, ANY sort of whip guidelines might have embarrassed him to a degree.

One of the best things about Ken was his nickname, because he started out as a window cleaner in Southampton, complete with bucket, bike and ladder, though I believe there was a van later on. Women liked him, there's no doubt about that, although maybe it was the van.

By golly, those were the days. Channon playing wide on the left, the ITV Seven, the Sally Annie band, the Woolston Ferry, people milling around outside St Luke's on Sunday mornings when church could still give Sainsbury's a run for its money. One day I bumped into my Logic teacher 'Basher' Barnett, who wouldn't say boo to a goose. He was impressed by the turnout and readily acknowledged the power of faith. There was a pause. "Not quite the same as proof, though, is it?" he murmured.

'All men are mortal; Brutus is a man; ergo, Brutus is mortal.' The classic syllogism, two statements of fact leading to an inevitable, logical truth. I'm not suggesting it would help you all that much with the Wokingham, say, but it's a start. Basher approached everything like that and you took his occasional silences to mean he disagreed with some conclusion you'd reached.

Some years later he asked for a tip, more in the interests of research as opposed to financial profit (I know, I know) and I gave him Striker at Salisbury. The great philanthropist and former Southampton FC president Herbert Blagrave was a very astute trainer and sellers were probably anathema to him. But old Striker, with his one eye, had become a little disappointing and there he was in this one-mile affair with Roger Wernham up.

He won by nearly half a furlong at 15/8 and I think I knew, as he galloped home alone, that I'd always be in thrall to days like these. Basher was pleased, too. He liked the bit about being dropped in class but suggested that racing could never quite match Brutus' mortality when it came to certainties.

Blagrave, a very rich man descended from a line of Berkshire squires, was a kindly philanthropist, totally without affectation. Southampton manager Lawrie McMenemy used to say that he owned half of Reading, which may not have been a huge exaggeration. Striker winning a seller would have brought a wry smile to the trainer's face because, many years before, he bought Royal Drake and Vic Day from France and saw them finish first and second in the Manton Stakes at the same course. His best horse, however, was Chinese Cracker, who won the Ribblesdale but was unluckily beaten by Neasham Belle in the 1951 Oaks after being badly squeezed against the rails.

Of fairly recent Southampton players only Mick Channon would remember Herbert Blagrave, but Ian Balding took over the training of his horses for a while many years ago. Sitting in the Blagrave Arms near Reading station I wondered if any of the regulars had ever asked how the pub came by its name. I should have taken a photo of Striker storming clear and had it blown up and framed.

Too late now, like so many things.

NOT A DRY EYE AS FRANNY NODS HOME
Racing Post September 2014

Now, here's a thing. Antonin Dvořák completes his Symphony No. 9 'From the New World' in 1893 and then, 80 years later, a little lad pushes his bike up a Yorkshire hill (except that it's in Dorset), his basket full of Hovis. The second movement ensures this will be one of the most famous advertisements ever made. It certainly did director Ridley Scott no harm.

You wonder what old Antonin would have made of it, just as you wonder what John Meacock makes of one of his horses appearing in a novel by William Trevor. John served with the British Army in the Gulf and, when he turned his hand to training in the 1960s, his runners bore the names of Persian kings, statesmen and poets. Most of them were very slow but, like a lot of seemingly cock-eyed optimists, the trainer knew when a surprise mightn't be such a surprise after all.

'Malacca was tipped to win at Harold's Cross, rumours about Yellow Printer's limitations were denied. At Brighton, the £35 filly Qalibashi had won at 20/1. Whisky Poker was selected for the 3.00 at Redcar, and Whisky Noggin for the 3.30. Privy Seal would win at Ascot.

'Eugene sat, considering a few of the facts that he had absorbed, listening to the ticking of the clock. Within a couple of minutes his head dropped on to his chest and he returned to sleep; he dreamed he was standing in Riordan's public house.'

This is from Trevor's *Mrs Eckdorf in O'Neill's Hotel*, first published in 1969. It's interesting for a number of reasons. The confident tips were probably on the *Life*'s front page, before racing politics took over, while Yellow Printer, also mentioned in a popular song of the time, was the most famous greyhound in training before Ballyregan Bob came on the scene. Qalibashi, well, Qalibashi lit up one of those unforgettable Brighton afternoons when summers were longer and hotter and we walked barefoot on the pavement, avoiding the cracks – or so Carly Simon sang.

The mare also makes an unlikely appearance in Julian Wilson's autobiography *Some You Win*. A very shrewd punter, he bought her and passed her on to Neville Dent with a view to landing a gamble in a minor hurdle at Southwell but she finished second. For some reason they'd painted the wings of the hurdles bright orange and she hesitated at every single one.

Karkeh Rud and Vakil-ul-Mulk (Meacock's Derby horse but more effective at Wincanton) did me proud but my dad never got used to the names and preferred horses trained by Eddie Magner, which he routinely referred to as 'pit ponies'. He followed racing but his real strength lay in finding likely draws on the football.

He used to study the coupon during the night shift at Pirelli in Eastleigh and it occurred to me the other day that, when he left the factory at 6am, Benny Hill was probably halfway through his milk round. Anyway, he thought draws represented the only value and I tend to agree with him, especially in local derbies. Our shared opinion was endorsed by Nottingham Forest and Derby ending 1-1 on Sunday.

I'm not sure what he'd have made of Saturday's Southampton v Newcastle match, given his Geordie background, but he'd have been all for Franny Benali, who came out at half-time and completed a lap of honour following his 1,000 mile run in 21 days (think about it) around all of the Premier League grounds in aid of Cancer Research UK.

The most heart-warming aspect was the way the Newcastle supporters, two-nil down and with little prospect of improvement, applauded him as he jogged past the away section. Benali was a long way from being Southampton's best left-back – a tall order in a list including Mick Mills, Mark Dennis, Wayne Bridge, Gareth Bale and Luke Shaw – but he was the archetypal one-club man and never let anyone down.

On one occasion he played in front of the back four with instructions to 'take care of' Eric Cantona. Unlikely to be fazed by any dark threats or oblique references to French surrealist poet Arthur Rimbaud, he accomplished this so thoroughly that Manchester United were 3-0 down at half-time and famously changed their shirts.

Or there was the time he scored his one and only goal, a vital, looping header against Leicester when Matt Le Tissier hit him squarely between the eyes with a free-kick from 35 yards. Whilst it's true that your granny would also have obliged, assuming she was lurking in the box, it was quite something to see grown men in tears. In that respect, Benali's goal is the only sporting memory I can set alongside Dawn Run's Gold Cup. (I believe I recovered from the latter a shade quicker, probably because I needed Jonjo O'Neill to win the next race as well, which he did on Jobroke.)

Some days you wonder why you gamble, other days you wonder why you do anything else. He was trained by Peter Easterby so, with Marvel Mason telling me at York that The Grey Gatsby without Australia was the bet of the season, Yorkshire has done me proud.

"Ee bah gum," as Dvorak would no doubt have said.

Part Nine

A Setback To Last A Lifetime

It was a great pity the *Sports Adviser* closed two or three years into the new millennium. Apart from anything else it had, on the back page, a 'spiky' exchange between High Roller and Low Roller – Julian Wilson and Mark 'Couch' Winstanley. When people suggested that Couch's copy was risqué, to say the least, Ed Chamberlin would respond that they should have seen it when it came in.

The problem, of course, was the usual one. The *Sports Adviser* was a classy item and had some excellent writers, including Simon Barnes, but it was essentially a tipping magazine and had to be up to date. Come the weekend there were too many non-runners and it wasn't the first publication to discover that most punters, especially those focusing on racing, needed something for today. I've lost count of the number of talented writers whose material graced the *Life* and the *Post*, but you wouldn't sell many copies without the cards and the tips.

I interviewed many gamblers over those three years, including Dave Nevison, a free spirit who never allowed serious form study to get in the way of a rich and varied social life. He is great company, as I learned when working briefly with him on talkSPORT a few years before his appalling stroke of bad luck.

I wrote 'appalling' there and I'm standing by it, despite some unsympathetic comments on social media and elsewhere. To summarise, in January 2009 Nevison named the first six winners in a Tote Super7 at Taunton, having laid out £84 – a very small 'tilt' by his standards – in pursuit of a bumper pot. The closing race was a 3m 3f handicap chase and his selection Topless made light of the task, leading three out and going five lengths clear on the run-in. You will know it's a short run-in at Taunton but it was still about 20 yards too long as Topless, tiring and drifting left, jinked sharply right when James Davies tried to straighten her out with a single smack of the whip. Unbalanced, the mare threw him to the ground and a potentially life-changing £360,000 was carried away on the breeze like so much confetti.

Six years later, Nevison told the *Racing Post*'s Peter Thomas that he still thought about the race 'once a week or so'. At Goodwood, he told me he went for a run in the immediate aftermath and covered about eight miles, remembering nothing of the route taken. At Chepstow the following day, Davies was still ashen-faced. Almost unbelievably, a man came up to Nevison and said: 'That's racing!'

It's best not to comment on that, although it goes without saying that the man had never suffered any serious financial setbacks through betting. Sometimes we have to remind ourselves that thousands of people play every day for humble stakes, indulging their hobby and never letting it come within a country mile of hurting them. When all's said and done they're just horses, as my dad would have said, meaning no harm.

When I spoke to Dave at Goodwood he was working for RUK. In the *Racing Post* I suggested it must be hard, even as a good old pro, forcing himself through the days after his own moment had come and gone, that moment when leaving the City to indulge his passion had looked like reaping the richest of rewards.

All I was trying to say was that I'd have found it virtually impossible myself. A correspondent (not the biggest Nevison fan, I think he'd admit) was quick to point out how many people would give anything to be on the box, talking about horses for a living. Well, all right. But very few people who hold down that sort of job, analysing in the minutest of detail, strike me as gamblers. I'm not saying experts have to feel pain for me to like or respect them, but I'd rather listen to Dave Nevison.

The exchange of letters with the forthright correspondent occurred the day before we were due to fly to Canada to see our elder daughter Cathy and family. Overleaf I include part of the column I wrote for the *Racing Post* but I was still mulling everything over on the plane, still trying to imagine getting seven things right in a row without receiving a cheque, still thinking about form students with furrowed brow and carefree pin-stickers. The pieces are from different years but the trotters at Calgary brought welcome relaxation every time.

THAT SONG ABOUT THE MIDWAY
Racing Post August 2017

'And a voice calls out the numbers, and it sometimes mentions mine;

And I feel like I've been working overtime.'

On the long flight to Calgary to visit family, one of the films available is *Winter Sleep*, a Turkish production which is too long to summarise here but at one stage the lead character Aydin is trying to write his weekly newspaper column, only for his sister to keep interrupting. I must say I'm already rather fond of old Aydin.

Given that it lasts for over three hours I stay with it quite doggedly, though I keep thinking back to Goodwood, an interesting conversation with Dave Nevison and, of course, the television documentary *Britain at the Bookies*. Old songs arrive unbidden, stay a few minutes and wander off until the next time but Joni Mitchell's 'That Song About the Midway' captures the gambler's malaise so perfectly that a few minutes have become several days.

I happen to endorse Sunday columnist Steve Palmer's typically frank observation that 'if a few million strangers now think less of me I'm honestly not bothered' but he doesn't need to look at it that way. Most documentaries stay in the memory about as long as the last edition of *EastEnders* and 'Steve Palmer' is actually 'that bloke' as in: "Did you see that programme last night where that bloke did in 75 grand in cold blood?"

Steve is quite right when he says that people see the loss without acknowledging the skill it took to build up the stake in the first place; it was ever thus. Rather more disturbing was this week's third and final episode, which laid bare the effect obsessive gambling has on the individual and the people he cares for (except that he isn't in a position to care for them at all). It's pure coincidence that a fortnight ago I mentioned boredom as a factor in Omar Sharif's inability to concentrate on bridge as opposed to horseracing – an obsession that all but wiped him out financially. Now here was Terry in the betting shop in Slough, two marriages gone and no improvement in sight. "I can't stop it. I couldn't imagine life without gambling. It'd be an absolute bore."

Yes, that's right. You can say you'll give up gambling but it doesn't mean you'll turn your hand to landscape gardening or interior decorating. Without gambling, the day proceeds like a hearse caught in a traffic jam. What will you do at two o'clock on a typical Tuesday afternoon?

I've worked in betting offices, I've written about them and I've broadcast to them, readily picking up the much-needed pay cheque at the end of the month. I've certainly met some interesting characters but in 50 years I've met hardly anyone I thought was a winner overall and I've never thought the shops were anything other than a way of killing time. A perfectly agreeable way some will say, and that's fine by me, but there will be casualties.

There are winners at the track, of course, and when the betting exchanges first came in the shrewdest players made a lot of money. As for more traditional gamblers, Dave Nevison is the unluckiest I've met by a country mile and I always wondered how he managed to carry on. I readily admit I wouldn't have had the heart for it myself, though I suppose Zoman's short-head defeat by Opera House at the Curragh in 1992 (not for anything remotely approaching Dave's massive, life-changing pot) persuaded me to tone things down and put up with the boredom.

'I Can't Go On, I'll Go On,' as Samuel Beckett wrote. I see Dave pushing himself through the stints with RUK and, by golly, I bet it seems a long day, a rare old week of Tuesdays, but he's a pro and he gets through it.

'So lately you've been hiding, it was somewhere in the news;

And I'm still at these races, with my ticket stubs and my blues.'

Blimey, old Aydin is getting a hard time from his wife as well as his sister now. Tell them about the deadline, Aydin. Go on, send it, man. It's not as if you're somewhere over Greenland, a million miles from anywhere.

HAT-TRICK FOR THE LOCAL HERO
Racing Post August 2016

It's good to see some of the old faces again – Honey Booboolina, Mystic Messenger, Medicine Hat. Especially Medicine Hat, who seems to have found a new lease of life in claiming races, winning twice recently.

Of course, I know very little about it but these trotters, or pacers, seldom win twice in a row at Century Downs and Medicine Hat will be trying for a hat-trick in the last. They handicap you by pushing you out wide – eight or nine in a typical nine-runner field, and very few win from there. Medicine Hat is in seven but there's an hour or so to wait.

Meanwhile my daughter Catherine, passing me the baby, opts for Trustee in the seventh. Place only, she says, the way women do. Trustee breaks well and races in second the whole way round. He is still second when they cross the line, a couple of lengths behind Keep Coming, my son-in-law Jaret's choice at 8/1. I spend much of the contest praying that nothing will change and nothing does. They are both very happy and so is little Henry Douglas. It's not a bad start in life at nearly four months.

My Uncle Ted took me to Southampton Greyhound Stadium when I was a little boy. Fontwell soon followed and then there was the bingo a few years later. I had very little chance, really. My mother favoured the Broadway, formerly a cinema where my friend Marvel Mason started on his first fortune, buying and selling comics on Saturday mornings.

There was a near miss on the bingo when my mother was waiting for one more number for a big cash prize, her hopes dashed by a familiar, guttural cry from a few rows back.

"Huh," she said. "Money goes to money. German Edie. And she's on the game, too."

I thought this a bit harsh, just because her numbers had come up, but there we are.

Jaret had fared less well at the Cowboys Casino in Calgary the night before. The American roulette wheel has both a single and double zero and the latter came up early on. It reminded me of *Mississippi Grind*, a gambling film which came out a few months ago and seemed to pass relatively unnoticed.

Although not as funny as the wonderful *California Split* (1974), it charts similar territory and has much to recommend it, especially Ben Mendelsohn's performance as Gerry, a gambler who is down on his luck and very near the edge. Enter Ryan Reynolds as Curtis, an altogether smoother individual who befriends Gerry at the poker table and effectively funds the rambling adventure which follows – greyhounds, horses, casino.

No two gamblers are quite the same. At the racetrack, Gerry believes they are both on the same horse – the one they're relying on to get them out. All the premature elation followed by despair are there, but Curtis (and it's his money, after all) has held something back for the successful favourite. This is not something he can easily admit, quite apart from the fact that, amidst all the joshing and the camaraderie, in that moment of defeat he sees Gerry as a terminal loser.

And so there is a measure of guilt followed by a brief parting of the ways. To say any more might spoil things, though the denouement revolves around an unlikely double zero.

If you've always viewed gambling – or, more correctly, betting – as a harmless pastime, you won't take much from *Mississippi Grind*. But if you've tasted the ashes and entered something akin to F Scott Fitzgerald's 'real dark night of the soul', you'll probably watch it twice.

He's a big horse, Medicine Hat, a six-year-old gelding who beat six of these last time but from that draw he's 6/1. However, he's got the taste for it now and, even though I leave him alone, I'm sort of pleased when he comes barrelling through and keeps on like the good old boy he is to beat them once again. He's a local hero, even though Medicine Hat is 270 km away. Big place, Canada.

"How did the trip go?" Marvel asks.

"It was great. Bit of reading, bit of racing and you'll have worked out the Ebor for me. By the way, do you remember that German woman who used to play bingo with our mums at the Broadway?"

"Blimey, that's going back a bit. Hang on a minute. Short name, not German sounding. German Edie! That's right! She was on the game, wasn't she?"

Sometimes I think life is a bit too hard for me.

IDEAL PREPARATION FOR THE BIG ONE
Racing Post August 2015

My mother said it would end like this although, as I recall, there was no mention of harness racing at Century Downs in Calgary.

I'm rather proud of finding the last winner, Too Ideal, in a weak-looking claimer over a mile. A seven-year-old mare, she was soon in front but dropped to second at halfway. My record with horses fighting back to win is pretty grim (Red Abbot for Vernon Cross in the City Bowl at Salisbury in the mid-sixties?) but this was Too Ideal's day and she rallied to get up and deny a 25/1 shot close home. It was hard work at 9/5 but paid for the day.

No one is about to compare what happens here with events at Vincennes when the brilliant Gelinotte was in her prime. The starts are a bit ragged, all the races are over a mile, blinkers and bandages are much in evidence and anything a couple of lengths to the good around the second bend will take some catching. But the prize money is quite attractive, with the winner of an Open the other day picking up 11,500 Canadian dollars – about £5,600 – and it costs nothing to go in, though you pay three dollars for a racecard.

Bookies, who used to do business out of truck tailgates, drifted away from up-country meetings around 1912 and were replaced by a pari-mutuel system. With only a couple of booths in operation this week, and no more than 30 or 40 punters watching the racing out front, you wonder how on earth the whole thing works financially, bearing in mind Century Downs is planning thoroughbred meetings from next year onwards.

The answer, of course, is the casino which dominates the complex. There were many more people in there, with a facility in the corner for betting on all the 'away' meetings in America and Canada. As for the roulette and blackjack, there are no croupiers or dealers and everything is computerised. Apart from slashing the wage bill, this speeds everything up; no chips, no handing over of cash, just a running total in the corner of the screen which you can redeem at any time, taking your slip to the counter.

There was no way the Too Ideal money was going back, so I merely watched my son-in-law build up the sort of profit he should have taken and pondered what Dostoyevsky would have made of it. There was no one for grandmama to shout at, for a start – no croupier, no pit boss, no manager unwilling to cash yet another cheque.

I wonder how long it will be before we experience something similar at racetracks in Britain. Those who dismiss the idea probably ruled out roulette machines in betting shops, as well.

Personally, I hope racing and casinos remain separate. Painful though it was in the end, roulette for me was always a night-time activity in the room with no clocks and the 5am beer at Smithfield Market to follow. There is that wonderful dawn feeling when everything seems possible – Audrey Hepburn looking through the window at Tiffany's; world-weary detective Steve McQueen arriving home in the brilliant San Francisco light in *Bullitt*.

Anyway, I've walked on a glacier, relaxed in the Miette Hot Springs Pool in Jasper and seen a female grizzly bear by the roadside in the Rockies. Add a charming, operatic version of Cole Porter's 'Begin the Beguine' by Thomas Hampson while Desert Law was winning at Nottingham and it's been quite a trip. 'Let the love that was once a fire remain an ember' just about sums up the way I feel about roulette, too.

In an ideal world the Hampson CD would arrive at home in time for me to play it on the way to Brighton, where I win enough on tomorrow's big race – a humble seller to you but a fascinating contest to me – to cover the champagne bill at my friend Ray Wilson's 70th birthday party on course the following day. Too ideal for it all to work out, I dare say, but it's much too late to stop dreaming now.

RIP AND I WERE CERTAIN TO FAIL
Racing Post March 2011

It's good to know the great god Fluke is still in business.

Like the Lotto or the hottest of streaks at the roulette wheel, pure chance and backing horses on a whim will sometimes count for more than endless hours of careful study. Steve Whiteley was more than happy to admit as much as Lupita gave him the sixth and final leg of the Tote jackpot rollover at Exeter on Tuesday and earned him a cheque for very nearly £1.5m.

There are many things I like about the story. He didn't even need to place a token losing bet afterwards, the way fruit machine players do when three bars or three golden money sacks or three pomegranates are up there on the screen. (It's good to see pomegranates making a comeback, isn't it? When I was ten an old lady dropped a whole bag of them in the street and I dutifully picked them up, receiving two shillings [10p] for my pains. It meant I could go and see *The Man from Laramie* starring James Stewart.)

Then we have the selections themselves. Well, Mr Whiteley and I certainly have something in common apart from the bus pass because I'd definitely have found Semi Colon and Tony McCoy in the opener. After that he'd have left me behind, though, as his subconscious took over. Semi Colon, the lull before the storm; Black Phantom some looming presence to be banished once and for all, hence the Ammunition. Afterwards it gets quite tricky. Mr Bennett the kindly schoolteacher who ran summer camp under the Lundy Sky? Lupita the sultry Spanish language assistant who tucked the boys in? Hm. Sometimes I think I could write something like that. Anyway, it's the kind of thing that would stay with you for 50 years or more, no doubt about it.

Sadly, the truth is rather more prosaic. Mr Whiteley said that Lodge (Lupita was ridden by Jessica Lodge) was a name 'that hangs in my head'. He seemed laid-back, euphoric and in a state of shock, all at the same time. It's something we should all experience before we go.

It's good when racing makes the news pages with stories like this but I couldn't quite see the link between Mr Whiteley's astonishing good fortune and the piece which accompanied it in the *Independent* entitled 'Why tired gamblers are the biggest losers'. My first thought was that several thousand people will need to be very careful at Cheltenham from this Tuesday onwards as their 'inbuilt fear of a negative outcome' (I think we can take that to mean losers, yes?) vanishes when people are deprived of a good night's sleep'.

I feel better now because I obviously didn't have a chance right from the start and nor did Rip Van Winkle. I'm always awake at 3am thinking about the past so I'm bound to be a bit jaded, while Rip fell asleep for 20 years. Obviously he felt wonderful when he woke up and it follows that he'd have given the bookies an absolute pasting but they'd closed his accounts.

Now that I think about it again I'd have got two out of six at Exeter because Lundy Sky would have reminded me of Word From Lundy, who was Grundy's dam. I'm not saying I habitually bet for sentimental reasons but I'm not immune to it and I do tend to stay with champions until they're beaten, which is why I'll be right behind Big Buck's in the World Hurdle. If he loses, I lose on the week and nothing can change that.

I back most abbots and abbesses, so I was on Talgo Abbess, third at 100/8, in the Champion Hurdle in 1967. I couldn't really bet the previous year because I was equally fond of Salmon Spray and Flyingbolt, who finished first and third. Flyingbolt, very nearly as good as his mighty stable companion Arkle, had won the Champion Chase two days previously and all but completed the double, though the late Johnny Haine, the best hurdles jockey I have ever seen, had things pretty much under control on the winner.

You never expect to meet your heroes but I bumped into him in a hotel just outside Bristol 20 years later. I doubt that either of us was going very far in life at that stage but he certainly had the edge because he'd taken a job as a long-distance lorry driver, though all he wanted to do was talk about racing.

I was thinking about him the other night and wondering how on earth Bob Turnell managed to keep everyone happy, because he had to find enough rides for his son Andy and Jeff King, as well. I thought about it for a long time and backed two or three losers the next day. Still, now that I know it had nothing to do with any lack of skill or judgement, and everything to do with tiredness, I'm perfectly relaxed about the whole thing.

Have a great week.

Part Ten

Water Is King For A Day

I never thought Bristol, or Nailsea, would become 'home' because a job presenting on HTV West after the BBC always looked a short-term affair. This was a correct assessment but I made good friends, including the group responsible for Limelight, who joined Portbury trainer Pat Murphy from James Toller at Newmarket.

She won twice over hurdles for us, including at Chepstow – 16/1 after a long lay-off, underlining how patient Pat was – but was retired afterwards and visited Master Willie at stud. The result was Lenny The Blade, a slow learner with Richard Phillips but subsequently a winner at Newton Abbot when switched to Sarah Robinson at Bridgwater. Lenny had the winner covered when falling with fatal consequences at Chepstow next time.

There comes a point in life when you know you won't be working full-time anywhere any more. HTV had me back as a freelance interviewer and the most memorable day came in 1998 when my wife and daughter picked me up outside the Bristol studios at noon the day after my 50th birthday and we somehow managed to miss only about eight minutes of Blackburn v Southampton.

Stevie Basham didn't score many for Saints but he managed one that day in a rare 2-0 away win and if I say it was memorable for me it was even more so for Roy Hodgson, who was sacked as Blackburn manager soon after the final whistle. (I wonder what price you'd have got about his becoming England manager after that.)

Things just ticked over after the *Sports Adviser* closure. There was always *The Irish Field* in the background and I worked the corporate boxes at Haydock and Doncaster with Roger Hart, who was a great supporter. There was interviewing work at Goodwood (for George Materna, who became a close friend) and Cheltenham and a memorable winner – Robert Stronge's Water King at 50/1 in the conditional jockeys' handicap hurdle on the Friday of the Cheltenham Open meeting in 2005.

It's quite a story. I knew Robert quite well because we played in a very modest poker school in the Swindon area. Water King wasn't a 'thinker' but he wasn't easy to win with, either. Anyway, Robert was going to give him a little outing around Uttoxeter and then on to Cheltenham where he'd be ridden by Shane Walsh, not well known here but very promising according to Robert, who'd be acting as his manager.

I made a note and told one or two people, including my great friend Howard Dawson. But Water King didn't go to Uttoxeter, he went to Chepstow and FELL when beaten. However, he wasn't hurt and I reasoned that nothing had really changed unless his confidence had been dented. Shane Walsh gave the horse a peach of a ride at Cheltenham, producing him at the last and driving him out to score by half a length.

Most of the people I told had the same bet. Indeed, they took 'worth a tenner each-way of your hard-earned' quite literally, so they all won well over £700, Water King paying 69/1 for a win on the Tote. At the course I was with Jeremy Scott of IG Index, his friend James and the award-winning writer Jamie Reid. It's fair to say we offered some vocal encouragement on the run-in.

Cheltenham is an easy journey but there are times when everything seems a long way from Bristol. Home games are at least two hours away and, where the Brighton sponsorship is concerned, I look for dates when a Goodwood or Salisbury meeting takes place 24 hours later so that we can double up, so to speak.

After 64 years without bothering the medical profession, I saw the Saints win 2-0 at Reading but woke up several hours later with my left arm more or less out of control. I think the flashing blue light soon afterwards was rather important to my continued existence, so too the three stents in my heart in the small hours. Apart from family and three close friends I couldn't see any point in telling anyone and just carried on as before without losing any work.

The new hip followed five years later and the main thing I remember is a phone call in hospital from my great friend Pat McElroy, who sorted out at least one of my remortgagings in the troubled times and continued to support the Carnaby seller, even when cancer was close to claiming him. A committed Arsenal supporter from the day he arrived in England, he even turned up for lunch before the Southampton game at the Emirates late in 2019 but was too weak to attend the match. You could say I miss him.

It's been suggested that I try to fit in too much and there were a couple of worried phone calls during the rain-soaked 9-0 home defeat to Leicester not so long ago. I can appreciate that a new hip, three stents and an ordinary pacemaker about to be replaced by an upgraded one might have made people anxious but the fact is I was more concerned with the result and the steam rising inside the car when I turned the heat on. I dried out a little at Brian and Lesley Truscott's place and all was well soon after Sutton Scotney Services, by which time I was consoling myself with the memory of the 9-3 beating we handed out to Wolves in 1965.

Their goalie was a chap called Dave McLaren. Of course, we signed him soon afterwards. How could anyone NOT love the Saints?

EPSOM THOUGHTS FROM THE WORKHOUSE
Racing Post May 2016

One way and another, I seem to be spending quite a lot of time at the Bristol Royal Infirmary – dropping people off, picking them up, visiting them and undergoing the occasional procedure myself.

Mercifully it's not far from the Botanist wine bar and the other day I discovered a pleasant café called the Workhouse Kitchen, where they favour CDs by Bob Dylan and The Band. I mentioned to the waitress that Manfred Mann had a hit in Britain with Dylan's 'Mighty Quinn', though I believe she may have missed it by a few decades.

Anyway, the Workhouse Kitchen is ideal for studying the Derby form and trying to win enough to finance another visit to Canada, where a third grandson has arrived. Fortunately I have a line to the Calgary harness racing form, especially the equivalent of a seller they put on at the end, though things may be a bit blurred after a year away.

On Thursday I arrived at the hospital via Old Market and Gloucester Road. I'd forgotten how many pubs, betting offices and massage parlours there are in close proximity. It makes sense, of course, having a wide variety of places to celebrate if you happen to back a few winners.

It occurred to me in the Workhouse that the ancient Romans had it all figured out. The word fornication comes from the 'fornices', the arches of great stadia like the Colosseum, where ladies of easy virtue plied their lucrative trade with punters already high on gladiatorial blood and betting on the chariots. We'd have been more than happy there, I think, even without Tote facilities. Actually, with only five or six chariots lining up the place dividends would have been pretty skinny anyway, so no change there.

I have not felt strongly about anything in the Derby since Authorized a few years ago and even then the stake probably wasn't all that much bigger than the Blakeney bet in 1969. It was all the years in between which did the damage. My view was partially obscured but I remember Blakeney and Ernie Johnson wriggling through against the far rails – a feat Ernie might have repeated on Barry Hills' Rheingold four years later, but for Lester Piggott's truly astonishing effort on Roberto.

Lester Piggott wins on Roberto

Major Dick Hern's Henbit is not generally regarded as a great Derby winner and came across as something of a bit-part player at West Ilsley following stable companion Troy's comprehensive victory in 1979. Even so, Henbit lives on in the memory because I travelled on one of the open-top buses from Denmark Street, just around the corner from Soho, to Epsom.

Denmark Street was better known as Tin Pan Alley, the centre of the popular music industry and you could always get a drink there, day or night, long before all-day opening was introduced. After midnight two clubs, one known as the Spanish Rooms, an unlicensed bar, and the other as El Dandy, favoured by Colombians who went there to dance salsa, did huge business.

The two places sat one above the other at number 18 – unrecognisable now and part of a vanished London. Personally I favoured the Mazurka Club, open well into the small hours, but as long as you made it to Frith Street for a coffee at breakfast time you caught the bus all right and travelled to Epsom in the company of some vaguely disreputable characters. And let's be honest, vaguely disreputable characters tend to have the best stories.

Two months after Henbit did his stuff, a man called John Thompson, having argued with staff at the Spanish Rooms, poured some petrol through the letterbox, lit a match and wiped out 37 people. It was one of the worst fires in London's history, which is saying something, and the amazing thing is that it's hardly ever mentioned now. Thompson's trial – he went down for life – took place at the same time as the Yorkshire Ripper's and was largely ignored. He died on the anniversary of the fire, in 2008.

Anyway, time to visit my friend Brian, 83, and give him his chocolate cake, which I have to spirit past the nurse. Speech gone, writing gone, teeth gone but a big gummy smile when he sees the cake. I don't suppose for a moment he'll have done any research on the Derby; there's more chance of a bumper place dividend.

EYE OF THE TIGER IN THE MIDNIGHT HOUR
Racing Post June 2018

Apparently, a cocktail of codeine and paracetamol is due at 2am. The pain from the hip replacement is far from serious but quite insistent. There is no stretching, which means I cannot reach the laptop and glory in Oeil De Tigre's win in the first at Goodwood. Another evening meeting gone.

There is some gentle snoring further down the corridor. The verb 'to snore' comes quite close to the actual sound, though maybe the French have the edge with 'ronfler', which is a shade deeper and possibly building to a climax. This chap is not French.

I should have brought more books. Still, Thomas Hardy's *The Woodlanders* and *The Smoking Diaries* by Simon Gray will help. You can't read *The Woodlanders* (1887) without finding the characters vaguely similar to those in *Far from the Madding Crowd*, though Giles Winterborne is no Gabriel Oak. Maybe that's unfair because Giles has no Alan Bates to play him in a film version, but *The Woodlanders* is too claustrophobic to lend itself to the screen anyway.

Most of the men are employed by Melbury, the timber merchant. Everyone is expected to marry within his or her social class. This is village life in Hardy's Dorset, though you might be forgiven for wondering if anyone in Little Melbury receives any outside news at all. The maiden Merry Hampton winning the 1887 Derby would be a long shot in all respects.

You cannot spend your life looking at racing every day without making literary connections. *The Mayor of Casterbridge* is one of Hardy's best novels and Michael Henchard one of his strongest characters. The really interesting thing about Henchard's wife Susan, leaving aside the fact that she was also a filly trained by John Francome during his brief spell with a licence (won at Bath, I think) is that some modern reviewers have little sympathy for her. Sold with a young child to a sailor when Henchard is in the grip of the dreaded furmity at a country fair, much is made of her weakness and subservience. Henchard himself is so ashamed he takes the pledge and turns his life around to a degree. Hardy is very perceptive on the subject of drink. At dawn the people have always gone and the room or tent is always smaller than you thought.

I first read *The Smoking Diaries* several years ago. Gray knew that cigarettes would claim him in the end and they did, though not before a string of hits in the West End and on Broadway had established him as one of the finest playwrights this country has produced. I'm not sure if the third of the diaries is suitable for hospital reading because he's just been diagnosed with prostate cancer but I can't really resist it. Here he is on 'urologist number one's bill'.

'See him now, sitting in his study, anticipating a smooth run to his eightieth birthday, when he will be found in his favourite armchair, slippered feet resting on his favourite cat, head bowed over his favourite poem, by Hardy of course. And outside the grandchildren dumping in the paddling pool, the butterflies humping in the woodshed, the plumple bees drifting drowsily on little eddies of insecticide, a life spinelessly lived, now supinely closing.' (Not one of Simon's favourites, urologist number one.)

The tablets arrive. The laptop is moved. It has taken Oeil De Tigre all this time to reach Goodwood but he has a gilt-edged chance of a hat-trick on Monday – another meeting I shall miss, sadly.

I can reach my bag with my other foot. I need to see an obituary of the volatile actress Margot Kidder, who was married to my favourite American novelist Thomas McGuane for a while. It would be wonderful to do something, anything, as well as McGuane and still have plenty of time for horses. In the first chapter of *Some Horses* (Vintage, 1999) we learn that only one horse, Comanche, survived the Battle of the Little Bighorn. 'There is a special grief for the innocent caught up in mankind's murderous follies.'

The nurse thinks sleep might be a good idea. I tell her I'd still be awake at home, as well, but I suppose I could give it a try.

FREUD SLIPS THOUGH THE INTERVIEWER'S NET
Racing Post August 2011

I think it's a great pity that Lucian Freud has gone. Quite apart from anything else, he provided an invaluable personal service. If you wondered whether your looks were starting to fade, you just got him to paint you and that removed all possible doubt. Given the time it took, you'd probably have deteriorated a bit more, as well.

He ate a bar of nougat for breakfast and drank vintage champagne, though not when working. I wanted to interview him about the old Soho days, those long afternoons with Bruce and Jeffrey Bernard when betting shops were very different from the spruce parlours they've become today.

He turned me down flat and it was only when I read several obituaries, most of them fascinating, that I realised you were meant to keep on asking. But he'd never have done a gambling piece anyway, because he left it all behind years ago. When the paintings brought in millions, there was no longer the desire to bet. "It doesn't mean anything unless it hurts," he once famously said.

Most people will find that sad or strange but some will know exactly what he meant. His grandfather, Sigmund Freud, was quite certain gambling was a substitute for this, that and the other – especially the other. At the last count, Lucian had 14 children, three of them born to different women in 1961, so I'm not sure the theory holds up all that well in his case.

Sir Clement Freud was quite a big gambler, but I formed the impression that everything was pretty much under control. We bumped into each other at the races two or three times before he died and talked about various things, writing mainly, though his long estrangement from Lucian, which is what interested me most, would certainly have been off limits.

An only child finds it hard to imagine having a brother and not talking to him. That's what I think when I'm being serious but in my more frivolous moments, which are many, I picture Lucian trying to get through a whole half-hour of *Just a Minute* and the radio ending up down the bottom of the garden. Not his cup of tea, I fear.

The other night I was lying awake and thinking about close finishes which had influenced things to a considerable degree. Opera House beating Zoman at the Curragh by the width of the proverbial cigarette paper in 1992 stands out because I realised, when that short-head defeat finally sank in, that it was time to step back from the edge of the abyss.

On the other hand, there was a selling plater of Les Hall's that did the business by a similar margin at Newmarket. The principals raced wide apart with Dennis McKay going like the clappers on the far side and getting there by a nostril. I'd forgotten the horse's name but I saw Dennis at Goodwood on

Wednesday and he remembered Liberty Lawyer in about three seconds flat. Not bad after 40-odd years. Dennis would have been of little interest to Lucian because he looks fantastic – well-turned-out, not a hair out of place and more than capable of getting up on one and doing us another favour at the drop of a hat. What a shame Les Hall is no longer with us.

After Frankel had given us that magical 'I was there' moment and a tearful Sir Henry Cecil had embraced his women with the kind of fervour that had me damp-eyed, envious and wishing I'd taken advantage of the £1.90 win dividend on the Tote, I wandered down to the furlong pole to watch Andrew Balding's Whiplash Willie come past in the mile and a half handicap. I'd seen him burst clear at Salisbury and thought he might win again, even off a 12lb higher mark. Maybe I'm getting the hang of it at last, or maybe I just liked the name. *Meet Whiplash Willie* started life as *The Fortune Cookie* in America and starred Walter Matthau. Walter made at least three films to clear gambling debts.

I used to watch quite a few races down by the furlong pole, offering up the odd prayer now and again. Brighton is a particularly good place for it because even after they've come past there's still plenty of time for things to change.

"Only get me out of this, God, and I'll live different, honest I will," you know the sort of thing. As an agnostic my own exhortations would not have carried religious overtones and I can't quite recall where I got that example from, but I think it comes at the end of Evelyn Waugh's *Officers and Gentlemen*, from the 'Sword of Honour' trilogy, when the exhausted, retreating soldiers are cast adrift in murderous seas off Crete.

They'd all but given up hope and several of them went over the side but a handful made it safely to dry land. Of course, they looked completely wasted and haggard. It's a pity Lucian wasn't there with his brushes.

STILL OBSESSIVE AFTER ALL THESE YEARS
Racing Post October 2017

Well, of course I can see there is something magnificent about Gregorio Allegri's 'Miserere', or 'miserere mei, Deus' – 'have mercy on me, O God' – but it does go on a bit and hardly perks you up in the morning after Signs Of Blessing has beaten only one home in the Prix de l'Abbaye.

They've revamped Essential Classics on Radio 3 and instead of a quiz question they play a piece of music and ask listeners to suggest a suitable follow-up, or ideal companion piece. The 'Miserere' still had several minutes to go and I thought everyone might need cheering up so I volunteered 'I Wish I Could Shimmy Like My Sister Kate'. They didn't read it out, though. Too facetious, I suppose. I have 50-year-old school reports in the garage suggesting much the same thing.

I always have Essential Classics on but they favour Radio 2 and Ken Bruce at the dentist's. He's been going for ever and must have reached three figures but that seems to be the way of it with DJs. Jimmy Young was playing 'Unchained Melody' by the Righteous Brothers nearly half a century after having the original hit himself in 1955. Meld hacked up in the Oaks and there was old Jimmy, or young Jimmy, really, warbling away in the background.

For a while they favoured piped music at the doctor's, Vivaldi of course. Nice and light. Well, you wouldn't want the 'Miserere' before you went in, we can all see that. People would stagger out before their name was called. My last doctor but one was Robin Lambert, who had a passing interest in racing. It picked up appreciably when Dr Richard Newland started training winners but it didn't stretch to buying a *Racing Post*, so it was only when I felt rough that he got the latest news.

Anyway, Signs Of Blessing beat one and Dark Red at Chelmsford on Saturday beat two but The Big Short at Goodwood last Wednesday week didn't beat any at all, so it came as something of a relief when Syrian Pearl turned up at 10/1 at Nottingham. By then I'd rallied anyway, having watched Robert Altman's beautiful film *Vincent & Theo*, about the last years of Vincent van Gogh's tragic life.

It is quite extraordinary that Altman, who directed *M*A*S*H*, *Nashville* and the very funny but seldom seen gambling picture *California Split*, was able to turn his hand to this study in obsession. As the troubled painter gradually loses his mind in Provence, his syphilitic brother Theo is still negotiating sales with largely unsympathetic art dealers in Paris.

Some of the locations in the capital are familiar to readers of Balzac or Proust. Obsession pervades the latter's Á *la recherche du temps perdu*, in which Proust tries to monitor Albertine's movements almost by the hour. Although Albertine seems very real to us, or to me anyway, Proust invented her as a substitute for his secretary Albert Nahmias, for whom he nursed feelings which were hardly platonic. We don't know much about young Albert, except that he was a keen gambler and speculator on the stock market, so we'd probably have liked him.

It matters little when you're well ahead and the coach is inching its way out of the Bois de Boulogne in early evening – somehow, Chantilly last week couldn't quite match that – but, like Proust, I can't help thinking about, or obsessing about, the 'early' events which shaped the way things turned out.

As a board man I rode the strongest finish with the help of a rolled-up *Sporting Life* that anyone had ever seen. Of course, that was back in the days when the people behind the counter had opinions of their own, no one minded the gaps between races and there were no machines. Sure, some shops were smoky boltholes, bastions of male escapism and the language could be fruity. I'm not reimagining some bijou little pied-à-terre with civilised conversation and sweet breezes wafting through an ever-open door. But there was atmosphere, and there were characters.

Would I have won overall in those days if I'd known what I know now? No, probably not. I might have learned how to shimmy, though.

WAITING FOR GODOT – AND LONGCHAMP

Racing Post October 2016

The reserve postman has spiky, steel-grey hair and plenty of it, brushed straight across and standing up slightly, though not alarmingly. With his sallow, lived-in face he is, you might say, a dead ringer for Samuel Beckett, though very few in Nailsea have passed comment.

He seems to have Beckett's stamina, too. I long for him to sit down on the wall for a rest. "You can't go on. You'll go on," I shall murmur, paraphrasing the great man. Nearly all posties are thin, wiry and indefatigable. 'As rare as a fat postman,' as Raymond Chandler put it in *The Long Goodbye* or one of the other Philip Marlowe private eye novels. I like to think it's *The Long Goodbye* because it's my favourite, especially the film version with its moody Johnny Mercer soundtrack.

With Longchamp closed this will be the first Arc I've missed for several years. I go back as far as Sea-Bird II in 1965 and, whilst I find comparisons between outstanding champions of different generations fairly pointless, I shall never see a better middle-distance horse than Sea-Bird.

I loved Zarkava, it's true, and rejoiced when she was retired after the Arc because there was that hint of temperament likely to dent her unbeaten record the following season. But Sea-Bird simply laughed at one of the strongest Arc fields ever assembled, beating Prix du Jockey Club winner Reliance and subsequent Washington International hero Diatome by six lengths and five.

Racing, like all sport, is covered in such comprehensive detail these days that it comes as a surprise when certain incidental points slip through the net. For instance, not one of Sea-Bird's five immediate dams won a race under Jockey Club rules in any country. As a sire his record was hardly prolific but he was responsible for Allez France, winner of the Arc in 1974.

The most bitterly disappointing result was Nijinsky's narrow defeat by Sassafras in 1970 although, coming to terms with it in a restaurant in the Place du Marechal Juin a few hours later, one could only reflect ruefully on Yves Saint-Martin's terse dismissal of all our hopes and dreams. "I don't know whether Nijinsky has been over-raced or overrated," he said. Here was a man who could shrug for France and never take the captain's armband off.

The Petrus on the Place du Marechal Juin became too expensive for most tourists (including this one) almost overnight. The last throw of the dice came in 2006 when Rail Link won the big race and Kevin Ryan's Desert Lord inched home in the Prix de l'Abbaye at 25/1.

In previous years it was the perfect place to sit outside on the morning of the Arc, sipping a cognac and a very strong, if minuscule, coffee. "Not enough to get in your eye, boy," as my mother would have said.

The jazz musician Miles Davis fancied himself as a painter, as well, and designed a logo for Hennessy brandy when they were sponsoring a lot of jazz events in Paris, while the great saxophonist Stan Getz divided his time between the capital and Saint-Jean Cap Ferrat. When *Rolling Stone* magazine asked presidential candidate Bill Clinton what band he'd like at his inaugural ball, he replied: "Too bad Stan Getz is dead." Somehow it's hard to imagine Hillary or the other chap coming up with something like that in a few weeks' time.

Paris doesn't smell the same these days and not merely because the street-corner 'pissoirs' have gone. General de Gaulle has generally been credited with their rapid decline from 1960 (Puissant Chef's year, appropriately enough), though it was Madame de Gaulle who took particular exception to them. The more genteel word for a pissoir was a 'vespasienne', which was rather like asking someone who has spent his working life on the land to refer to manure as fertiliser. (Not that he was bound to say manure in the first place, of course.)

Where the Metro was concerned, there used to be a rather wonderful smell of garlic, dust and tobacco wafting up through the gratings in the street. Buying a *Paris-Turf*, ordering that first cognac on Arc morning and studying the impossible, divided handicap at the end offered an early taste of paradise.

There are few, if any, mentions of racing in Beckett's correspondence, though he sometimes wrote from 6 Rue des Favorites. *Waiting for Godot* closed at the Hebertot Theatre just before Ribot obliged for the second time in 1956. I was going to mention it to the postie, but Bristol City had just prevailed against Leeds the night before. More of an *Endgame* man, I suspect.

A CHANGE OF TRAINER THE UNKINDEST CUT OF ALL
Racing Post August 2012

I try to stay with a barber until he dies or I do.

As a child I went to a place called the Elite in Southampton where one of the barbers was called Mr Shearing. Look, it can happen. There used to be a dentist on Chiswick High Road called Mr Phang and for years the *Guardian*'s health correspondent was John Illman. He's still going strong, I think.

In our first 27 years in Bristol I had only two hairdressers, Lillo and Carmelo. Lillo had a place on the Bath Road and we talked about football (Juventus) and racing (don't back favourites) all the time. I only ever saw him get angry once and that was when a large, middle-aged lady, who required the combined attentions of Vidal Sassoon and Teasy-Weasy Raymond to counter the ravages of time generally and the previous 24 hours in particular, plonked herself down and asked him for a miracle.

This wasn't what made Lillo cross – he relished a challenge – but when he excused himself she looked over her shoulder and said: "Darling, I'm absolutely desperate. You couldn't possibly get me a large vodka and tonic, could you?"

Well, I don't see how you can refuse a request like that – I'd expect someone to do the same for me – so I wandered down to the Three Lamps on the next corner and surprised them with this 11am windfall. We needn't dwell on the attractions of the Three Lamps. Suffice it to say that it was boarded up soon afterwards and wasn't the sort of place where you asked for a slice of lime.

I must have been quite quick because she was sipping the vodka like someone given an unlikely hold on life when Lillo came back in. All in all, I think 'dumbfounded' is not too strong a word to describe his expression.

"Never, ever do that again," he said, when she tottered off in search of fresh adventure. "She can buy her own vodka and tonic. And besides, I'm not licensed!"

Lillo died too young and the brandy didn't help. It was very sad because his family had been told there was no immediate cause for concern but he suffered an abdominal rupture when they left the hospital. His son Tony didn't want to run the business and fancied taking up riding again. I arranged for him to go down to Jeremy Naylor's at Shrewton, where Bob Sievier trained the legendary Sceptre to win four Classics, but he wasn't strong enough after missing so many years and was too old to claim an allowance anyway.

Jeremy is an interesting character who used to run the Bristol University Equine Research Centre whilst also working as Martin Pipe's vet. As a trainer he deserves better horses, which might be said of a few dozen others, as well. At Shrewton he followed John Bolton, who gave him a few rides in amateur riders' races, John having taken over from Richmond Sturdy.

No mean historian where the yard is concerned, Naylor can give you chapter and verse on Ashurst Wonder's 50/1 success in the Stewards' Cup in 1954. Ashurst Wonder had recently left to join Les Hall and Sturdy (being Sturdy) recommended a couple of quiet outings with a major coup in mind. However, Hall realised how well the horse was, went for the big one straightaway and saw him blown in by the wind under 6st 12lb.

The pair of them would have enjoyed last Saturday, not merely because Hawkeyethenoo defied a big weight but also because an upgraded selling plater won the nursery. Dandy Nicholls, responsible for the winner four times in the last six years, allowed Jamesbo's Girl to win a seller and a claimer by the same margin, seven lengths – whereupon Richard Fahey claimed her.

Presumably, had she remained in Dandy's stable, she would have started at nearer 6/1 than 16/1, a price which put Marvel Mason off. In the White Swan near Newbury a few hours later he admitted he'd have backed her at sixes. He's in therapy, apparently.

"How much does that cost?" I asked.

"An absolute bloody packet," he said. "If I backed a few winners I'd cheer up and give it a miss."

I think that's the right move. If I'd ever needed to be told I drink too much, gamble too much and dwell in the past, I'd have asked Lillo. It would only have cost a haircut and we could have gone for a brandy afterwards.

SUNNY SIDE UP – LET'S HOPE SO, ANYWAY
Racing Post March 2015

"There's no point in giving anyone Faugheen," Marvel Mason says. "When people ask you, they're looking for something around 12/1."

This is quite true, of course, though a while back, a little weary of all the analysis, I decided to back Big Buck's and nothing else. I did it two years in a row and both times he fooled the commentator by hesitating briefly before storming up the hill to a thunderclap of approval. I wondered why I didn't bet like that all the time; too long between races, probably.

Marvel and I have had a cough for about three weeks and this strange-tasting brandy, possibly German, is not helping.

"I went to see the quack this morning," he says. "New chap, knows his racing. He's got a framed Gary Larson cartoon on his desk. That one where the middle-aged woman looks quite perplexed and is saying to the copper: 'Well, when I got home, Harold's hat was gone, his coat was gone, his worries were on the doorstep and my neighbour, Gladys Mitchell, says she saw him walking off down the sunny side of the street.'

"I gave him Faugheen. Told him to make his money on the first day and then stop. I was hoping for some linctus or something but he says there's no need to worry yet. Things change with the passing of the years. When you're at school the quack turns up – Scottish bloke, what was his name? – and you struggle to cough because you're distracted but now you could cough for England, no problem."

Alan the Buddhist chuckles softly. He has a look of fixed concentration on his face and a few more lyrics from 'On the Sunny Side of the Street' will surely issue forth at some point.

The name suddenly comes to me.

"McCaffrey. Angus McCaffrey. Very strange man. When you went into the surgery he'd look at you and shake his head. 'Ah, dearie dearie me,' he'd say, which wasn't the best of starts. He liked a bet and backed Rockavon at 66/1 in the 2000 Guineas in 1961. After that he backed anything trained by George Boyd and ridden by Norman Stirk or Norman McIntosh. George let anyone ride his horses as long as they were Scottish and called Norman."

"I sold Angus some comics, you know," Marvel says. "A complete set of Wally Brand: The Ball of Fire, all about an English centre-forward banished to the Scottish Second Division, who comes back to help a team battling relegation from the old First Division. He was barrel-chested and not very tall but frighteningly fast – 'his feet going like trip hammers' comes to mind – and he wanted the ball played in fast and low, so that defenders would fall on their backsides as they chased back and this very fast barrel would come between them, scoring vital goals to keep the team up. It was wonderful stuff, though no one remembers old Wally now. At least Alf Tupper, the Tough of the Track, had two horses named after him."

Archie, his bookshop closed for the day, has been studying form for at least an hour. He is on good terms with himself, thanks to a Nigel Twiston-Davies treble, and will try to go one better on the opening day of the Festival with Douvan and Un De Sceaux already pencilled in, though I suspect Marvel's words will make Faugheen the vital cog in a wheel fast gathering pace.

"What happened to old Angus in the end?" Marvel says.

"He saw out his time and avoided dreadful platitudes like 'just pop your things off' but after 50 years of intimate examinations you're bound to become a bit world-weary. Sighing deeply and saying: 'Right, it's troosers doon time, laddie,' didn't meet with universal approval."

This leads to such a fit of coughing from old Arthur Sears that we look at him in some alarm. He's just caught sight of *The King and I*, which is on in the other bar. "Hello Young Lovers – You're Under Arrest!" he splutters, wiping his face.

Alan the Buddhist stares at him intently. "Just direct your feet, to the sunny side of the street," he smiles, not without a hint of pride.

"I love you, Alan," Marvel says.

GREAT OAKS, LITTLE FISH ... AND LOVE TO FOLLOW
Racing Post May 2014

The cheapest return fare I could find from Bristol Temple Meads to York, even with my old timer's card, was £153. Gone are the days when I could write out an expenses claim. An old Fleet Street friend used to fill out the form, humming the words to 'I'm Hans Christian Andersen' by Danny Kaye as he went along. (For younger readers, Hans Christian was a Danish writer, famous for fairy tales and fables ...) Anyway, there is no outside help. I'm on my own, living on my wits and the occasional Placepot dividend.

So I thought I'd better drive, though when you hit the roadworks on the M1 just north of Nottingham it's hard not to think of the rattler, what passes for coffee and a relaxed, in-depth perusal of the sprint handicap and an ordinary-looking Musidora. At such times I ponder going all the way to Blyth, where my Uncle Tom played for the Spartans the better part of 80 years ago. Blyth and Venice, those are my big two. A round trip is in the offing. Croft Park followed by the dark, eerie streets trodden by Donald Sutherland before his encounter with the dwarf in *Don't Look Now*. I shall do it soon. After all, when the autumn weather turns the leaves to flame, one hasn't got time for the waiting game.

"Is that a song?" Toni says, wondering how to make a haircut last longer than four or five minutes. (That's the thing with life, isn't it? You used to have enough hair for an in-depth discussion of Milton's *Paradise Lost*, but now …)

A connoisseur of minor setbacks, I have recently seen Jim Old's Witch's Hat come down at Towcester and QPR fail to beat Wigan in 90 minutes at Loftus Road but Toni, only my third-ever Bristolian barber, has just landed a fairly major football accumulator, all at short prices. He looks a little weary after a late-night poker session at the casino but is buoyed by a happy marriage; Mrs Toni is very keen on staying in, apparently.

"You come in here and give me good advice but you don't take it yourself," he says. "Why 90 minutes? Go for the shorter price and make sure. Little fish are sweet, yes?"

I must say I never thought an Italian barber would remind me of my mother but if you live long enough these things come around. 'Great oaks from little acorns grow,' that was another of hers after a minor coup at the bingo. I've never discovered how far in advance you have to plant them but I'd give a few bob to hear her say it again.

"You would love Venice and also Sorrento," Toni goes on. "I can recommend a couple of restaurants." I promise him a couple of badges for Chepstow in return and we start humming 'Torna A Surriento', which Pomus and Shuman turned into 'Surrender' for Elvis Presley, though I think Toni is more than happy with the Italian version. Marco does not join in and continues reading the *Sun*, which makes me think of racing correspondent Claude Duval and highwaymen in general.

Not that Claude is a highwayman, of course, though his near namesake Claude Du Vall certainly was and people fondly imagine that he was up and down the old A1, aiding and abetting Dick Turpin. It's a good story but Du Vall, originally a dashing Parisian footman who once ambushed Charles II's master of hounds in a thicket and relieved him of 50 guineas, was hanged at Tyburn in 1670 at the age of 27, some 36 years before Turpin was born.

Dick suffered a similar fate on the Knavesmire in 1739. Horse theft would have seen him hanged eventually, though in fact he was arrested for the minor offence of shooting a cockerel. Then, very foolishly, he wrote a letter to his family from York Castle prison which gave his identity away when intercepted.

I was going to tell a rapt audience all of these things on Wednesday but Astaire was running in the Duke of York Stakes and I'm torn between him and Es Que Love, who'll go like the clappers, start to hang fire inside the final furlong and probably give best to one or two, but not three, making him a very good each-way bet. (He was indeed third at 12/1, having been held up for the first time in living memory and come between horses late on. Sometimes my head hurts with it all.)

"Well, at least you'll look smart," Toni says. "Want to see the top and the sides?" I want this as much as I want an extra armpit but he is too quick for me.

"Torna A Surriento," he smiles as I reach the door. I wonder what it costs from Temple Meads.

THE FIVE PER CENT SOLUTION
Racing Post May 2018

Ever since Problem Child bolted up at Newbury I've carried with me a small yet highly significant statistic: Alzheimer's is hereditary in five per cent of cases.

It was a long time ago, of course. Ron Smyth and Sir Peter O'Sullevan were still with us, Problem Child had shown nothing on the Flat and was making his debut over hurdles and my mother wanted a cup of tea. She always wanted a cup of tea and her face would light up when it arrived. She also thought there was a bus stop nearby with a regular service from Nailsea to Southampton. I have often wished for such a bus stop myself, whilst keeping quiet about it.

You'll have worked out the rest. It was probably the only time in a long and chequered punting career that the line to Coral was busy – I tried twice – and in the background I could hear The Voice, a gentle yet insistent lapping of waves over light shale, building to a crescendo and calling Problem Child home at 25/1. "Good tea, boy," my mother said.

I keep an eye on myself, just in case. No problem with the Seven Dwarfs or the Magnificent Seven (always kick off with Brad Dexter) but the other day I couldn't remember the name of the actor who played Tinker in the television series *Lovejoy*. Round face, dark beret, fond of a drop. My wife couldn't remember either and Google was mentioned but you mustn't cheat. Gamblers approach things differently and set themselves a specific task. Driving down North Street in Bedminster, what are the odds about recalling Tinker's name before reaching Nailsea some seven miles away?

Now and then I solve problems by invoking racing or football memories. Also, I imagine the sort of bet I'd need to place to settle an unexpected bill or sudden setback. We continue to bring up our eight-year-old granddaughter Matilda and she shows great promise at judo. I'm not sure if being half-Chinese helps. Recently, the club she attends went ahead and bought some brand new mats, relying on subsequent sponsorship – it was the 10k Bristol road race last week – to offset the cost.

Now, I am not about to set new levels in hypocrisy by suggesting it might have been advisable to get the money in first; you can't live with risk for 70 years and suddenly come up with boring strategies like that. You just have to get on with it and my wife promptly donated £100.

So did I, of course, but here is the difference between men and women. She handed it over with good grace, an immediate withdrawal from our mutual bin, not that she used that particular word, whereas I was thinking, 'Well, there's a Class 2 sprint at Haydock tomorrow, it's absolutely perfect for David O'Meara's Intisaab, especially if Dancing Star just needs the race. 11/4 should do it.' Which it did.

It's not big money, needless to say. Indeed, by comparison with my colleague Steve Palmer's most recent investments I'm not sure any of us is playing for big money, but it just about squared the train fare to York, as well.

Before I left I bumped into Marvel Mason and told him about Tinker and the five per cent problem. With Marvel you have to put up with some gentle ribbing and the suggestion that, after all the frazzled days and nights, it's amazing you can remember anything at all but he tried to help.

"Two place names," he said. "And the giveaway, *The Leather Boys*."

It's not, though. I remember Tinker in the 1964 film, which was about bikers who congregated at the Ace Café on London's North Circular Road and was actually quite ground-breaking because it treated gay men seriously. The Ace Café was famous in its day and reopened recently, so we've forced a one-all draw around that section of the A406 – Park Royal greyhounds gone for ever but the Ace and the bikers back. Tinker was one of them.

Anyway, I'm on the rattler to York, approaching Birmingham New Street and thinking of the year I drove to Haydock and nearly gave up in appalling traffic on the M6 before Wolverhampton. Soon I was hopelessly lost in a sea of old red-brick industrial towns beginning with 'W'. But then, studying form with the Knavesmire still a couple of hours away, I vaguely remembered there was an exception. And I shouted out: 'Dudley! Dudley Sutton! Yes!'

And I was mighty relieved.

A SHORT-PRICED DOUBLE, BY GEORGE
Racing Post November 2015

"There's a man at the bar who says he needs a winner," Marvel Mason says.

Marvel has just got them in, having made his first mistake for quite a while, betting old Arthur Sears that he couldn't name the piece of classical music which inspired the 1978 hit 'If I Had Words'. Marvel would not have known the answer himself, had it not been on Radio 3 earlier on.

"Saint-Saens' Symphony Number 3," Arthur murmurs. "Cognac, please, Hennessy if they've got it. I stay loyal to the old brands."

Marvel continues in excellent form otherwise and will make quite a lot of money as long as Dickie Johnson stays fit and well but he seldom relaxes and says the bookmakers' advertisements on television are starting to get him down. They just wash over me, though I must say I thought Victor Chandler was a natural and probably missed his vocation.

"The point is, no one can afford to be left out," Arthur Sears said. "Mind you, they have to tread carefully where the various lobbies are concerned. We didn't have that problem in the 1970s because the drinks companies got together and had a gentlemen's agreement not to advertise spirits on the box. Everyone kept to it, as well. Cinemas yes, television no.

"Of course, those of us in advertising had to find an alternative. That's why, if you watch old episodes of *Minder*, you'll see that all the drinks in Arthur Daley's lock-up are Gilbey's products – Gilbey's Gin, Smirnoff, Hennessy and the rest. It cost a packet but it was worth it. Why doesn't that fellow come over? I've been looking at Seychelloise and Man Of Harlech at Lingfield."

In all the years I've known Arthur (he is 93 now), he has never bothered with form but he loves the names and the breeding. Glancing at the paper, I see that Seychelloise is out of Starlit Sands and Man Of Harlech's dam is Ffestiniog. And somehow I feel the double will come up, because there is no way Sir Mark Prescott would ask a three-year-old filly, penalised 6lb, to give weight to older sprint handicappers unless she happened to be slightly different class, while Man Of Harlech was fourth in the Cambridgeshire and this looks quite a bit easier.

I find myself wishing I could be there, heading south from London and turning left off the main road where there was a corner shop with (probably) the last W & A Gilbey sign in the country outside. Alfred Gilbey was the grandfather of celebrated racing correspondent Quintin Gilbey, whose father, strangely enough, detested the sport.

Quintin's autobiography, *Fun Was My Living*, is an engaging read and pulls no punches. He took an instant dislike to Winston Churchill, for example, but warmed to Lord Beaverbrook, whom many thought something of a martinet. Under the circumstances it's surprising that 'Quinny' never worked for the *Daily Express*, though he remembered Peter O'Sullevan being taken on by Cyril Luckman (wonderful name for a tipster), who'd been the Scout on the paper for donkeys' years.

Marvel shakes his head sadly. "I think we've lost Ian, Arthur," he said. "It's happening more and more, I find. Anyway, I've given that chap the two tips. Partly on your say-so and partly because they're both favourite. Seems rather worried but he's gone off to back them."

The George in Backwell has undergone complete refurbishment. Scruffy for years and ignored by drivers on the A370, it's much smarter now and the ideal place to mull things over. There aren't many pubs offering Barolo at £48 a bottle.

"Do you remember Thames Trader, Arthur?" I say. "Won for all the top jockeys and Peter O'Sullevan used to tip him in the *Express*, even at very short odds. 'Never mind the price, just make sure you never go too long without tipping a winner,' he used to say."

"Moët & Chandon Silver Magnum at Epsom, John Oaksey up. I only remember it because we had the Moët account. Must have been about 1963 and I think Brough Scott may have ridden in the race." He pauses. (It's the 'I think' I love, just that scintilla of doubt, the mark of a true professional.)

"Brough Scott never rode against John Oaksey at Epsom," Marvel says.

And I look at him and I say: "Marvel, I really, really wouldn't bet on that."

Arthur chuckles softly, then the phone rings and there's no need to bet anyway, because the barman says the young man is on his way back, the weight miraculously lifted from his shoulders in half an hour. Apparently we're not to buy any drinks ourselves.

"Couldn't fail with breeding like that," Arthur says.

KIPPERS AND GIN ARE BOTH ON THE MENU
Racing Post January 2017

Happy New Year.

It's just possible you need a pick-me-up on New Year's Day and I'd rather hoped that Pink Gin would be running somewhere. We shall have to be patient because there is little doubt Jim Old will place him to advantage before long.

No matter what anyone tells you, there is no cure for a hangover. However, people have favoured some interesting delaying tactics at breakfast-time and one of the senior tasters for the CAMRA – Campaign for Real Ale – organisation used to force down a couple of cream buns, thereby forcing glucose into the bloodstream.

Sir Winston Churchill liked a brace of cold snipe and a pint of port. A pint! I wonder how much that would cost at Cheltenham today. Horatio Bottomley preferred a pair of kippers and a tumbler of brandy and water but Samuel Taylor Coleridge opted for six fried eggs with a glass of laudanum – an alcoholic tincture of opium – and seltzer. I expect you already knew this but fizzy alcohol drinks hit the spot faster than still ones.

Anyway, today's the day because Samuel opted for this special treat on Sundays only. I imagine the laudanum has much the same effect as the tried and trusted Bolivian marching powder but I confine myself to soluble aspirin and have no personal experience.

As Ecclesiastes said quite a long time ago, 'Wine maketh merry, but money answereth all things,' so you might want to place your bets first. I don't know if Tenor Nivernais will turn out in the BetBright Handicap Chase over 2m 5f because he wants very soft ground but he's 7lb better off with Village Vic on their running last year. The tips are on the other pages, I think.

As a confirmed Scotch drinker there is no chance of J A B Old pouring a pink gin today but, if he did, it would have to be right; no more than half a dozen drops of Angostura bitters and some ice. Also, the gin should be Booth's, which has a yellowish tinge to it, or Plymouth.

Years ago I used to call on a pub in Feltham out Heathrow way where the Irish manager had a gallon bottle of Booth's on optic. It was going out of fashion and the label had seen better days but three old girls who'd trodden the boards at the Windmill Theatre asked for it by name. It was back in the days when you could call someone 'darling' without getting a stiff right-hander and they were lovely.

Under the tie with the brewers Watneys, the manager was supposed to order Gilbey's Gin and always did. Finally, rash youth that I was, I asked him about the yellowish tinge and he gave me that pitying look that people a few years older reserve for a true greenhorn.

"I didn't think we'd be getting into this but it's 95 per cent Gilbey's and five per cent Gilbey's Royal Anchor Brown Sherry," he said. I grew up a bit that day. We became firm friends and used to sit outside with the planes coming in to land. Deafening but fun. Everyone was very happy, especially the old girls, one of whom nursed an abiding passion for Warren Beatty.

Talking of Warren, it has long been assumed that Carly Simon's song 'You're So Vain' – 'You had one eye in the mirror, as you watched yourself gavotte,' etc., referred to him. But no! Whilst there is no doubt they were lovers at one stage, her recent memoir *Boys in the Trees* makes it clear it's a composite of three chaps.

So, there you are. Make 2017 the year of kippers, pink gin and port, go easy on the Tennent's and the laudanum, leave out the cream buns and write a song about three of your lovers, leaving them to ponder which one you meant. If you can't manage something as straightforward as that, my name is not Matt Le Tissier.

UNSURE OF THE VOCALIST? ME TOO
Racing Post March 2016

I was thinking about 'me too' products the other day. Anyone selling a 'me too' product acknowledges that the brand leader is well clear but it's still worth carving out ten per cent of the market. Betdaq is a pretty good example, though from its sponsorship at Kempton the other Saturday I assume it's going along quite well, if a long way behind Betfair.

In the 1970s I sold a drink called Bowies Rock & Rye, with a Jim Bowie figure and some crossed muskets on the label. It was made up of rye whiskey, neutral grain spirits and natural fruit flavours. It was 77.5 degrees proof and did very well in the West Indian pubs in Shepherd's Bush, despite giving Southern Comfort the better part of 100 years' start.

There was a problem, of course. By law the bar staff were supposed to tell the customers that they were being served an alternative brand, like Dry Cane instead of Bacardi, and the sheer hassle and threat of litigation spelt the end for a lot of 'me toos'.

It was good while it lasted, though. Jimmy Deans out Heston way shifted any amount of Rock & Rye and we'd celebrate by taking in Kempton on lazy Friday afternoons.

Jimmy was mainly a casino player, however, and would fit in a trip to the West End and hit the blackjack tables quite hard before returning in time for the evening shift. He was remarkably relaxed, even under strong financial pressure. Old Harry would be sitting at the end of the bar, sipping his half of Guinness, and out would come the crumpled betting slip, probably a 10p Yankee. "I had some bad luck today, Jim …" he'd say, and Jimmy, a few hundred adrift, would smile and ask which one had let him down.

I was sitting in the Botanist in Bristol this week, nursing a South African Chenin Blanc, listening to 'How Insensitive' and wondering why I never had Diana Krall ahead of Etta James, Julie London and Dinah Washington as the likely vocalist. Age, probably. It's a very sad song, 'How Insensitive', but the odd quotation here and there can help sometimes. 'Man is born, suffers from love and toothache, and dies.' There you have it, the Spanish writer and philosopher Miguel de Unamuno at his best. 'We can't forget the past, any more than we can change it.' No, indeed. I thought that might be old Miguel as well, but after careful consideration I think it was probably Jack Nicholson in *The Two Jakes*.

Archie the bookseller came in while 'What a Difference a Day Makes' was playing and that definitely IS Dinah Washington.

It's a song that always reminds me of Malcolm Allison. During his early days as a player at West Ham he was deeply into greyhound racing and one night he was all but wiped out at the track.

It was December and, upstairs on the bus heading back to his digs, he could see people dressing Christmas trees and generally preparing for the big day. And for a few moments he'd have given anything to be like that, to be like them. But in those days there was greyhound racing in London every night of the week; back he went 24 hours later, everything came right and it was champagne, cigars and a taxi ride home. And in THAT moment he realised that nothing would ever change because, deep down, he didn't want it to.

I haven't seen Jimmy Deans since bumping into him in Hounslow one day, when he said the blackjack had all but finished him. I wanted to help and told him Jack Holt's sprinter Coppermill Lad would win at Goodwood as long as the ground remained soft. It rained and rained and I thought he'd win easily but there was only a head to spare at the line. Jimmy's bet almost certainly eclipsed mine; down by the furlong marker I discovered you can sweat freely in a downpour.

Malcolm has gone, of course. Always a maverick, he had Plymouth playing in two arcs of five when we went to see them one night. It was entertaining stuff and the opposition took a while to figure it out before scoring five without reply.

"What's this wine?" Archie asked.

"It's a Chenin Blanc. They're hoping to sell it on the back of Kleine Zalze coming back into fashion."

"I think I'll have another one."

"Me too," I said.

Part Eleven

And The Seasons They Go Round And Round

'And the painted ponies go up and down; we're captive on the carousel of time. We can't return, we can only look behind from where we came. And go round and round, and round in the circle game.'

A Joni Mitchell song from many years ago; poignant, sad and therefore likely to irritate, even infuriate an army of keyboard warriors. No matter. I like it because it fits. I'm not saying nothing changes in a long life – the shaving mirror might have something to say about that – but interests and obsessions stand their ground pretty well.

Fifty-three years since Foinavon found the only available gap at the 23rd fence and 35 since Last Suspect confirmed my time at the BBC was coming to an end, I look at the list of Grand National winners since Sundew and Fred Winter in 1957 and can't quite believe how long it is. All those years, all those horses, all those heroes.

I remember a day, couldn't tell you the year, when Southern Television broadcast a couple of races from Plumpton. I think

Shepherd's Plaid and Jim's Tavern won. He was a long way in front and I wanted him to hold on. At a very early age and with no financial involvement at all, it really mattered to me. Jim's Tavern in the afternoon, James Garner as *Maverick* in the evening. You could write your own script from then on.

A couple of points. When I said earlier on that there would be no detailed record of bets made, I meant it. Tales of near misses have something in common with strange dreams: they both have the listener or reader stifling a yawn. Even so, I don't think there is anything boring about Dave Nevison's near miss and I hope I've done it justice. As far as my own betting record is concerned, let's just say the roaring days of the eighties and early nineties involved bets of four figures rather than three and leave it at that. Duggan, an easy winner at Catterick in 1990, may have netted £3,700 but he started at 8/13. So I think we can see that I've been there, and I don't mean Catterick.

Enough already. There are many regrets but at least I've learned to laugh at myself, out loud sometimes, and have never imagined I was centre-stage in any way. Punchestown in 2019 provided a timely reminder of that when there was a presentation to mark the end of my 32-year stint as British correspondent on *The Irish Field* and one or two cameras clicked away among raised glasses, only for Ruby Walsh to announce his retirement about 20 minutes later. A slightly bigger story, perhaps.

My time at the *Field* ended at much the same time as the column in the *Racing Post*. It was time to go and no hard feelings. It's also most agreeable to attend Cheltenham without the responsibility of all those interviews for the crowd. In the early days I never knew who was coming up next. This was rather worrying for someone whose knowledge of soap opera faded with the departure of Ena Sharples and Minnie Caldwell from *Coronation Street*, though I do remember Minnie's cat was called Bobby. Not bad after half a century.

For the final *Post* column I imagined being back in Marylebone High Street all those years ago, even though 'the memory of a particular image is but regret for a particular moment. And houses, roads, avenues are as fugitive, alas, as the years.'

Who wrote that? Marcel, of course. Stayed awake all through the night more often than not, you know. I wonder what that's like.

Be lucky.

THE SWEET LIFE IN PARIS
Racing Post May 2015

Arthur Sears, who bets sparingly on the horses, sometimes considers a rather more serious wager when a general election is called.

He can vividly recall Winston Churchill's shock defeat in the aftermath of World War II but this time around, having decided that the Conservatives would record a modest overall majority, he wagered that there would be two resignations in the hours following David Cameron's likely triumph in 2015.

Hard luck gambling stories are ten a penny but this one takes some beating, because Arthur could hardly have expected Nigel Farage to upset the proverbial apple cart by resigning, only to change his mind. Some bookmakers might have offered 'money back as a free bet', noting the punter's shrewdness, but not in this instance. "Dear heart, there were three resignations, end of story," Arthur shrugs.

A happier tale comes from my good friend David Ashforth. A lady he knows has a brother with terminal cancer. This chap had one specific bet in mind, namely £50 on a Conservative majority of between 10 and 15 seats. His plan, if it came up, was to pay for a holiday for his sister and her husband. They struggled to find a price and asked David for his assistance. Well, I think we all know that D Ashforth would be the man for that and he duly obtained some 25/1 with Coral. Holidays do not come cheap these days but £1,250 is a pretty good start.

"If one of the bets had to go down I'm glad it was mine," old Arthur says. He means it.

"I thought Miliband and Clegg were both very likely to go, albeit for different reasons. But I'm bound to say, in all my 91 years, I've never known such unrelenting bias in the press. To me, Miliband never looked a winner but when you've got *The Times*, the *Telegraph*, the *Mail*, the *Express* and the *Sun* queueing up to bash you every day it must wear you down eventually."

"Did you have a big bet?"

"No, not really, but it would have paid for lunch in Paris. I still went, of course, because at my age you don't put things off and it was a trip I'd been promising myself for a while.

"It was wonderful, just wandering around by myself, like the old days when I went to see the trotters at Vincennes. We had an ad campaign going for Pretty Polly stockings, I think, and I used to go over when Gelinotte was running. She was an amazing mare and the crowd went wild. You know what a gelinotte is, of course?"

"I believe it's a hazel grouse, or in her case a hazel hen, Arthur, and if that was the first quiz question it's one-nil." (This will not last, needless to say, but I celebrate with a generous sip of manzanilla.)

The manager in the Failand Inn has belatedly discovered Radio 3 and Essential Classics is on. The guest is film director Mike Leigh, who has already chosen Elisabeth Schwarzkopf singing 'Soave sia il vento', 'May the winds be kind', from *Cosi Fan Tutte* and is moving on to Mahler's 5th.

"I'd be happy to bet my Mecca's Angel winnings that this will be the fourth movement, the Adagietto from *Death in Venice*," Arthur says. "Even money?"

I'll only ever bet with friends for a round of drinks and, in any case, it's no use playing when you don't want to lose and you don't want to win, either. In fact I'd have won for once because Leigh chooses the first movement, the funeral march. Arthur looks quite distracted, probably because some of his friends, maybe even a lover or two, watched *Death in Venice* on a regular basis. All gone now, of course.

"Oh dear oh dear, Arthur," I smile, sounding like Terry McCann in *Minder*. "I think you're two-nil down. But just to give you a chance, all or nothing, what is the link between Elisabeth Schwarzkopf and the film *Tell Me That You Love Me, Junie Moon*?"

Gradually he starts to connect things up as his extraordinary memory clicks into gear, his forehead finding room for a few more wrinkles. He will nurse his manzanilla before answering and the game will be up. I want him to live for ever.

"*Desert Island Discs*!" he says, startling an old boy nodding off in the corner. "Elisabeth Schwarzkopf asked for seven of her own recordings and Otto Preminger, who directed *Tell Me That You Love Me, Junie Moon*, when asked what book he'd like to take, said: 'Vell, zere is zis ver' fine biography of Otto Preminger!'"

And he bursts out laughing, and we wonder how to fill in the time before lunch, and then they'll be racing somewhere or other later on. Life is sweet, as Mike Leigh would no doubt agree.

ON THE RIGHT TRACK WITH LYDIA
Racing Post March 2016

In the end, I left the car quite close to Bishops Cleeve.

It cost £5 and meant crossing a few fields and a railway line but the fact is I'm a bit tired of being turned away from the press car park with all the spaces occupied by the *Abergavenny Argus*, the *Cleveland Advertiser* and the *Kuala Lumpur Times* soon after nine o'clock.

If you've worked at a place for over 20 years I think you should be able to enjoy a pint of bitter at 11am and turn up as a humble punter an hour before the first, no questions asked. All right, I invented those three publications but you know what I mean. Maybe retired broadcasters could have a blown-up picture of themselves on a pole above one of the spaces. They had them outside football grounds in the old days. 'Desmond Hackett Is Here Today!' The *Daily Express* was still a newspaper then, of course. To be honest, if obliged to look at a big picture of myself for four days I'd probably head for Bishops Cleeve anyway.

We had to wait by the tracks while a racing special retraced its steps. It was quite wonderful, six Pullman cars in the familiar old brown and cream livery hauled by 7820 Dinmore Manor, preserved and lovingly cared for since its days on the old Western Region. I seem to remember it steaming into Swindon, its birthplace, many years ago when the world was young and everything seemed possible.

If they'd opted to keep 7821 instead, that was Ditcheat Manor, and everyone would have taken it as an omen and backed Paul Nicholls' horses during the afternoon, including 13/2 winner Diego Du Charmil. I would, anyway.

By and large I find the racing at Cheltenham much too difficult and spent most of Wednesday catching up with old friends, one or two of whom have acquired extra chins. In the hospitality tents they rely on RUK coverage rather than Channel 4 and there was a moment, following Sprinter Sacre's unforgettable triumph, when Lydia Hislop admitted to viewers that she'd been crying.

No doubt this was lost in all the hubbub but here was a fine broadcaster completely caught up in something she loves. For those few seconds, Sprinter Sacre's winning meant more to Hislop than anything else in the world and that sort of emotion can sometimes make for exceptional broadcasting. It's hard to say whether the switch from C4 to ITV will have much effect on viewing figures but, however it turns out, someone who mixes a deep love of the sport with a willingness to ask awkward questions deserves a bigger stage.

Lydia versus Rich Ricci on the subject of Vautour's late switch would have made for essential viewing. Not that anyone in a suit like that is likely to be fazed by much. The double initials come into it, of course. You can get away with anything if your double initials roll off the tongue. Max Miller, Charlie Chester, Rich Ricci, all in the same suit. Never let anyone tell you that music hall is dead.

A committed gambler might have looked for a bookmaker paying out on the first four in the cross country. Given that I thought Quantitativeeasing would finish either third or fourth I should have shouldered my way through the crowd instead of settling for the Tote counter nearby. We need not dwell on the outcome.

Almost as painful was my failed attempt to find the car, though not the railway line. At one stage I reasoned that walking alongside the track would eventually bring me out above the field in question but the barbed wire was a worry, so too the sign threatening a £1,000 fine for trespassing on private property. In the week when we lost a dear friend, a talented journalist and one of the old school in John Santer, his more limited colleague might have been flattened by Dinmore Manor in full view of that floating airship thingy. Imagine the embarrassment. Worse still, imagine the jokes.

So I walked back to the course and a very kind man called Chris, who lives nearby, drove me to Bishops Cleeve to start over. I even made it back to Nailsea in time to hear the Andy Champion Big Band in the masonic hall. And the answer to your next question is no, even supposing I could master the funny handshake.

For me the glass is always half-full, though I thought of asking the vocalist if she knew Peggy Lee's 'Is That All There Is?' ('Cos if that's all there is my friend, then let's keep dancing.')

But I suppose I was a bit tired by then.

BOBBY DARIN A SAFER BET?
Racing Post April 2019

I think it fair to say that Archie has yet to recover from Benie Des Dieux's last-flight fall in the Mares' Hurdle at Cheltenham.

It was the final leg of a particularly ambitious treble and, in Archie's words, 'would have made a difference'. Whether he meant a little place in Juan-les-Pins, a minor work by Lucian Freud or a woman with Bristol Rovers in her heart I have no idea, but I can see he is still hurting. Clearly there have been one or two attempts to put things right – the gambler's role in life, whether we like it or not – but these have proven unsuccessful.

Life for a small independent bookseller cannot be easy. I never allow potential usurpers like Tesco or W H Smith to enter the conversation and we move on to the Arc, where Archie once risked an alarming sum on Avenir Certain, making the future anything but certain.

Alan the Buddhist, who once saw a clear leader fall at Fontwell and promptly made a vow making it impossible for horses ever to hurt him again (which they haven't), was sympathetic and liked the name.

"Was that because you're certain we're all coming round again?" I ask Archie, innocently. I'm all for anything that gets us through to the end, especially if it turns out not to be the end after all. I once attended a series of talks on the difference between Buddhism and Hinduism; the lecturer ended up as general manager at Swindon speedway stadium, so he'll probably want it quieter next time.

Alan and Archie do not know each other well and I fear one of those 'why do you do it?' conversations that gamblers face every now and then, so I wander over for another bottle of Italian Chardonnay, not bad in the Botanist, abandoning all thoughts of the Bath Placepot or trying to work out whether it's Bobby Darin or Mel Tormé singing 'Beyond The Sea'.

It would make things a lot simpler if they played the original 'La Mer' by Charles Trenet but you can't tell them. I knew a chap who took his own CDs into the Sawyer's Arms in

Nailsea. *Cat Stevens' Greatest Hits* was one of them, though I think Cat had become Yusuf Islam by then.

No one in my experience has ever drunk a glass of wine more slowly than Alan the Buddhist so I'm relieved in a way that he is due to chant in half an hour or so. He is a kindly soul and has promised to visit Archie's shop but the conversation has come round to doubts and certainties again.

"Have you got anything to get me out?" Archie says.

I've been in this position often enough myself to know that 2/1 on is no good because the man under pressure can't raise the requisite stake, although if I were a bookmaker Sir Mark Prescott's High Secret would be 2/7 in a very weak Bath handicap later on.

"I think it's Bobby Darin," Archie says. "It's not flashy enough for Mel Tormé. Mind you, it could be Harry Connick."

"It couldn't be Sammy Davis Jr., could it?" says Alan the Buddhist and we gaze at him with no little affection, as we might a child that we love beyond all measure who is still struggling with maths homework when all the other children have gone to bed.

"That's right," Archie says. "It really, really couldn't be Sammy Davis Jr. And it's not bloody Burl Ives, either." And suddenly he bursts out laughing, quite possibly for the first time since Benie Des Dieux came to grief.

"You'll be all right," I tell him. "You're good at the jumps, all you need is a little rest. Just think of all the winners Twiston-Davies will have between now and the next Mackeson meeting. I see a major payday coming."

I think we can all see that I offer excellent advice. One of these days I must work out why I fail to take any of it myself.

KEEPING THE FAITH IN A FAVOURITE PLACE
Racing Post December 2012

The carol singers have come round earlier this year.

Netley's winter light fades quite rapidly. Julio, his Father Christmas hat slightly askew, has weathered the storm of three Christmas lunches and glances down at the monitor behind the bar. Every now and then he looks at me and raises an eyebrow, a clear sign that he is pleasantly surprised by the way things are going. I take it we are still in the Placepot. 'O Come All Ye Faithful' seems quite appropriate.

"*Adeste Fideles*," Alfred murmurs. "That's one thing you never forget, you know. The Latin they teach you at school." He hasn't forgotten much else in 91 years, either, though some of it he keeps locked away. His mind is as sharp as a tack, whereas some of the others wander a little, shall we say.

Lunch has gone rather well. Esther has organised things in her usual, no-nonsense way. Party hats, crackers, presents. One year we did it all at the home and there was a pianist. Edward had lived in his own private world for years but, upon hearing the first few bars of Al Bowlly's 'The Very Thought of You', he stood up and sang the whole thing, pitch perfect. I seldom pray but there's a very tricky high note towards the end and I remember making various promises if only Edward could be allowed to get it right, which he did, so maybe there's something in it.

Esther, about 50 I suppose, has her hair scraped back even more severely than usual and favours the kind of stockings seen quite recently in *Foyle's War*. Lenny and Maurice are playing dominoes, a game punctuated by Lenny's occasional cries of delight. "Soft drinks or halves of bitter," Esther says. "No spirits, of course." She fixes me with a stare. "And no gambling."

Having firstly fallen down a well at Bouchoir and then been blown up by a shell while sleeping, the war poet Wilfred Owen came to the military hospital at Netley to recuperate in the summer of 1917. He visited his cousin in the Hazeley Down area but was so mentally scarred that the blameless Winchester Downs became the trenches and inspired the famous poem 'Asleep'.

"It was four years before I was born," Alfred says. "He must have passed quite close to Littleton. Do you remember the Littletons? Littleton Lad, Littleton Lass, Littleton Queen. Les Hall lost his licence over Littleton Queen and she went to Ken Cundell but never did anything. Good trainer, Cundell, but I couldn't believe it when Stalbridge Colonist beat Arkle."

Lenny looks up sharply. "Arkle?" he says. "Is Arkle running? He'll win. He's bloody good. Always wins, Arkle. We should back him."

Choosing my moment, I approach the bar with a tray. "Gin! Gin!" Lenny shouts. Julio looks at me enquiringly and I indicate the smallest possible measure, topped right up with tonic. On the way back I sniff it and it seems the most perfect blend of juniper berries, orris root and coriander seed I have ever experienced in my life. Esther is emerging from the ladies. Mercifully she stops to talk to someone.

"Between the wars it was all Booth's Gin with that funny yellow tinge," Alfred smiles. "She'd have had you straightaway."

"Has she always been on her own?"

He frowns and shakes his head. "Lost her young man in the Falklands," he says. "Not remotely interested in anyone else after that."

I expect more on this but you never really know with Alfred.

"It's a funny thing, but I've never actually done it with a Jewish woman, you know," he says.

A pause seems in order.

"What about that club you used to go to in Shirley? They played kalooki there all the time, didn't they?"

"I never learned. Are you saying that would have made the difference?"

"Well, I'm not sure about Southampton but you'd have been odds-on in Manchester. It's a long way to go, though."

Setting off within sight of Netley, Siegfried Sassoon returned to the Front, also in 1917. 'My mind was unperturbed when we steamed out,' he wrote. 'I watched the woods on the Isle of Wight hazily receding in the heat. And when the Isle of Wight was out of sight – well, there was nothing to be done about it.' He was on his way to Arras, doubting that he would ever return.

There is a burst of Spanish from behind the bar. Politeness personified, Julio has put Henry the historian and a tricky question about Guernica on hold to roar home the last leg of the Placepot. Musselburgh, mysterious and quite possibly fictitious a few hours ago, is suddenly his favourite place on earth.

All of the glasses are empty and I lean over to pick up the tray, winking at Lenny as I do so. "G & T all right?"

He looks at me keenly, his china-blue eyes alive with mischief and wonder, the child reclaiming the man.

"Who are you?" he says.

WAYS AND WAYS TO RECOVER
Racing Post July 2017

I bumped into Jimmy Deans in Brighton on Tuesday. The wind was getting up, there were a few spots of rain and he was walking the wrong way along the front, unless Hove had more to offer than a handful of Class 5 and Class 6 handicaps up the hill.

Jimmy had pubs in Hounslow and Heston when the world was young. The top brewers are loyal employers and I'd seen him once or twice before on John Smith's day, in the marquee down by the furlong pole. He was a big punter in the old days but Coppermill Lad getting him out of serious trouble in a quagmire at Goodwood was a one-off.

He was very grateful but it was always blackjack which fascinated him, leading to long and punishing sessions in the midnight hour. He was very, very good but the house still enjoyed a mathematical edge. When the casino bosses started worrying about people 'counting' cards – a lot of high ones left in the shoe favoured the punters – they introduced a machine to feed the 'deads' back in prematurely. You could get the same six of spades twice in three hands. Time to stop, but Jimmy didn't.

Omar Sharif and Charlie Benson, both hooked on racing, should have stuck to bridge and backgammon and Jimmy might have made money from film quizzes. We repaired to the Regency Tavern where the Shepherd Neame Spitfire continues its truly remarkable recovery after several years in the doldrums and Stan Getz was tootling away in the background – 'Girl from Ipanema' with Astrud Gilberto on vocals.

"They used to play Astrud Gilberto tracks late at night in the Victoria Sporting Club," Jimmy said. "'Fly Me to Brazil',

I remember, which often seemed a very good idea, always supposing you had enough money left for a taxi to Heathrow. And they liked a sad little song called 'Who Needs Forever?'. If you listen hard you can just pick it up in a film called *The Deadly Affair*. Simone Signoret plays a nymphomaniac. Who needs forever, see, if that's what you have to have right now. The only thing that will do," he added, glumly.

I did a selling job in Rio about 40 years ago – graphic arts materials, about which I knew very little indeed – and stayed in a little hotel overlooking Ipanema beach. When you open the curtains in the morning there are literally hundreds of people bending and stretching. In need of some exercise myself, I was pleased when the agent took me racing later on. To be honest, I thought the jockey on the favourite in a claimer wasn't terribly busy but you don't say anything when it's all free. Apart from the bet, of course.

"I've got a little place down here I can rent and I don't play seriously any more," Jimmy said. "Getting out of trouble was always the most wonderful feeling and Coppermill Lad was great but when I hit the skids I couldn't get to grips with things the following morning and there was still a pub to run."

We're all different, I suppose. I used to play a lovely, melancholy track by Stan simply called 'Her', which I always took to be about love lost, though I believe it may actually have been dedicated to his mother when she was seriously ill. Or there's 'My Foolish Heart' by Bill Evans, or you can watch that bit in the Marx Brothers' film *A Night at the Opera* where Groucho loads them all into the cabin and then opens the door suddenly so that they fall out. I'm bringing up an eight-year-old and she was helpless for five minutes. You're probably not a terminal case so I dare say you'll rally if you watch any clip of John Belushi and Dan Aykroyd dancing in *The Blues Brothers*.

"I don't suppose there's another Coppermill Lad?" Jimmy said.

"No, but conditions will be just as wet when The Stalking Moon goes in the 6.45. Very, very long way for John Quinn to send a horse when it's also engaged at Catterick tomorrow. Don't go mad."

"*The Stalking Moon*? Gregory Peck and Eva Marie Saint? All this and Stan Getz as well. We were meant to bump into each other, my son. Do you believe in things like that?"

Well, no, not really. But I like to think Jimmy discovered The Stalking Moon was a non-runner, then waited all day on Wednesday to see it bolt up at Catterick. If so, he'll have woken up a very happy bunny the following morning. And sometimes we'd give anything for that.

ALL DRESSED UP AND EVERYWHERE TO GO
Racing Post December 2015

I stand on the corner of Sussex Gardens and Edgware Road, assailed by alternatives.

Turn left, head north to Maida Vale and beyond, past the BBC studios and the cinema where a young man might have sat entranced by *The Garden of the Finzi-Continis*, the achingly sad story of a well-to-do Jewish Italian family, living an almost dream-like existence until Mussolini's henchmen close in.

On and on, past the Irish pubs in Kilburn and so to Hampstead and the Flask, just along from Al Alvarez's place. The poet, broadcaster and long-time Flask Walk resident was a proud Londoner of many years' standing. "We had to leave Spain in 1492, but turned up here soon after Cromwell let the Jews back in in 1656," he told you with a smile.

Or turn right and opt for a shorter journey to Marble Arch, past the Lebanese restaurants and the old boys with their hookah pipes, past the twilight betting shops with American racing that no one wants and the silent, programmed spin of the roulette wheel. The late George Wigg, former chairman of the Horserace Betting Levy Board, made this journey often enough and it occurs to me that this is the only thing we had in common: we both needed a *Sporting Life* at 11.30pm the night before the following day.

I used to buy one and read it in Charlie Chester's Casino in Archer Street, Soho but Lord Wigg, well, who knows? He was arrested for allegedly approaching six ladies of the night (six!) but told the judge he was simply on his way to buy the *Life*. As one wag pointed out, there weren't many *Sporting Life* sellers wearing high heels, short skirts and shiny red PVC macs; even so, we should mention that the noble lord was acquitted. As Mandy Rice-Davies probably remarked at the time, "Well, he would be, wouldn't he?"

In what became known as the Profumo Affair, Wigg, then MP for Dudley, played a leading role in bringing down the Secretary of State for War, placing him under intolerable pressure in the House. Profumo resigned, having lied about his relationship with Christine Keeler, who was also entertaining the Russian naval attaché Yevgeny Ivanov. 'Irony' is an overworked and misused word these days but, having labelled Keeler a prostitute (which she wasn't) few would have missed the irony had the Park Lane/Marble Arch case gone against Wigg. As for Profumo's liaison with Keeler, a fleeting fascination cost him just about everything, though not his marriage.

Or turn around and go back down the Gardens, all the way to Notting Hill Gate and the little 'tucked away' pub, the

Uxbridge Arms, where they used to serve Brakspear's bitter, in a class of its own now that Young's Special has gone the way of most wonderful things from our youth.

From there, on down Holland Park Avenue, past the restaurant which used to be called Au Caprice des Dieux. There can't be a gambler alive capable of resisting a place which translates as In the Lap of the Gods; personally, I wouldn't even try. Playwrights Harold Pinter and Simon Gray used to dine near here with their wives, conversation sometimes strained because of Harold's progressive cancer. And yet, when it struck, it hit Gray so hard and fast that he went first. There are no certainties.

Or I can stride straight on, maybe as far as Marylebone High Street, where Lord Howard de Walden owned 110 acres of land, and I wonder if that took all the fun out of betting. No I don't. How could anything possibly be fun with that much money? Where is the pain? Where are the 3am thoughts? I cross the Edgware Road, mindful of the fact that the Victoria Casino is only yards away.

And I don't need to play, I really don't, because Jim Old has Valid Point running at Leicester on Wednesday and the Christmas expenses will soon be under control. Then again, Wednesday is so far away. I push the revolving door. Colin is on the desk. "Mr Carnaby!" he says. "Colin!" I say. And my coat is off and I'm up the stairs, ignoring the still small voice pointing out that I really haven't travelled very far at all.

THE LONG ROAD FROM PORTMAN SQUARE
Racing Post Final Column June 2019

At 25, it's probably time to face up to a few things.

I've reached that age now and need something a bit more permanent. The trainee scheme at the Jockey Club was all right, even if I was the only punter, and reporting games down the Orient and Cold Blow Lane is enjoyable but you need to be very careful up the fire escape steps to the press box at Brentford, especially on a wet and windy night. At £7.50 a go the phone never stops ringing and I must have worked for half the local radio stations in the country but it's hardly *Grandstand*, is it?

Towards the end of my time at Portman Square I was walking further and further up Marylebone High Street in my lunch hour. Anyway, now that I'm in the wine trade at the other end it's hardly surprising that I do most of my thinking in the Baker & Oven. Morston wins the Derby at 25/1 but I can't get last year out of my mind.

It's probably the way Lester sways back, like a bareback rodeo rider, and administers those final staccato cracks with the whip that gets Roberto up to beat Rheingold. It's just astonishing and no journalist's words can match Fred Winter's message to beaten trainer Barry Hills: 'Suppose just bad luck on all concerned to be born same century as L Piggott.' Of course, Piggott himself acknowledges the thunderclap of approval which greets his return with a wan smile. Not so much a jockey, more a force of nature. I wonder what it's like to interview him. Pretty hard work, I should think.

1973 is turning out all right. Bill Wightman has won three races with Mick Channon's Cathy Jane and Mick can't stop scoring. A dozen goals and it's not even Christmas but the

Saints' defence looks rickety to me and this will be the first season that three go down. Something tells me this may make all the difference. Odds against, needless to say, like lots of things that end up hurting you.

I celebrate minor triumphs. Racing on radio and television is all very well but there's nothing quite like picking up the paper and seeing that the horse you've backed has won. At school I always had the *Sporting Life* furled up in the inside pocket of my blazer. Denys Smith's Doubtful Character winning at 20/1 at Carlisle and Augur on the front page with his Pontefract nap no matter what else was going on. The *Life* will last for ever, thank goodness, and I sit here in the Baker with Cathy Jane's latest success writ large. When Bill finally calls it a day I want to write the retirement piece somewhere, anywhere, because he's my hero.

I shall never see another ride like the Roberto one but it's sometimes rash to sound dogmatic. Until *Don't Look Now* came along a few months ago I thought *Sunday Bloody Sunday* would always be the film I turned to first when life was cutting up rough. Most of all I love Peter Finch as the agreeably world-weary GP vying with Glenda Jackson for Murray Head's favours against a north London background of bar mitzvahs and Mozart's *Cosi Fan Tutte*.

Oh well. Luton on Saturday and then three days' racing with David Ashforth – 'the student', as Jeff Connor and I used to call him at college, which was daft because we were all students. I think it had something to do with his long hair and even longer scarf. I keep telling him he should write an article and send it in, because you never know.

I can sell most things, you know. I can certainly sell Lagunilla rosé wine in Shepherd's Bush, for a start. It's just that I can't imagine doing anything all the time, as it were, which probably means I'm waiting for the card 'that is so high and wild I'll never need to play another'. Leonard Cohen, of course. Even so, better send off a few applications for jobs I don't really want. I doubt some of them will last very long but there's always the long walk up Marylebone High Street afterwards, the old boys with their Carlsberg Special, the comfort of strangers.

That's how it works. Then one day, 45 years on, you come to the final piece of work and hope that, by some quirk of fate and often working out of a dimly lit bar with Stan Getz tootling away in the background, you've stayed in the game and managed a few bits and pieces that weren't too dusty. Like Peter Finch at the end of *Sunday Bloody Sunday*, with the language tape spilling out phrases he'll never use, because Murray has chosen a business opportunity in the States instead of the longed-for Italian trip, leaving both lovers to Mozart and Hampstead's empty elegance.

"All my life I've been looking for someone who was courageous and resourceful, and it wasn't him," Finch says to camera. And there's a pause before he adds: "But it was something."

Yes, that's right. It was something.

Index

301